# AFTER TEHRAN

ALSO BY MARINA NEMAT

*Prisoner of Tehran*

# Marina Nemat

## AFTER TEHRAN

### A LIFE RECLAIMED

VIKING
CANADA

VIKING CANADA

Published by the Penguin Group

Penguin Group (Canada), 90 Eglinton Avenue East, Suite 700, Toronto, Ontario, Canada M4P 2Y3
(a division of Pearson Canada Inc.)

Penguin Group (USA) Inc., 375 Hudson Street, New York, New York 10014, U.S.A.
Penguin Books Ltd, 80 Strand, London WC2R 0RL, England
Penguin Ireland, 25 St Stephen's Green, Dublin 2, Ireland (a division of Penguin Books Ltd)
Penguin Group (Australia), 250 Camberwell Road, Camberwell, Victoria 3124, Australia
(a division of Pearson Australia Group Pty Ltd)
Penguin Books India Pvt Ltd, 11 Community Centre, Panchsheel Park, New Delhi – 110 017, India
Penguin Group (NZ), 67 Apollo Drive, Rosedale, North Shore 0745, Auckland, New Zealand
(a division of Pearson New Zealand Ltd)
Penguin Books (South Africa) (Pty) Ltd, 24 Sturdee Avenue, Rosebank,
Johannesburg 2196, South Africa

Penguin Books Ltd, Registered Offices: 80 Strand, London WC2R 0RL, England

First published 2010

1 2 3 4 5 6 7 8 9 10 (RRD)

Copyright © Marina Nemat, 2010

Manufactured in the U.S.A.

ISBN: 978-0-670-06462-5

Library and Archives Canada Cataloguing in Publication data available
upon request to the publisher.

Visit the Penguin Group (Canada) website at **www.penguin.ca**

Special and corporate bulk purchase rates available; please see
**www.penguin.ca/corporatesales** or call 1-800-810-3104, ext. 2477 or 2474

*To Shahnoosh Behzadi*
*and Neda Agha-Soltan*

## Author's Note

Although this is a work of non-fiction, I have changed names and some details to protect the identity and privacy of individuals.

*N*ineteen years after leaving Iran, I began to have recurring dreams about putting different items in a suitcase to take to the next world with me. I was getting ready for death.

In my waking life, I knew that I would like to wear a red dress to the grave and to keep my wedding ring on.

This book tells the story of every one of those dream items. Each object (sometimes paired with another) stands as the title of a chapter.

There are other things I would have liked to take to the next world with me. But during moments of anger, frustration, madness, or surprising sanity, I have given them away, thrown them out, or buried them.

# My Grandmother's Silver Jewellery Box

"**L**ook what you've done now! You've killed your mother!" my father said to me in Persian as paramedics carried my mother on a stretcher down the narrow flight of stairs in my suburban Toronto house on a cloudy day in October 1998. Standing in the tiny foyer with the front door wide open, I shivered in the cold wind that held the scent of winter, relieved that the paramedics didn't speak our language. But one of them looked at me with questioning eyes, and I guessed that he had felt the anger in my father's voice, as cutting as broken glass. My father was trying to place blame, as if finding a person responsible for my mother's sudden illness would fix things and make her well.

The paramedics rushed my mother past me, and I caught a glimpse of her face. It was paler than usual, and the lines around her brown eyes seemed deeper. But there was more: her eyes were different; they were not as stern and condemning as they had always been. She looked like a defiant child who had been caught red-handed but didn't regret what she had done, not even for a moment. I followed the paramedics and my parents out the door, and tears rolled down my face. I wiped them with the back of my hand. I was stronger than this. Yet here I was, a thirty-three-year-old woman, feeling as if I were eight again and back in Tehran.

I watched the lights of the ambulance disappear around the corner. Then I went back into the house. My husband, Andre, and I had bought it in July 1993, two years after our arrival in Canada as landed immigrants. My parents had joined us in the fall of that year. The top half of the wall next to the stairs was painted yellow, the bottom half a pistachio green, and a wide border of blue and white flowers separated the two. I had wanted to paint that wall as soon as we moved into the house, but because I was working part-time at McDonald's and then Swiss Chalet in addition to being the mother of two young boys, I didn't get to it for a while.

I locked the door behind me and, unable to carry my weight any longer, sat on the floor in front of it. I was grateful that no one was home; my children were at school and Andre was at work. I knew I had to call him, ask him to pick up the kids and come home so we could go to the hospital and find out what had happened to my mother. But I couldn't move.

*"Look what you've done now! You've killed your mother!"*

Was my father finally reacting to what had happened in Tehran sixteen years earlier? In 1982, at the age of sixteen, I was arrested for so-called political crimes, then locked up in the notorious Evin prison. I knew my incarceration had taken its toll on my parents. But it had taken its toll on me, too. I hadn't thought about Evin in years. My past was a ghost that I, like my family, had chosen to ignore, even though its presence was undeniable. I had never talked to my parents about what happened to me in prison, because not only did they never ask me, they also made it clear they wanted the experience forgotten. Immediately after my release, I didn't *want* to talk about my imprisonment, but I would have felt reassured to know they would be willing to listen when I was ready. Now my mother was dying, and my parents still had no idea what had gone on behind the walls of Evin. How could I tell them that I had been tortured and had come close to execution? How could I describe being forced to marry one of my interrogators and spending nights with him in a solitary cell? And there was more, much more—

The phone began to ring, but I didn't dare answer it. What if my mother had died? What if my father was right and I *had* killed her?

I soon learned that I had not caused my mother to have a heart attack. She had gallbladder cancer and had to undergo surgery. My mother had known about her cancer for a while but had not said a word to any of us. When later we asked her why she hadn't told us, she said she hadn't wanted us to worry.

My parents and I had never communicated, never gotten along. As a punishment when I was a child, my mother sometimes locked me out on the balcony of our apartment in downtown Tehran. We rented two connecting apartments above a small restaurant and a furniture store on the northwest corner of Shah and Rahzi avenues. Our three bedrooms, small kitchen, and bathroom lay on either side of a dark, narrow hallway between my mother's beauty salon and my father's dance studio.

I can clearly remember why my mother locked me out on the balcony the first time. It was shortly after the death of my paternal grandmother, Xena, and I was seven years old. My grandmother Xena—or *Bahboo*, as I called her—lived with us and ran the household, cooking and cleaning and caring for me. She took me to the park every day and read to me. She was my best friend. I hardly ever saw my mother. She worked in her beauty salon all day and usually went out at night. *Bahboo*, like my mother's mother, was of Russian descent and Christian. My Russian grandmothers had married Iranian men who had gone to Russia for work before the Communist revolution of 1917. After the revolution, both families had to leave the country; the men were not Russian citizens, and foreigners were no longer allowed to remain there.

Xena and Esah, my grandfather, left Russia for Iran when Xena was pregnant with my father, and my father's only sibling,

Tamara, was four. My father was born in the city of Mashad in 1921, shortly after the family's arrival in Iran; soon after his birth, they moved to Tehran. Only weeks later, Esah, a jeweller, went out to sell the jewellery he had brought with him from Russia to buy a house for his family—but he was murdered, and everything he had with him was stolen. Xena, who didn't speak Persian and was a stranger in Iran, managed to survive. She eventually opened a boarding house and provided a decent living for her two children. She never married again.

Esah had given Xena a silver jewellery box. After his death, she used the box to store sugar and kept it on the kitchen table. Every time she sweetened her tea, she was reminded of him. I loved that box, and after her death, I wanted it to be only mine, so one day I dumped all the sugar onto the kitchen table and hid the box under my bed. My mother soon discovered who had made that mess, and she locked me out on the balcony to punish me. Of course, this would not be my last time there. I was a curious, opinionated, and articulate child who wanted to know everything and never took no for an answer. "No" always set up an intriguing challenge for me, and I always responded to it with "Why?" My mother, who was beautiful, busy, and short-tempered and was going through a difficult menopause, simply didn't have patience, so she came up with the perfect punishment to keep me out of her way: locking me out on the balcony. My brother wasn't around to help. Alik, my only sibling, was fourteen years older than I was. He had left home at the age of eighteen to go to university in another city.

I hated the balcony. It was either too hot or too cold, and, worst of all, it was lonely. However, this was where I learned patience, a virtue that didn't come naturally to me. One thing I hated even more than being locked away was being humiliated, so I never made a scene; I never screamed, banged on the balcony door, or stomped my feet. I cried silently and watched the street below from above the bamboo shades encircling my eight-by-four-foot roofless cell.

The paved four-lane street seethed with traffic during rush hours and the air smelled of exhaust fumes. Across the street, Hassan *Agha*, the vendor who had only one arm, sold sour green plums in spring, peaches and apricots in summer, cooked red beets in autumn, and different kinds of cookies in winter. At one corner of the intersection, an old blind man held out his bony hands to passersby and cried, "Help me, for the love of God!" from morning till night. Opposite our apartment, the large, mirrored windows of a fifteen-storey office building sparkled in the sun and reflected the movement of the clouds. At night, the neon lights above the stores came on and coloured the darkness.

My sentence on the balcony would last from half an hour to several hours. For most of this time I could hear a waltz or a tango through the windows of my father's dance studio, and sometimes I heard my father counting. "One, two, three … one, two, three …" In my mind, I could see my father's students, elegantly dressed couples, spin and glide to the music, and I wished I could be a part of the forbidden world of the studio. But my father never let me in when he was working. Often when I awoke very early in the morning and everyone was still asleep, I would go into the studio and swirl to an imaginary waltz until I became dizzy and collapsed on the cool brown linoleum floor that smelled of wax.

As a child, I was afraid of my father. I would watch him while he sat on his favourite black leather chair in the waiting area of his studio every evening, reading the paper. His posture was always perfect—as straight as a ruler. If I disturbed him by saying something or making a sound, he would look at me with his serious amber eyes, his mouth an unbending line that seemed incapable of ever breaking into a smile. He, too, had no patience for young children. I knew quite well that if I misbehaved, he would slap me on the face, which was the most humiliating thing I could experience.

This was how I grew up, an outsider, observing my family from a distance, as if a brick wall that became thicker with each passing day stood between us. I found refuge in books, school, and friends, and I spent most of my time reading and studying. Having always been one of the top students in my class, I decided when I was twelve to become a doctor. All my teachers encouraged me, telling me that with my perseverance, I could become whatever I set my mind to. Meanwhile, in other ways my life resembled that of an average North American girl. Every Thursday night, I watched *Little House on the Prairie* (dubbed into Persian), and every Friday, I watched *Donny & Marie* (in English). At the age of twelve I was madly in love with Donny Osmond! We owned a cottage by the Caspian Sea; there I spent my summers riding my bike, sunbathing on the beach, partying with friends, or dancing to the tunes of the Bee Gees.

The Islamic Revolution succeeded when I was thirteen and changed my world beyond recognition. From my window, I watched the gathering storm. It was a drizzle at first, but then it turned into a flash flood, engulfing the streets, washing away the normalcy of our lives. Our street, which had always been congested with cars and crowded with pedestrians who strolled or rushed along or haggled with vendors, was empty and silent. Even the beggars were gone. Soon, military trucks shadowed every corner. Once every few days, hundreds of angry demonstrators filled the street, bearded men leading the way and women wearing *chadors*\* following them; with their fists raised in the air, they screamed,

---

\**Chador* is a cloaklike garment worn by some Iranian women in public and is only one way in which a Muslim woman can follow the Islamic dress code known as *hejab*. A *chador* covers all of a woman's body so that only her face remains visible.

"Down with the shah!" and "Independence, Freedom, Islamic Republic!" For the first time in my life, I heard gunshots; the military had opened fire on the demonstrating crowds. My mother ordered me to stay away from windows, and now I obeyed her without an argument.

Even though the revolution was gaining momentum, my parents believed that a bunch of mullahs and unarmed civilians would never defeat the shah's military. But they were wrong. The shah went into exile; Ayatollah Khomeini, who had been in exile for years, returned to Iran; the Islamic Republic of Iran was born, and with it, our world and all the rules that had held it together collapsed. The people of Iran wanted democracy, but that is not what they got. Soon, dancing was declared satanic. My father closed down his studio and began working as an office clerk at a friend's stainless-steel factory. He hated his new job but was hopeful that the new Islamic government would not last very long. Makeup, pretty clothes, and Western books became illegal. Before I knew it, my dream of becoming a doctor slipped away, because fanatic young women of the Revolutionary Guard, most of whom didn't even have a high-school diploma, gradually replaced our teachers. These unqualified new teachers spent most of the class time spouting political rhetoric. When I protested to the new calculus teacher and asked her to teach calculus instead of enumerating all the great things Khomeini had done for the country, she told me to leave the classroom if I didn't like the new order. I left and unintentionally began a school-wide strike that went on for three days.

During the next few months, I started a school newspaper and wrote articles against the government. Our new principal, who was about nineteen years old and a member of the Revolutionary Guard, came to know me as one of her worst enemies. Most of my friends were now supporters of anti-government Marxist or Marxist-Islamist political groups, and I tried very hard to fit in with them. But even though I hated the new government, I was a devout Christian who attended Mass every day, so I soon found myself isolated and depressed. My parents were aware of most of my activities, but they never tried to stop me; after all, by normal standards, I wasn't doing anything wrong. All I wanted was to study math, science, and literature instead of government propaganda. Finally, the principal gave my name and the names of many other "anti-revolutionary" students from our school to the Courts of Islamic Justice.

I was arrested at about nine o'clock at night on January 15, 1982, just sixteen years old. My imprisonment lasted two years. During that time, my mother and father suffered a great deal. They knew that political prisoners were tortured in Evin. They had heard about the rape of young girls and the daily mass executions. Every day, they waited for the phone call that would tell them to go to the prison gates to collect my belongings because I had been executed.

Evin was a country within a country. It had its own unwritten rules, and in a way, it had its own government and army. Its guards and interrogators had extreme powers. Evin prisoners were stripped of every right and were considered less than slaves. Most prisoners were allowed regular visits with close family members, so I saw my parents for five to ten minutes once a month. A thick glass barrier divided the large visiting room in half. For the first few months of my time in Evin there were no phones in the visiting room, so we couldn't talk and used a sign language instead. Armed members of the Revolutionary Guard stood in every corner and monitored our every move. My parents cried constantly, and I tried to smile and assure them I was all right. At one of the visits about six months after my arrest, I told them I had converted to Islam. They didn't ask why. They knew I had been forced to. No one dared question what went on in Evin.

When I was released after two years, two months, and twelve days, my parents behaved as if I had been away on an extended holiday. The first night I was home, we all sat around the dinner table, and I listened with astonishment as my parents talked about the weather. I almost felt locked out on the balcony again. It took me a few days to understand their behaviour. I finally decided that their silence was their way of protecting themselves as well as me; they didn't want to know about the pain and horror of my time in prison, so they pretended it never happened, hoping we would all forget it. But I did not forget anything. I pushed my memories into a dark corner of my mind, where they would remain dormant for many years. I became a prisoner of silence.

After my release in 1984, for about six years the government of Iran refused to give me a passport. Finally, they agreed to let me leave the country, but only if I guaranteed my return and put down five hundred thousand *tomans*—about thirty-five hundred U.S. dollars—as a deposit. If I returned within a year, the money would be refunded. If not, it would go to the government. At the time, Andre's salary was seven thousand *tomans* a month—about sixty U.S. dollars. We didn't have enough money, and it took us a while to gather it. Once we did, the government let us go. However, since I did not return to Iran after the year was up, there was the chance the Revolutionary Guard would decide to arrest my parents to punish me. After all that had happened in Iran, I couldn't rest until my mother and father were safely in Canada. So, shortly after our arrival in Toronto in August 1991, I asked my brother, Alik, to sponsor my parents. He had immigrated to Canada in 1979. Andre and I would have sponsored my parents ourselves, but legally, we couldn't until we were Canadian citizens—a process we knew would take more than three years.

My mother passed away from cancer in March 2000, before I was able to tell her my secrets. But the past had come back to life and there was no escaping it. It had built up like a volcano for sixteen years and an eruption was imminent. When members of the Revolutionary Guard had come to my house to arrest me and pointed guns at my face, I had felt nothing. It was as if I had left my body and was watching a movie. At that terrible moment, I entered a never-ending state of shock. Without realizing it, I'd lost the ability to feel anything deeply. Fear, love, anger, and hatred brushed my skin but never penetrated my flesh. This mechanism became my key to survival in a prison where ninety per cent of the thousands of prisoners were teenagers who had been dragged out of their warm beds and lashed on the soles of their feet until they were so badly swollen that they could not walk. The crimes of these children ranged from having read Western novels or works of Marx and Lenin or publications of illegal political groups, to having dressed the wrong way or having spoken against the values of the Islamic Revolution. Some had participated in protest rallies against the regime and some had distributed pamphlets of "anti-revolutionary" political groups. Evin was like high school in hell.

I HAD MY FIRST psychotic episode right after my mother's funeral in mid-March 2000.

Bundled up in our parkas, hats, and gloves, Andre, my father, my seven- and twelve-year-old sons, Thomas and Michael, and I got into our gold Toyota Camry. Even the children were silent, somehow aware that all had to remain unsaid. Silence had become a member of my family; like a weed, it had crawled into all the spaces between us, its sap a thick, stubborn emulsion of secrets, pain, and anger. The car moved along grey streets under a grey sky. Spring still felt a world away, and people walked briskly with their backs hunched against the wind. I wondered if my mother was watching us, if God had told her about what happened to me in

Evin and if she finally understood how lonely I had been. Would she embrace me now and murmur soothing words to take away some of my sadness?

A wave of guilt washed over me. How terribly selfish of me to think of myself on the day of her funeral.

Except, she was gone, and I still had to deal with this world. Should I ask God to forgive her? Had *I* forgiven her? Forgiven her for what? For a lonely and often terrifying childhood, for one thing. She sometimes threatened to leave me forever if I misbehaved. A few times she even pretended to go, grabbing her purse and rushing angrily down the stairs as I hung on to her skirt or her legs and begged her to stay. She never truly left, but every time she went to the grocery store or to run an errand, I sat by the window and cried until she returned, worried that I would never see her again. But I had forgiven her for that many years ago, I guess when I turned thirteen. By then, I had grown into an independent child who had come to understand that she had to rely on herself for survival. I had finally lost my fear of losing my mother. Did I blame her for not asking me about what had happened in Evin? No, I didn't exactly blame her, but the sadness and loneliness of carrying the burden of the past made me feel, in a way, that I was still in prison. All I wanted was for her to understand how I felt and know the truth. I didn't want her to feel sorry for me. I didn't feel sorry for myself. It would simply have comforted me to know that she knew.

We stopped at the Loblaws at Yonge Street and Steeles Avenue to buy flowers. Pink and white gladiola. My mother's favourite colour was blue, but the store didn't have any blue flowers. A few days before she died, during one of her rare moments of lucidity, she asked me to make sure that she would be buried in the purple dress she had worn to my wedding.

"I ask *you* because your father is too emotional right now, but you're sensible and I know I can count on you," she said to me.

*Sensible?*

I had always believed that if she had to find one adjective to describe me, it would be *stupid*. Cancer had changed my mother, as if, like her body, her soul had been affected. But the cancer wasn't the only thing devastating her; it was also the morphine.

One day she awoke from her medicated sleep and looked around like a terrified, wounded animal.

"What is it, *Maman*?" I asked, jumping out of my chair, which was next to her bed.

"They're coming to get me ... they're here ... look, over there!" she said, pointing into the empty space in front of the door and then the window. But nobody was there.

She grabbed my hand with her cold bony fingers. Her skin was dry like desert sand. I remembered when she was young and healthy and beautiful, when her hands, warm and soft, always smelled of roses.

"Marina, tell me you can see them! Look! There!"

"Who do you see, *Maman*? If you tell me what they look like, I might be able to make them go away."

When I was six, *Bahboo* had said the same thing to me to get me to talk about my nightmares, which used to make me shiver and cry without saying a word—and, very quietly, I whispered everything in *Bahboo*'s ear. If I spoke any louder, *they* might hear and punish me. I told *Bahboo* about the shadows walking around my room. I believed that I saw them when I awoke in the middle of the night. With their bodies covered in long black cloaks, they were tall and darker than the darkness surrounding us. They walked in a circle in a slow, steady pace. I couldn't see their faces because they always bowed their heads. I knew that they were chanting, but it was as if their voices were made of darkness. I could almost see their song but couldn't hear it; clearly, it was a well-protected secret that wasn't made for my ears. After I told *Bahboo* about them, she looked at me thoughtfully, and then her amber eyes inspected my room. It was daytime and there were no dark shadows.

"Monks," she said reassuringly, and smiled.

"Monks? Who are they? Are they bad? Will they hurt me? They're scary!"

"Have you ever heard what they say?"

"No."

"Have they ever hurt you?"

"No. They just walk around."

"They will never hurt you."

"You sure?"

"Yes."

"But how do you know? Do they walk around your room, too?"

"No, but I've had my own nightmares."

"But I see them, *Bahboo*. They're not a nightmare! They're real!"

"I know. I know. I've had real nightmares, too. Trust me. *Bahboo* knows. What you have told me sounds exactly like monks. They're good. They walk around and pray. Maybe they pray for you."

"Really?"

"Who else can they be? If the Devil wanted to hurt you, do you think he would send such a useless bunch to walk around your room and do nothing? What's the point of that?"

She was right. The Devil probably had very scary monsters. Much scarier than my monks. It felt good to know their name; "monk" was much better than "dark shadow."

"So ... what should I do?" I asked.

"You should acknowledge them."

"How?"

"Talk to them."

"No way!"

"Why not?"

"They're scary!"

"Scary? You told me they never hurt you."

"Well ... I don't know ... What should I say?"

"How about a Hail Mary?"

"Okay ... I'll try."

"You can't run away from shadows and nightmares, Marina. You have to face them."

I swallowed.

It took me a few nights, but I did whisper a Hail Mary to the shadows. My every word was a little more than a breath that crawled reluctantly out of my mouth through my trembling lips and helplessly floated into the night, disappearing in the black nightmare that lived in my room. The shadows stopped moving for a moment but soon resumed at the same pace as before. However, I heard something. Surprisingly strong, my own voice echoed back to me: "'Hail Mary, full of grace, the Lord is with thee. Blessed are thou amongst women and blessed is the fruit of thy womb, Jesus. Holy Mary, Mother of God, pray for us sinners now and at the hour of our death.'" As the prayer touched my face, my fear began to melt away. "Good night," I said to the monks, then turned around and soon fell asleep. I was not afraid anymore. At least, not as much as before. *Bahboo* was right. They were just silly monks who had nothing better to do than walk around my room.

Now my mother was seeing shadows. We had switched positions: I was the adult and she was the child.

"*Maman*, if you tell me what you see, I'll be able to help you," I said.

"They're coming for me. They want to take me away and lock me up. They will suck my blood."

"Who?"

"*Pasdarah.*"

"*Maman*, there are no Revolutionary Guard here. What you see is from the past. We're in Canada. It's safe here."

"But they're here, Marina, and they want to take *me* this time!"

"I won't let them take you, *Maman*."

"But they're here for *me*. I know it!"

"No, *Maman*. They're here for me, and I will tell them that they have already had me, and they will go away."

"Yes, you do that," my mother said exhaustedly.

"Go away!" I said sharply. "You've already had me. Leave us alone!"

My mother was suddenly still. Was she breathing? I put my hand on her chest. Her rib cage rose slightly under my fingers. She was alive.

This was the closest my mother and I ever came to talking about Evin.

Soon after this hallucination, she didn't recognize any of us. She was awake but dead. Her eyes were not the ones I had known all my life. They had turned into glass. Cold, fragile, and without nightmares or dreams. Her soul had left her body.

At the funeral home my children and I warmed ourselves by the fireplace, but at that moment, all the fires of hell could not have stopped me from shivering. I reluctantly took off my coat. I wasn't wearing black garments but rather a beige sweater and a brown skirt, the nicest clothes I owned. When dressing to come to the funeral home, I realized that I didn't own any black outfits. "What kind of a woman never wears black?" I asked myself. After the success of the revolution in Iran, they made women wear only dark colours. Was this why I hated black and avoided it, and was this why I had painted my living room an "interesting" shade of yellow, as Andre put it politely? Why was I thinking these stupid thoughts at my mother's funeral?

We had to climb a flight of stairs to get to the visiting room. My feet were already hurting in my high heels. Wearing pants and boots would have been so much more sensible. My father walked

ahead of me. He was seventy-nine years old, but his posture was
still perfect; he still had a dancer's elegance. His every movement
was light, as if gravity didn't apply to him. As he extended his hand
for people to shake, I could almost hear the waltzes and tangos of
his dance studio in the background. How had he felt when the
Islamic Republic of Iran took music away from him? What does a
nation become without colour, music, poetry, and literature? What
do *we* become when beauty turns into a crime?

People were nodding, smiling, and looking sad. I knew a few
of them, but most of them were Alik's friends I had never met.
I felt guilty standing there, greeting strangers and accepting their
condolences. They didn't know I was a terrible daughter who went
to prison for two years at the age of sixteen and made her parents
suffer. Were they wondering why I had not worn black? I saw a
few of my own friends and sighed with relief. Even if they didn't
know the details, they knew I had been in prison, and still they had
chosen to come to the funeral.

My mother's flower-covered casket sat on the other side of the
room. I knew that she was wearing her purple dress. She had looked
great in it at my wedding. She never cried that day at the church the
way some mothers do when their daughters get married. She had
been angry with me for marrying Andre; she couldn't understand
why I was doing something so illogical. However, she tearlessly
played the role of the proud, happy mother, and I was grateful for
that. I myself hadn't known why I was marrying Andre, but I was
quite sure that I had to do it. It was as if I were starving and had
to eat. Even though I returned to my church immediately after
my release, the government of Iran still considered me a Muslim
woman. Since a Muslim woman is not allowed to marry a Christian
man, by returning to the church and marrying Andre, I would be
automatically condemned to death. Did I want to die? Was this
why I married Andre? Or was marrying him an act of defiance,

showing the world that even though the Islamic Republic had tried to destroy me and almost succeeded, I was still me?

From the cemetery, with family and friends, we went to Alik's house for lunch. Given the fourteen-year age gap between us, Alik and I had never been close. And we don't look alike: he is six-foot-seven and thin, with clear white skin, deep amber eyes, and a large nose; I'm five feet, with dark hair and dark eyes. The caterers had prepared a Persian meal of basmati rice and chicken and beef kebabs, but I wasn't hungry. People were eating and chatting. For dessert, there were cups of *sholeh zard*, a Persian rice pudding made with rosewater, saffron, and cinnamon. I took a pudding—I needed some sugar in my system—and sat next to my father.

The scent of cinnamon made me close my eyes and think of happiness. Was I happy with my life? I had survived Evin, married the man I loved—even if under strange circumstances—had two beautiful children, a nice house, and, altogether, a wonderful Canadian life. Was happiness supposed to be an intense emotion? When I thought of happiness, my memories carried me back to my childhood days by the Caspian Sea when I munched on cinnamon cookies on the beach, watching the sunset.

"Marina, your mother forgave you before she died," my father suddenly announced.

"What?" I heard myself say.

"Yes, she forgave you."

I stared at him and a strange feeling rushed from my stomach to my chest. It saturated my heart and lungs in what felt like a thick, chalky liquid, and for a moment I thought I would vomit. But I didn't. Instead, to my own astonishment, I began to scream. I wasn't saying anything; I was just screaming. I had not screamed while being tortured. Not because I was resisting, but because every lash that landed on the bare soles of my feet somehow drained every ounce of my energy. Under torture, I couldn't breathe properly, as if I had forgotten how. The man who was beating me, Hamehd, thought my silence was a sign of resistance and flogged me even harder. Why was I screaming now? I didn't know, but I couldn't stop. I expected to bleed from my eyes and nose and ears and my skin to rupture. Anger. An emotion I had not felt since I could remember.

My screams became so urgent I couldn't catch my breath. I ran to find air.

Faces around me were a blur of colours and lines that blended and moved, but sometimes a face came into focus and all I could absorb from it was a sense of shock and fear. I landed in the front yard, still screaming. I needed someone to help me stop, but everyone was staring at me. I collapsed. A friend of mine who is a medical doctor bent over me. "You're okay," she said. "Everything is okay. Look at me and breathe." I gazed into her familiar brown eyes. I trusted her, had always trusted her. Her husband had been Andre's colleague in Iran, and she had been our family physician there. I concentrated on her voice.

I can't remember how I got home, but in the days that followed no one phoned to see how I was doing. No one asked why I had behaved the way I had. I guessed they assumed that I was upset because of my mother's death. Except, that kind of an outburst wasn't like me at all. What I had done was not normal in any way. *That* was not grief. Why didn't people ask me anything? Maybe they were doing the right thing. Maybe I had to continue doing what I had done for all those years and look ahead. I had a job, a family, a life, and I had to attend to them. So I tried to do just that. I kept on serving quarter-chicken dinners at the local Swiss Chalet where I worked, and I smiled at my customers and inquired if they wanted fries or salad with their meal. Then, every weekday after my lunch shift, I picked up my kids from school, went home, did laundry, and made dinner.

# Ed's Receipt

In the spring of 1994, I began working part-time at a McDonald's. Even though Andre's salary wasn't too bad, we had been unable to save any money. My parents were now living with us and my children were growing up; expenses were on the rise. Michael was five and a half and in kindergarten at the time, and Thomas was a year old. My mother agreed to look after Thomas while I was at work. She was good to my children and gave them the love she had never given me. With my first paycheque—about three hundred dollars—I bought a swing set for the boys. I was so proud of contributing to my family's finances.

When my parents first arrived in Canada, they were happy to be with us. But they had expected life here to be easier than it was. I simply couldn't meet their expectations. I was too busy working, and when I *was* home, I spent most of my time with my children. I had vowed to be a good mother, and I tried to accomplish this by being present in my children's lives. The boys and I went to the park, swimming pool, library, and movies when they were old enough. We biked and took long walks. Eventually, I signed Michael and Thomas up for soccer and piano lessons, and Andre coached their soccer teams. I wanted them to have the opportunities I had never had. Still, I tried not to spoil them. They knew they couldn't have everything they wanted. Andre and I worked hard, and we made it clear that we expected them to do the same. As a result, they did well in school.

My parents soon began to feel isolated in Canada. My father coped better with his adopted country than my mother did because he spoke English, but my mother's English was so limited that she stayed at home most of the time. She quickly became bored. In Iran, she had had friends and relatives to fill her time; in Toronto, she had no one except Alik, my father, Andre and me and our two boys. She couldn't make new friends because she spoke so little English and our neighbourhood was predominantly "white," with few Persians other than us. As well, we lived in a small semi-detached house, which didn't give any of us much privacy from one another. All these problems together with the long, harsh Canadian winters took their toll on my mother. She once told me she felt as if she were in prison. I wanted to say that she had no idea what being in prison was like, but I bit my tongue. Before long, she grew irritable and got upset over little things. I prayed she would come to see that if she and my father had stayed in Tehran, their lives would have been much more difficult. Before Andre and I left Iran, and even when Andre's work caused us to live away from Tehran, across the country in the city of Zahedan, we'd paid half my parents' rent because we knew that if we didn't, they would be unable to live in a good neighbourhood. Prices had soared after the revolution, and middle-class families found it hard to pay their bills. My parents might not have a life of luxury in Canada, but they were safe and relatively comfortable. At least, this was how I saw it. Yet my mother was not happy. We had fight after fight, and after a while, we were barely talking to each other. My parents informed me that if I wanted them to babysit Thomas when I was at work, I had to pay them. I agreed. The situation became increasingly tough to bear, but I kept up hope that their dissatisfaction would pass. Andre was very patient, but my parents' behaviour caused him a great deal of stress, too.

In 1997 when I heard that a new Swiss Chalet would soon open close to my house, I applied for a job there and was hired. Every day, I went straight to work after dropping Michael off at school, then picked him up after my shift ended. For the first three years or so, I usually walked to the restaurant, which took me about half an hour; when the weather was good, I rode my bike—I had bought it for five dollars at a garage sale. After arriving at work, I did the morning prep: chopped and diced all the vegetables for the day and made salads and coleslaw before the restaurant opened at 11:00 a.m. At lunchtime on weekdays, I waitressed. I now earned tips, and compared with McDonald's, I had a better income. I liked my boss and co-workers, and before long, I had regular customers who would tell me about themselves and their families.

My customers often remarked that I had a "cute" accent and would ask me where I was from, and I would encourage them to guess. Most thought I was Italian, or South American, even French. When I said that I was from Iran, they were surprised. Some knew a few things about Iran, and said I must be very happy to be in Canada. I told them I was. Many people, however, did not know much about Iran at all, and believed that it was similar to Afghanistan, when in fact the two countries are very different. Others thought that because I was from the Middle East, I was an Arab. I found this frustrating and explained to them that Arabs and Persians are two distinct peoples.

Historically, Persians are the people of the Great Persian Empire, which became the first superpower of the world about twenty-five hundred years ago. Persia is the land of the great Achaemenid kings (circa 550 BC to 330 BC) Cyrus and Dariush; they made Persia the largest empire the world had ever seen. These kings were not mere conquerors; they showed respect and tolerance toward other cultures. Arabs trace their ancestry to the tribes of Arabia, who were the original inhabitants of the Arabian Peninsula and the Syrian Desert. Arabs speak Arabic; Persians (Iranians) speak Persian (Farsi).

After two years of working at Swiss Chalet, I seemed to know most of the people in the community. It felt good. My biggest disappointment lay in not being able to return to school. I only had a high-school diploma and wanted to go on to university. However, that was impossible; we couldn't afford it. I had to think about my children's futures.

Living in a "normal" town and working a "normal" job almost made me believe that I was a "normal" person. People told me that I was cheerful, friendly, and kind. Why would anyone be any other way living in a country like Canada? No one ever asked me about the details of my life in Iran, and I was relieved that they didn't. The last thing I wanted was to revisit the past. However, life has its ways of reminding us about what we do not want to remember.

One winter day a few months before my mother's death, the first customer who came into the restaurant was a man in his late sixties. His grey hair was thinning and he was wearing a navy suit and a white shirt.

"Table for one?" I asked him from behind the hostess stand.

"No, two," he answered.

People waiting for people—this was usually the case at lunchtime. I always ended up having four or five tables with people waiting for someone to show up. Then everyone would arrive at once, and I'd have to deal with customers who wanted their food served immediately. Canadians, I discovered, were always in a rush.

"Would you like to sit by the window?" I asked the man.

"Sure," he replied.

I seated him at table five, put the menu in front of him, and walked to the kitchen. It was almost 11:30 a.m. Jimmy, the other daytime server, had just arrived. He was supposed to be in at 11:00, but he was always late. I didn't mind. Our lunch rush didn't start until noon. Although my shift ended at three, Jimmy would let me leave earlier if the restaurant wasn't busy. We had a give-and-take. We got along. He was in his late twenties, and trying to decide what to do with his life. Most of our servers were students. For them, working at Swiss Chalet was a passing moment. For me, it had become destiny. I wasn't unhappy about that. I knew my children would have the opportunity to follow their dreams far from wars and revolutions.

Putting on my name tag, I walked back to table five. The man was looking out the window. It had started to snow.

"Something to drink while you're waiting?" I asked.

"Two waters and two of your specials."

"Would you like me to place your order right now? The food won't take more than ten minutes to get here."

"The sooner the better."

By the time I delivered the meals, the man's friend—predictably—still hadn't arrived.

"Would you like me to take your friend's food back to the kitchen to keep it warm?" I said.

"No, leave it."

I put both orders on the table and walked away. A couple of minutes later, as I was seating another table, the man at table five, who was still eating alone, waved me over.

"Yes?" I said, guessing that he probably wanted me to remove his friend's food.

"Can we have two glasses of your white house wine? And the ketchup bottle is almost empty. My wife likes ketchup. Can you get us another bottle?" he said.

"Sure."

I poured two glasses of wine at the bar, watching table five. The

man was talking to himself. Something was not right. I delivered
the wine.

"Thank you," he said with his mouth full.

I walked to the hostess stand to greet the elderly couple waiting
at the entrance. They were regulars, and I knew that the husband,
Mark, had Alzheimer's disease. Helen, his wife, was small, delicate,
and still beautiful, with deep blue eyes and short grey hair. Mark
was tall and handsome, with kind brown eyes, his well-made suit
always perfectly pressed. I seated the couple at table six and looked
at the man at table five. He was still alone.

"Heather, don't do this," I heard him say softly, and I knew for
sure that his wife would not arrive.

I went to table six to take Mark's and Helen's orders.

"We'll have the quarter-chicken special," Helen said, "but salad
instead of fries. I'll need extra napkins. Oh—and you remember
that Mark likes extra Italian dressing on his salad."

"Of course," I said, nodding.

Mark stared vacantly at me.

"How are you today, Mark?" I asked, but he didn't reply.

The man at table five had finished eating. Both wineglasses
stood empty on the table. He waved me over again.

"Yes?"

"We're done. I guess Heather wasn't too hungry. She hasn't been
eating much lately. I think she's on a diet. She doesn't listen to me
when I tell her to eat more. She's always been stubborn. Today is
our fortieth wedding anniversary."

"Maybe Heather would like to have her food later. I can wrap it
to go," I said. My voice sounded weak and distant to me.

"Thank you, but she doesn't like the taste of leftover chicken."

"Can I get you anything else?"

"What's your name?" He narrowed his eyes, trying to read my
name tag.

"Marina."

"Thank you, Marina. You've been very kind."

My face felt hot.

"Maybe Heather would like a slice of apple pie," I suggested, uncertain why I was playing along.

"That's a good idea. I think she would. One slice of apple pie with two forks, please, and two coffees."

I went to the kitchen. Table six's meals were ready. I delivered them.

"Who are you?" Mark asked me.

"Mark, this lady is our waitress. We're here to have lunch. See? Your favourite. Chicken and salad. I'll cut your chicken for you."

"This is nice," he said, and smiled at me. "Are you coming with us?"

I smiled back. "Can I get you anything else?"

"No, thank you," said Helen.

I took one slice of apple pie and two coffees to table five.

"My name is Ed," said the man, glancing down.

"Nice to meet you, Ed."

"You're probably wondering ..."

"I understand."

Ed looked up. "She died six months ago." He started eating his pie.

I gazed at his sad, clean-shaven face. A man having lunch at a Swiss Chalet restaurant with the memory of his wife. Where were my memories? What had I done with them?

Fighting my tears, I ran into the walk-in fridge and stayed there a few minutes. The silence and the cool dark air calmed me down.

By the time I returned to table five, Ed had left. On the back of the receipt, he had written "May God bless you—Ed." I put the receipt in my pocket.

It was snowing heavily now. The world resembled a snow globe.

Up and down Yonge Street, cars and pedestrians inched along, burdened by the heavy whiteness. I felt trapped. There was a big knot in my chest.

I had to get out of the restaurant.

"I'm going home," I said to Jimmy.

"You okay?" he asked.

"I have a headache."

I almost raced to the old green Ford Escort I had bought a few months earlier. Once I had closed the door behind me, tears rolled down my face. Deep inside, I knew that the normalcy I had been clinging to was not real. I envied Ed. He was brave enough to face his loss. He was grieving. I had never grieved. I had fled from my pain, pretended it didn't exist. Maybe Ed was crazy, but at least he acknowledged the ghosts that haunted him. I felt like a fraud. I thought about Mark. What if one day I was condemned to forget like him? But I had a family, a job, and a life, and I had to keep on going.

When I got home, I secured Ed's receipt to my fridge door. I needed to see it every day so that maybe one day I might become brave.

ONE LATE-JULY EVENING in 2000, I was making spaghetti and meat sauce while the boys were busy playing upstairs. Shortly after my mother's death in March of that year, my father moved out of our house to a small apartment in a quiet and well-maintained seniors building, and in early July, we moved into a detached house, the picture-perfect suburban Canadian dream home, with four bedrooms and two and a half baths. Before our move, whenever I had a few minutes after work prior to picking up the kids, I would drive to the new house, park around the corner, and gaze at our future home. I'd imagine my children in their freshly painted bedrooms and Andre and me in our spacious master bedroom. What colour would I paint the living room? No more crazy yellows. A lilac, maybe?

The meat sauce came to a boil, and the scent of onions, tomatoes, and beef filled the house. I added a little oregano to the sauce, and my mind drifted.

*Evin. One of my interrogators, Ali, is reading to me from the Koran. The chapter is about the Virgin Mary. She's blessed. Why doesn't she help me go home?*

*They have tied me up to a bare wooden bed and are lashing the soles of my feet. Pain and nothing else. What have I done to deserve this? "Where's Shahrzad?" they keep on asking me. I don't know, or I would have told them.*

*It's dark and cold. I just want to go home and sleep in my bed, but I'm in a solitary cell, and a dirty, smelly military blanket is covering me. When I close my eyes, I can smell my mother's scent—a mix of Chanel No. 5 and cigarettes—and feel the warmth of her body.*

*Someone is kicking me. My whole body is aching. "Get up! Get up!" someone yells. It's my interrogator Hamehd.*

*I'm tied to a wooden pole. There are other prisoners like me here. Armed guards have surrounded us. My feet hurt. I'm tired. So tired.*

*The small body of my friend Sarah is hanging from a noose made of head scarves. Her face is blue. "Marina! Run! Get scissors! Hurry! Now!" Sheida yells. I run.*

*Ali is ripping off my clothes. He's on top of me and is holding down my wrists with his hands. I try to push him away but can't. I feel a terrible pain between my legs. I scream.*

*I'm walking away from Evin. They have finally let me go. It's raining, and it's cold.*

*Why did I leave my friends behind?*

I jolted back to reality at the sound of the fire alarm. Smoke was everywhere. The sauce had hardened into a strange black substance. I turned off the burner and opened all the windows. How had this happened? I was standing right at the stove!

My children ran down the stairs. "Mom, what's going on?"

"Don't worry. I just burned the food."

I hadn't thought of Evin since my release—had avoided it at all costs. Why was I thinking about it now? Why were my memories as clear and fresh in my mind as if my imprisonment had occurred last week?

That night, after a hot day that ended with a thunderstorm, I opened one of our bedroom windows before going to sleep. I had already kissed Andre good night, and, as usual, he had fallen asleep immediately. He snored mildly when he lay on his back, and I listened to the peaceful sounds he made. He was very handsome, maybe even more than when I had met him a few months before my arrest. He had matured, lost his boyish, shy look. I gazed at his perfect face: the gentle curved lines of his closed eyes and his blond eyelashes, his nose narrow and straight, his lips not too thick and not too thin. I fell in love with him the moment I saw him at our church in Tehran, and I think he fell in love with me the moment he laid eyes on me. Then Evin happened. In the prison, I hung on to his memory to survive. I hung on to my recollection of his perfect face and the thought that someone beautiful was in love with me. Before Evin, Andre had never told me he loved me, but I chose to believe it, and his love became my hope, a light that would guide me back to him one day. It would have been so much easier for him to forget me while I was in prison and move on, but he didn't. He waited for the girl he loved. Except, the girl who walked out of Evin was different from the one who'd been led in. Yes, different. But I didn't want to be. I wanted to be the same. I wanted everything to be the same.

"I was ready for you to come home with a baby in your arms," Andre said to me shortly after my release, "and I would have loved you just the same. Nothing would have changed for me."

Back then, he had no way of knowing just what had happened to me in Evin, but he had heard rumours about the rape of young women. Those two sentences he uttered to me in March 1984 were the closest anyone came to acknowledging my ordeal. Andre didn't ask me to marry him. Instead, he asked, "When should we get married?" And I would have married him on the spot had it been possible.

Perhaps I betrayed Andre by marrying him. I hadn't told him the truth. Except, how could I have? How could I put my experiences in Evin prison into words? When I married Andre, did I truly love him, or was I just following a memory? How can you live a lie with someone you love?

I watched the curtain in front of the open window swell in the breeze, pregnant with the light of the full moon. The delicate fabric fluttered and rose. I imagined a silver angel trying to enter the room to tell me something that would lift the terrible weight I felt. Where was my angel? The angel I dreamed of when *Bahboo* died. The Angel of Death, who, to my surprise, didn't look scary at all; the one who comforted me and held me in his gentle arms. Maybe I had disappointed him, too.

That night I dreamed I was standing by a road in the middle of a desert. There was no one around. The road was a grey line on a sea of sand that covered the world. There were no trees, no plants, and no animals, and the sky was a dome of intense blue, as hostile as everything else. I was waiting for Andre to pick me up, but I didn't know why I was in the desert or where I was supposed to go. Andre was late. After a while I began to feel frightened, thinking he had forgotten me. Then a black car appeared on the horizon, and I became even more frightened because I knew the driver was not Andre. I thought of running, but there was nowhere to go. The black car, a Mercedes, stopped right before me, and the front window on the driver's side rolled down. Ali sat behind the wheel.

"Waiting for someone?" he asked.

"Andre is picking me up," I explained.

"Get in the car, Marina. No one is coming," he said, smiling.

And I awoke, covered in sweat.

I didn't dare remain in bed any longer. I slipped out and went downstairs to the kitchen. I had not dreamed of Ali in years. What did he want from me? I took a deep breath and tried to collect myself. He was dead. He wasn't going to show up at our door and claim me back. I had just had a dream, a stupid dream. But what if the dream meant something? I began to sob.

Only a few days after my arrest, Ali saved me from execution. In 1982, court in Evin prison was a Sharia judge who sat behind a desk in a hallway or in a room with a pile of files in front of him. Every day, tens of young people were being arrested and the prison was operating far beyond capacity. Evin had been built for a few hundred prisoners, not for thousands. As a result, prisoners had to be processed quickly. The Sharia judge would spend moments on each file and pass verdicts as fast as he could. If a prisoner had not cooperated and had talked back to the interrogators, he or she could easily receive a death sentence or many years in prison. I had two interrogators: Hamehd and Ali. Hamehd lashed me as Ali watched. Hamehd believed I was lying, but Ali thought I was telling the truth. Ali later told me that he had used his influence to reduce my death sentence to life in prison. Then, five months later, he forced me to marry him, threatening to arrest my parents and Andre if I refused him. I hated him for it. I was so terribly ashamed of our marriage that I kept it a secret. As long as I was a prisoner living in the world of Evin, my family didn't need to know that I was sleeping with my interrogator.

After I married Ali, I spent several months in solitary confinement. One has a great deal of time to think in solitary. I wondered why Ali had saved my life and married me. Was he truly in love with me, as he claimed? At the time, the only books available to prisoners were the Koran and books on Islam, so I read them to pass the time. In the Koran, I found this verse (Koran 4:3): "Marry such women [captive women taken in war] as seem good to you, two and three and four; but if you fear that you will not do justice, then only one, or what your right hands possess [captive women]."

A war waged between the Islamic government of Iran and the "anti-revolutionaries," and I had become a prisoner of it. As I understood it, according to the laws of Islam, I had literally become Ali's property. I wondered if he had married any other girls. Maybe it was common practice in the prison. I asked Ali, and he said I was his only wife, but could I trust his word?

Ali took me on short leaves of absence to see his parents and sister. His mother told me that he had been a political prisoner during the time of the shah. I saw the lash marks on his back. He had been a victim like me. I gradually realized that the man I considered evil was human after all. His parents, always kind and generous to me, knew that he was a torturer in Evin, but they were proud of him and his job. From their perspective, their son was protecting their way of life, his country, and Islam. They were blind to the cruelty of what he was doing because they were able to justify it. His family accepted me only because I had agreed to convert to Islam. In their belief, my conversion washed away all my sins.

Fourteen months after our marriage, Ali resigned from his job. He told me that he had clashed with the prosecutor of Tehran, Assadollah-eh Ladjevardi, who was also warden of Evin prison. A month later, as we were leaving his parents' house after dinner one night, Ali was gunned down by a man on a motorcycle and died in my arms. With his last breath, he asked his father to make sure that I was returned safely to my family. The Mojahedin-eh Khalgh, a Marxist-Islamist group that had murdered many government officials, was blamed for the assassination. But Ali's father believed that it was an inside job and Ladjevardi had ordered it. Ladjevardi, known as the Butcher of Evin and responsible for the torture and execution of thousands of prisoners, kept me in the prison for six months after Ali's death and wanted to marry me off to another guard, but Ali's father used his connection to Ayatollah Khomeini to secure my release. He probably even bribed a few Evin officials to get me out. Apparently, Ladjevardi was removed from his post sometime in late 1984 or early 1985, but, to avoid assassination, he lived in Evin with his family for a while afterward. He was murdered in broad daylight in the Grand Bazaar of Tehran in 1998.

*Not* dreaming of Ali would have been abnormal. How could I just forget and move on? I had betrayed Andre and my prison friends—and I had betrayed God. Was there a way I could make things right?

# My Mother's Crocheted Tablecloth

One nightmare followed another, and eventually, I didn't want to go to bed. Except I had to, because if I didn't, I would have to explain to Andre what was going on, and I wasn't ready for that. So every evening I kissed him good night and tossed and turned until at last I fell asleep. Then the nightmares came. I had the road dream at least twice a week. Sometimes I was in a desert and sometimes in the middle of a snowstorm, waiting for Andre, a friend, or my mother or father to pick me up—but Ali always showed up, instead. Sometimes I dreamed of being tied to a pole and lashed, or being locked up in a cold, dark cell. After a while, I realized that I had to do something or I would lose my mind. Yet what could I do?

One night as I lay sleepless in my bed, staring at the ceiling, I felt a presence in my bedroom. I looked toward the foot of my bed and saw a figure in the faint yellow light seeping in from the hallway night light. Someone stood there. It was my mother. She was wrapped in a shroud, which was covered with one of the delicate tablecloths she had crocheted from silk yarn. I tried to reach out and wake Andre, but I couldn't move a finger. I tried to cry out, but it was as if my lips were sealed. I stared at my mother. She was still and didn't say anything. I don't know how long I lay in that frozen state, but when I could finally move, she disappeared.

The next day, I told Andre what I had seen.

"You have to let her go," he said.

"I *have* let her go."

"If you had, she wouldn't have come to you. There are unresolved issues between you. You have to forgive her."

"I have!"

"Have you?"

"I thought I had."

"Why don't you think of all the things you wanted to say to her but never did, and say them as if she were in the same room? Or write her a letter. I don't know. But do something, or neither of you will have peace."

He was right. I had to face my problems.

Eight years later, as I was researching the effects of torture on young people under the age of eighteen, I had a conversation with Dr. Jean Wittenberg, a University of Toronto professor who is also a project director in the Research Institute as well as the head of the Infant Psychiatry Program at the Hospital for Sick Children in Toronto. I was hoping that my research would make it possible for me to better understand myself and help others who had been tortured at a young age. Dr. Wittenberg told me that he didn't have any experience with young victims of torture, but he *had* worked with children who had been badly abused, so we talked about the effects of trauma on young people in that context. I mentioned that for a long time after my release from Evin, I felt normal. I never thought about the prison, and for many years, I had no nightmares or flashbacks. But then nightmares and flashbacks began to plague me. I wanted to know if this was common. Dr. Wittenberg noted that it was not at all unusual for children to behave normally after a traumatic experience. He explained that they sometimes enclose their trauma in a bubble, put the bubble on their shoulder, and walk through life that way. They avoid anything that threatens to burst their bubble. As a result, they avoid what may be important parts of life. They can live like this for many years, until one day, somehow, that bubble bursts and they are forced to face their trauma. This is when symptoms appear. Each individual has a different way of dealing with trauma and its aftermath. The methods depend on many factors—genetics, the environment, and upbringing. I think the reason I chose to write as a way of coping goes back to my childhood.

As a child and then a teenager, I had always taken refuge in books. At the age of nine, I discovered a bookstore within walking distance of my house in downtown Tehran that sold only secondhand English-language books. The owner, Albert, a kind Armenian Iranian, knew I didn't have much money, so he lent me books. I devoured them. Within three or four years, I'd developed a pattern: I would read Jane Austen whenever I was sad or stressed—which, after the success of the Islamic Revolution in 1979, was frequently. Austen's writing transported me to a world much simpler and more predictable than my own. I became especially addicted to *Pride and Prejudice* and read it many times. Now I realized that I had not touched her books in years. Maybe she was what I needed. Except, what was the point of hiding in a fictional world? It would make me feel better for a few hours, but then I would have to return to reality. I was thirty-five years old. If I died tomorrow, half my life would be a lie, a desperate attempt to escape the truth. I had wanted to become a medical doctor. Instead, I became a political prisoner. After my release from prison, I spent my life trying to forget the horror I had witnessed.

"What would Jane Austen do?" I asked myself. The answer was clear: she would write. Could *I* write? I used to be able to. I wouldn't have to write for an audience; I could write for myself. As Andre had suggested, writing could help me.

Even though I was fluent in Persian and loved Persian literature, in a way Jane Austen, Charlotte and Emily Brontë, Emily Dickinson, Charles Dickens, and Mark Twain were my best friends. I decided to write in English.

I went to the local Business Depot and bought a notebook. Then, every day after my shift at Swiss Chalet, which now ended at 2:00 p.m., I went to a Second Cup coffee shop close to work and wrote until 3:20 p.m., when I had to go pick up my kids from school. I didn't write at home because Andre sometimes worked from home and I didn't want him to know about my memoir. I wasn't ready to share secrets I had protected for seventeen years.

My first draft was eighty pages long. Like a nightmare, the writing was raw and disjointed, and anyone reading my memoir at that stage would not have been able to understand much. It would have been like looking at a stranger's photo album.

I had expected to feel better once I'd put everything down on paper, but I felt worse. I could hardly sleep at night and became withdrawn and irritable. Maybe I was going crazy. Then I began to question what use my story served if my memoir remained hidden in my underwear drawer and no one ever read my words. My secrets would still be secrets; nothing would have changed, and I would still suffer. But I was terrified to go public. Yes, this was it. I was terrified. Fear had become my prison—a prison only I held the key to. I asked myself why I had survived. Was it because I was better than those who had died? I knew very well that wasn't the case. They were the heroes, not me. Yet I was here, and they were not, and no one could change that. Did this mean that I should continue being a smiling mother, a good housewife, and a hard-working waitress living the Canadian dream? The thought made me feel sick. I couldn't keep up the charade any longer. It was suffocating me. I had to find air. The only way was to share my story, even though the prospect scared me to death.

I started to worry that my memory wasn't as accurate as I had always believed it to be. Maybe I had forgotten things or didn't remember them exactly as they had happened. Maybe I should write my memoir as fiction and tell the world it was only partly true. Except, I wasn't a Jane Austen, much as I wished I could be. Besides, hiding behind fiction would undermine the reason I had decided to share my story: at last I had chosen to be unafraid, and concealing the truth under layers of imagination would be cowardly. More important, it would give the government of Iran an opportunity to dismiss my testimony, claiming I had made everything up.

My memory might be flawed, but hundreds of people with imperfect recall have written memoirs. These people have told their stories because they believe that what they have to say is worthwhile. Many Holocaust survivors, for example, have written their memoirs years and years later. I believed I had the right— maybe even the duty—to do the same.

I looked up *memoir* in the *Oxford English Dictionary*: "a historical account or biography written from personal knowledge." I wasn't a historian or a journalist, but this didn't mean I was insignificant. I had been in Evin without pen and paper. Even if I had had them, in Evin I would never have been allowed to write anything down. The prison authorities never permitted documentation of any of the atrocities they committed. Yet now that I thought about it, I knew that even if they had let me, I would probably never have written a word as the horror unfolded: I wanted it obliterated from existence. Now, many years later, I had had time to understand the importance of memory and the right to bear witness.

In early June 2002, I gathered enough courage to share my manuscript with Andre. Before I shared my story with the world, I had to put things straight at home. I had no idea how Andre would respond. He had every right to become angry. He might even hate me for having married Ali and keeping it secret. I was aware that my confession could end our marriage of seventeen years.

When I first told Andre I was writing about Evin and promised him I would share my work with him when I was ready, he didn't react to the news; and he never asked me about my work or how it was progressing. A part of him still didn't want to know. But there was no way out for either of us now.

I finally gave him the manuscript, rewritten and typed, and he took it from me without a word and put it under his side of our bed. I asked him the next day if he had read it, and he said no, that it was too difficult for him. He promised, though, that he would read it as soon as he was ready.

On a Saturday three days later, I was at work at Swiss Chalet—instead of my regular day shift, in the summertime I worked four or five nights a week and on weekends in order to spend summer holidays with my children—when I saw Andre and our two sons walk into the restaurant. I seated them in my section, brought them their drinks, and wrote down their orders. As I was putting their quarter-chicken dinners on the table, Andre said, "I've read it."

I froze. "You have?"

I recognized the expression on his face. It was sadness.

"We'll talk at home," he said.

The rest of my shift was unbearable. I couldn't concentrate. My co-workers thought I was ill. I said I had a headache and left the restaurant a little earlier than usual.

The streets floated by as I drove home. I parked the car in the driveway but couldn't move for some time. The light in my elder son's bedroom was on; he was probably playing video games. I gazed at my house, and it was as if I were looking at it from a distance. I considered my life. I had most of what I had dreamed of as a girl: I had wanted Andre, and I had wanted to have children with him and live in a nice house in a free country. Yet now that I had those things, I hated myself and felt like an intruder.

The sweet scent of the phlox in the garden enveloped me as I stepped out of my car and approached the front door. I turned my key in the lock—and I knew that my world was about to change.

I found Andre in our bedroom.

"Why didn't you tell me earlier?" he asked with a look in his eyes I had never seen before, a combination of pain, sadness, disappointment, and confusion. My silence had walled him protectively, but now the sheltering walls had collapsed.

"I couldn't. Will you forgive me?"

The hurt in his eyes melted away.

"There's nothing to forgive. Will you forgive me?" he said.

"For what?"

"For not asking."

He still loved me. I should have known that he would not turn his back on me. As he put his arms around me, I felt a huge relief, and some of the weight I had carried for so long dropped away. My good, dear Andre was so kind and faithful to me. Yet I didn't deserve it. If he had asked me about Evin right after my release, I probably would not have told him much. What I had needed most back then was to know that when I was ready to talk, someone would listen.

"What do you want to do with the manuscript?" Andre asked.

"I've decided to publish it. Except, I don't think it's ready. I want to take a few writing courses. The School of Continuing Studies at the University of Toronto offers some and there are no prerequisites, but each course costs about five hundred dollars. Can we afford it?"

"Yes, we can. Go ahead. I understand that this is something you have to do."

After all those years, Andre's goodness still astonished me. He could have said no. Financially, we were doing okay, but we didn't have much extra money. Yet this was Andre's way. Our marriage had not been an entirely smooth ride—we had had our fights. But he always came through for me when I needed him most. He'd waited for me while I was in prison and he'd married me. In doing so, he'd put his life in danger. With his relentless support and hard work, he'd made it possible for us to leave Iran, come to Canada, and start a new life. Our arrival in Canada was a huge victory. But after we arrived here, we still had a long way to travel before either of us could feel almost at home in our new country.

# Chocolate-Chip Cookies

W hen I was fifteen years old, Alik, who had immigrated to Canada in 1979, wrote to me about Yonge Street. He told me that it began at the foot of Lake Ontario in downtown Toronto and ran northward some nineteen hundred kilometres, making it at the time the longest street in the world. This was unimaginable for me, and as I tried to picture it, I saw the Yellow Brick Road leading to the Emerald City in *The Wizard of Oz*. Yonge Street had to be full of mystery and adventure.

On August 28, 1991, as our plane flew west over the Atlantic Ocean toward Canada, I wondered what our new country was truly like. Alik had sent me photos of his house in the suburbs of Toronto. The house was big—very big compared with the small apartments I had lived in most of my life—and it looked so beautiful that it seemed fictional, but Alik told me that according to Canadian standards, it was an average-size house. He had also sent me photos of Niagara Falls, the CN Tower, and the University of Toronto, but he might as well have sent me pictures of Narnia or some other imaginary land. Alik's photos all seemed alien. Even Canadian colours looked different from the colours in my life: the blues were deeper, the browns stronger, the reds more vibrant, the yellows sharper, the greens more alive, and the pinks and purples dreamier. In my mind, Canada was a cold land where it snowed and snowed in winter. The short summer unfolded on the shores of a blue lake surrounded by the emerald green of pine-covered hills. Except, how friendly was this magical land? Could we find our way in its strange vastness?

Michael was two and a half at the time of our trip from Hungary to Canada, and fortunately, he slept for most of the flight. When he awoke, we were close to Toronto. I told him to look out the window at the beautiful clouds.

"Is that Canada?" he asked, pointing at an enormous cumu-lonimbus cloud. I had told him so much about our new country that he was quite excited about it. I had promised him that we would make big snowmen in winter and swim in crystal-clear lakes in summer.

"No, honey, that's a cloud. Canada is down there ... below the clouds ... we can't see it yet."

"Snowman!" he cried, pointing at another cloud.

*Even God makes snowmen here,* I thought.

That day, the day we arrived in Canada, I wore my nicest dress, which my mother had made. It was burgundy and very stylish. I had even bought new shoes to go with it. They were black and had three-inch heels. I wanted to blend with the crowd. I wanted to look Canadian. I believed that the people who lived in a wealthy country like Canada had to be fashionable. As we made our way through Pearson Airport, I was surprised to see that most women were wearing blue jeans or khaki pants. But it didn't matter. One should be well dressed when beginning a new life. I wanted to mark the occasion properly.

I can't remember much about Pearson Airport. My memory is a jumble of images: rushing along hallways with Michael in my arms, standing in lines, and answering a customs officer's questions. Once we made it to the public concourse, I wanted to scream Alik's name, but I contained myself. Although I had not seen him in twelve years, I spotted him immediately. His hair had greyed and thinned, but he looked the same. At six-foot-seven he was easy to notice. His head bobbed enthusiastically above the waiting crowd. We hugged and couldn't let go.

I sat in the back seat of Alik's car and stared at the scenery as we drove to his house. We were to stay at his place until we could find an apartment. The sky was an indigo blue, as unrealistic as the sky in a child's painting. And the horizon seemed so far away, farther than I had ever seen it. It was August and the fields were a luminescent green; the cornfields seemed to stretch all the way to the North Pole. Buildings were scarce, and the scents of grass, water, and soil saturated the air.

"Where's Toronto?" I asked Alik.

"Toronto!" Michael exclaimed, pointing at horses in a farmer's field.

"My house is in the suburbs," Alik said, as if this explained everything. We had suburbs in Tehran, but we had almost no open spaces between them. What I now saw were farmland and wilderness.

The car moved along the highway, and after a few minutes, a town with rows of almost identical brick houses came into view. They all had front yards that, unlike the ones in Tehran, were not fenced in behind tall walls. Flower beds overflowed with reds, oranges, and pinks. We had arrived. I was worried but hopeful. How could I not find my way to a good life in a land of so many intense colours? As we walked into Alik's house, I felt like an astronaut on her first Martian expedition.

I had expected Alik and his wife to ask me about Evin, but they didn't. The silence I had faced in Iran, the one I had helped sustain after my release from prison, had stretched all the way across the ocean. I could almost see it now. It looked like a giant poisonous jellyfish that had swallowed the world. I did not want pity, but I needed acknowledgment—not only of my own experience, but also of all I had witnessed. My cellmates and I had suffered, and deep in my heart, I was desperate to know that our suffering had not been meaningless.

The day after we arrived, Andre began looking for a job and Michael and I set out to explore our new country. The first time I took Michael to a park in Canada, it was drizzling, but we went anyway.

Before coming to Canada, we had spent ten months in Hungary. In Budapest, people sometimes called me "Gypsy" and swore at me on the bus or at the park. I didn't take it personally. I had nothing against Roma people, but I was not a Gypsy. I had dark eyes and long dark hair, and I guessed that Hungarians had never seen an Iranian, so I couldn't blame them for their ignorance. After all, they had lived in a closed society for many years (we arrived there in 1990 shortly after the fall of Communism). I hoped that things were different in Canada and that I wouldn't be judged because of the colour of my hair or skin.

I put Michael in a swing and pushed him as hard as I could, and he laughed in delight, crying, "Higher! Higher!" No one else was at the park, but after a few minutes, a man with a girl about Michael's age joined us. I decided the man was the girl's grandfather. Michael got off the swing and went to the slide, and the man put the little girl in a swing. I watched them. The man smiled at me. I smiled an uncertain smile in return. He wore black casual pants and a beige jacket. Unlike me, he seemed very much at ease. He and the child blended with Planet Canada, not at all aware of its strangeness. Their every step told me that they knew what they were doing, when my every move was full of doubt and insecurity. I wondered how many times they had already come to this park. They had probably both been born in this country. This place belonged to them, and the truth was that I was an outsider—but at least I was sure that Michael would soon feel as though he had always lived here.

The rain had become heavier. The sky was an impatient shade of grey, the colour of a storm.

"Do you need a ride?" the man asked me.

I shook my head no and mumbled, "Thank you."

"Cookies! I want cookies!" Michael now cried. He had had his very first chocolate-chip cookie two days earlier, and we had no more left. I knew there was a convenience store around the corner, but I had not bought anything in Canada yet, since we were still staying at Alik's house.

"Cookies! Please, please!" Michael begged, and I scooped him up in my arms and ran toward the store as the rain drew puddles on the sidewalk. "'Rain, rain, go away, come again another day!'" I sang. I was teaching Michael to speak English, and he loved nursery rhymes.

They had so many different kinds of cookies at the store that it took me a few minutes to find the right kind. I felt dizzy. The abundance astonished me. I prayed that Michael wouldn't want to try them all. Wide-eyed, he stared at the overflowing shelves. My eyes filled with tears as I put the package in front of the cashier, a young blond woman, and gave her a twenty-dollar bill. I couldn't believe that I had become emotional buying cookies. She had no idea how treacherous my life had been and how long I had waited to come to this country.

"What a cute little boy," she said, handing me my change. "Nice shoes! Where did you get them?"

Michael was in my arms, wearing the pair of multicoloured suede shoes I had bought in Hungary.

"In Europe," I said.

"I guessed so. They don't make them so nice here. Where in Europe?"

"Hungary. We've just immigrated here."

"Do you like it so far?"

"Yes. Very much. People are nice."

I had gone to the park and now I was at the store, and no one had sworn at me. I had not been beaten up, arrested, or both for not wearing the *hejab* or for any other reason. And we had bought cookies. What more could one ask for? Michael and I skipped all the way home, singing nursery rhymes. I knew that our life in Canada would not be a fairy tale. Those require a kind of innocence that I had lost at sixteen, and since then I had not believed in "happily ever after." But here we could hope and work hard for a better life.

Andre found a job as an electrical engineer a few days after our arrival; this was close to a miracle because Canada was in a recession at the time. We rented an apartment, paid our first- and last-month's rent, and had two hundred dollars left in our bank account. Alik bought us a blue loveseat and a chair, and we purchased a cheap dining table, six chairs, a bed for Michael, and a queen-size mattress, which we put on the floor in our bedroom. Andre's boss gave us an old TV that he didn't need, and we bent a metal clothes hanger and used it as an antenna. That gave us six channels, which was much better than the two channels available in Tehran. We were grateful.

As it turned out, our apartment was on Yonge Street. I will never forget the first time I stood at the pedestrian crossing at the intersection of Yonge Street and Baif Boulevard. It was early October, and the sun still had a bit of warmth. Michael was clinging to my hand, waiting, as impatiently as I was, for the helpful little white man in the signal light to appear and indicate that it was safe to cross the street to go to the grocery store. Even though my house had not fallen on a wicked witch and a good witch had not given me ruby slippers, I was like Dorothy at the beginning of her journey. The difference was, I knew that the wizard, no matter how powerful he happened to be, could not take me back home. Even though I missed my home terribly, it didn't want me any longer.

One of the first things Andre and I did after moving into our apartment at Yonge and Baif was go to our local Catholic church. We had to give thanks to God. At the church, we met people who eventually became our good friends. One day after the Mass, Andre went upstairs to meet the organist, Flavia, and told her that he had been an organist in Tehran. Flavia invited us to her house for dinner and asked me if I would like to join her book club. Soon, the monthly book-club meetings were one of the highlights of my life. This wasn't only because of the books we read, which I greatly enjoyed, but because the book club gave me a sense of belonging. I think it was during the first meeting I attended that I briefly told the members I had been a political prisoner in Iran. They didn't ask me any questions. Ten years later, I would present them with a first draft of my memoir, *Prisoner of Tehran*.

At the church, I met a couple named Lynn and Joe, who had two young daughters. The youngest was Michael's age. They invited us to their home for our first Thanksgiving dinner in Canada. Lynn was a dental hygienist and worked part-time. We saw each other regularly and grew to be good friends. She had a car and sometimes picked up Michael and me at the apartment, and we took the kids to the library, the park, or the mall. Lynn also took us to Canada's Wonderland, which soon became Michael's favourite place to visit. With Lynn's help, I slowly began to feel I could belong in Canada.

# The *Sunday Star*

I started to improve my writing by asking my book-club friends to read my manuscript. By then, we had been meeting once a month for more than ten years. They were all very curious to read it—and once they had, their feedback and encouragement gave me the confidence I needed to take the next step and enrol in creative-writing classes.

At various events these days, Lee Gowan—my very first writing instructor at the School of Continuing Studies at the University of Toronto—sometimes tells people about the first time we met in February 2003. That day, after my shift at Swiss Chalet ended, I rushed to the store, bought two large pizzas for the kids and Andre for dinner, got changed, and then drove to Finch subway station to catch the train to the St. George Campus of the U of T. The entire trip took about an hour and a half. When I got off at St. George station and walked out onto Bedford Street, it was windy, frigid, and grey. I had checked the map and memorized my route, but I was extremely nervous, so I stopped at every corner en route and carefully looked around to make sure I had not taken a wrong turn. I was wearing my parka, hat, gloves, and my warmest boots, but my face was numb from the cold. The wind had managed to penetrate all my layers of clothing.

"What am I doing?" I asked myself somewhere along the way. Panic had crept under my skin. I was a woman from Iran with just a high-school diploma. I was only a waitress, and English was my second language; I was certain that all the students walking past me were smarter than I and much better educated. I didn't belong there at all. Then I reminded myself that I was on a mission.

As I turned onto Hoskins Avenue, I spotted the old stone building that is University College. It resembles a castle. I remembered a photo of it that Alik had sent me shortly after his arrival in Canada in 1979. On the back of it, he had written that University College was built in the mid-nineteenth century and then restored after a disastrous fire in 1890. He also mentioned that, allegedly, it was haunted. What I found most interesting about it was its asymmetry: the left half of the building is quite different architecturally from the right. I had examined the photo and thought about the people attending the University of Toronto. I had been fourteen then, living in post-revolutionary Iran: a time of slogans against the West, rhetoric against Western culture, the removal of women's rights, and the beginning of the ban on music, dance, and literature. To me, students at the University of Toronto were among the luckiest on earth. Now I was in Toronto, as unworthy as I had ever been. I chastised myself: I had to stop thinking this way. The truth was that I had to write my book and get it published. This was my second chance. This was why I had survived prison.

Standing in front of University College, I gazed up. The right tower had a window near the top, and I suddenly had an image of Rapunzel leaning out of it, throwing her thick long golden braid to the ground for Prince Charming. I pulled open the heavy wooden front door and stepped into the poorly lit foyer. A map of the building stood posted near the entrance, but I found it too confusing. I knew the room number for my class, and I knew it was on the second floor, so I followed the wide staircase, my right hand on the smooth old wooden handrail. My boots echoed against the walls and ceiling in the musty air that felt a thousand years old. Had I come here as a little girl, I would have expected a wicked witch to jump out from behind every closed door. I followed one hallway after another, until I finally found my classroom.

Lee Gowan walked into the room right on time. I had seen his photo, but he was taller than I had anticipated. He was wearing a black sweater and black pants. The desks stood in a square around the room, and I was one of fourteen students. Lee sat on the chair left empty for him. One by one, he asked us to introduce ourselves and briefly explain why we were taking a creative-writing course. Most of the students were either lawyers or office workers, and said they had always wanted to become writers. When my turn arrived, I looked down and told the truth.

"My name is Marina Nemat. I was arrested in Iran at the age of sixteen for political crimes and was tortured and came close to execution. That was almost twenty years ago, and now I want to write about it."

My heart was racing, and I felt as though every blood vessel in my body was ready to explode. Everyone was staring at me. I put my hands under my thighs and sat on them, hoping my classmates wouldn't see how badly I was shaking. I was afraid I might become too emotional. But I did not. In Evin, we had to hide our emotions from our interrogators, or they would use them against us—and we sometimes had to hide our feelings from our cellmates because we didn't want to upset them. I rarely cried in front of my friends in Evin. Instead, I saved my tears for prayer time when I covered my face with a *chador*. Most of the girls behaved the same way.

I can't remember what Lee said, but he seemed at a loss for words. He later told me that he had never heard such an unusual introduction and had been shocked.

Our first exercise was writing about an onion. The smell of onions reminded me of *Bahboo* and her cooking, so my piece ended up being about her. Exercise after exercise I became more confident with my writing and began to share bits of my memoir with the class. Lee and my fellow classmates appeared genuinely interested in my work, and their critiques helped me view my story from the perspective of a reader who didn't know much about Iran. I became aware that I needed much more detail in my story. Things that were basic knowledge to me were foreign concepts to most of my classmates. I had to explain an alien culture to the average Western reader. My story was not only about coming of age under difficult circumstances; it was about a child political prisoner who, like thousands of others, wasn't particularly political. How politically aware can you be at sixteen? Evin was a dark world of horrors, a real nightmare, and I had to make this strange concept comprehensible. The task overwhelmed me, but what I learned from Lee and later my other instructors was that I had to write the book one scene at a time, then fit the scenes together like a puzzle—which is exactly what I did.

As I wrote each scene, I felt as though I were travelling back in time. When I wrote about the lashing, I was back in Evin, feeling each lash on the soles of my feet. I remembered the strange numbness that came over me the moment I was arrested, which some people mistook for bravery, but I knew I wasn't brave at all. I had just detached myself from my body. As I recalled being tied up to a pole with armed guards pointing their guns at me, I didn't feel afraid; instead, I felt sad and tired. I just wanted them to let me go to sleep.

I had been healthy before my arrest, but in prison, I suffered from migraines and stomach problems. I developed severe acid reflux accompanied by horrible pain. After my release from Evin, I went to a specialist in internal medicine, who diagnosed me with stomach ulcers and prescribed medication and a special diet. My condition gradually improved and eventually disappeared altogether. However, once I began writing, all my physical ailments returned, and I had to see a physician again. This time medication and diet were not as helpful as they had been, probably because I was constantly reliving the same terrible experiences.

I had never talked to a psychologist or psychiatrist, and even though I had heard about flashbacks, I didn't know exactly what they were. But one day after I had begun writing, as I watched an episode of *CSI* about the rape of a young woman, I had my first flashback: Ali was there with me. I couldn't see him, but I felt him; his skin brushed against mine. I panicked and ran to the kitchen, my heart racing. Fear flooded my every cell. I gathered my strength and told myself it was only a memory. The shame I had felt so many years ago rose in me, real and present. I fought back, telling myself that *I* was in control. The shame retreated, then disappeared—but I was left shaken.

Describing flashbacks is not easy. For me, they are usually not images but extreme emotions—fear, disgust, or both—and they come out of nowhere. I am amazed that I have never had flashbacks of the torture I endured in Evin. The pain of the lash landing on the soles of my feet was beyond any I have ever experienced. Not only was the lashing painful, but it was humiliating. I never had any flashbacks about being in front of the firing squad. Even though it was terrifying, a part of me knew that death was something everyone has to face sooner or later. At that moment, if someone had given me the choice of being either lashed or killed, I would have chosen death, not because I was brave, but because I had given up. When Ali raped me on our wedding night, even though the pain was more bearable than the pain of the lash, it wounded a part of me that lashing never could. The truth is that I broke under torture; I would have told them where Shahrzad was had I known.

What Ali did to me had absolutely nothing to do with extracting information from me. When I married him, I felt I had become an object. Property. Something the world had completely forgotten and didn't care about. Ali had unlimited power over me and could do to me as he pleased. That was how I felt on my wedding night, and even though I got to know Ali better and began to feel some compassion toward him, the memories of our wedding night and the nights that followed have remained in my subconscious.

I'D HEARD that a few ex-prisoners from Evin had published their memoirs in Persian in Europe. To my knowledge, only two or three of these books have been translated into another language, and none has had much success. Even though I was aware of these books, I read them only after I completed my manuscript, mainly because I didn't want to be influenced by anyone.

At a Persian bookstore in Toronto, I found four memoirs about Evin. All had been written by members of different extremist political groups, and all the writers had been adults at the time of their arrest. They had chronicled the horrors of Evin, but, unlike my memoir, their works were ideological. All the writers claimed that they had never broken under torture and never been affected by the intimidation and brainwashing techniques common in Evin. Apparently, all of them were heroes. Even though these books were published as memoirs, they were painfully dry and impersonal, and I found them difficult to follow. I was more interested in the human experience of the writer than his or her ideology. Yes, the Evin we had all written about was the same, but the way we saw it and the way it had affected us were vastly dissimilar. I suspected that our age difference played a big role in this. The adult prisoners had had much more life experience than the teenagers, and this experience supported them when facing torture. Where my young friends and I felt shame and fear, the adults felt anger and hatred.

While we blamed ourselves, they blamed the regime. For them, prison was all about resistance; for us, it was about survival and going home to our parents.

I found these memoirists' frequent use of the word *tavvab* interesting. It is an Arabic word that means "repentant." The prison authorities employed this word to describe the prisoners who had broken under torture: those who had denounced all opposition groups and had confessed to the "righteousness" of the regime. A *tavvab* was a prisoner who had seen the "truth" and had realized that all he or she had said and done against the government had been "evil." The government of Iran had gone so far as to call Evin and other political prisons "universities" where prisoners were "educated." Of course, the regime never mentioned that the "educational" methods included physical and psychological torture and extreme intimidation.

The writers of the memoirs divided the prisoners into two groups: *sarehmozei*s and *tavvab*s. *Sarehmozei* is a Persian word that means "those who are firm in their ideological beliefs." *Sarehmozei*s were the heroes and were good; the *tavvab*s were the traitors who had betrayed their comrades and the cause and therefore were evil. That more than ninety per cent of *tavvab*s were teenagers didn't seem to bother any of these writers, and they demonized their young cellmates. A few of the writers believed that all *tavvab*s were the same, but the rest categorized them into four different groups: those who pretended to be *tavvab*s in order to fool the officials; those who had broken under torture but minded their own business and didn't cause any trouble for other prisoners; those who spied on others and informed the interrogators of what they heard in the cells; and those who made life miserable for all the other prisoners and even took part in interrogations and executions.

While in Evin, I had heard about a handful of adult prisoners forced to take part in the execution of their friends as proof of their repentance. However, neither I nor any of my cellmates knew such prisoners. Reputedly, these prisoners had been important members of anti-government political groups, so the interrogators made them do horrible things to prove that they had changed.

In 246, the cellblock in Evin where I spent most of my time, more than ninety per cent were girls like me. As far as I know, their biggest crime was having sold the publications of opposition groups or having taken part in demonstrations against the government. For this, the majority of them received ten- to twenty-year sentences.

Most of us in Evin were well behaved. We prayed the Namaz, watched the prison's "educational" programs, and said nothing against the government. We never harmed anyone or spied on anybody. Breaking under torture doesn't mean you lose your humanity, and those who did lose theirs were definitely a tiny minority.

My visit to the Persian bookstore in Toronto convinced me that my work was important. The heroes had told their stories; now it was time for someone to tell another side of what had gone in Evin. My prison friends and I were not traitors; we were Iran's children who had been tortured and had broken. But I had faith that we had enough strength to mend our lives and speak out about what had been done to us.

Even though my manuscript was still raw, things began to happen in December 2004. One of my creative-writing instructors at the School of Continuing Studies read it and introduced me to a *Toronto Star* reporter named Michelle Shephard, who wrote about Middle Eastern issues. She was interested in talking to me and maybe writing an article about me for the *Sunday Star*. We arranged to meet at the King Edward Hotel in Toronto. As I stood in the foyer waiting for her, my whole body began to shake. Was I ready for this? The world would know all my secrets and flaws, and once the story came out there would be no going back. Yet despite all my fears, a strong force was pushing me ahead.

Michelle was a petite woman. When we shook hands, I looked into her eyes, and they reminded me of my closest prison friend, whom I had not heard from in almost twenty years. I clearly remembered her happiness when the guards called my name over the loudspeaker just before my release from Evin came. She was so happy for me that she couldn't stop crying. "Marina, you're going home!" she said. "I know it! They're letting you go!" Then she told me to run. She pushed me down the hallway toward the barred door, and I watched her small hand waving to me through the bars as I walked to the office at 246. Where was she now? Had she survived Evin?

Four years later, in July 2008 during an interview in Italy, a journalist asked me which day had been the worst of my life. I considered for a moment.

"The day I went home from Evin," I replied.

"Why?" he inquired, surprised.

"The day I went home from Evin I left my friends behind. Girls closer to me than sisters would be. I left them behind. I shouldn't have, but I didn't know any better. I was a young woman who wanted to go home more than anything. And that was the biggest mistake of my life."

Michelle and I sat down at the hotel restaurant and ordered lunch. I wasn't hungry and had soup. She asked me about my life in Iran and the process of writing my book. I had believed that reporters were aggressive, but Michelle was gentle and soft-spoken. I expected her to ask me for the name of someone reliable who'd known me in Iran and could confirm that I had truly spent two years in Evin—and she did. I gave her contact information for a few people who'd known me quite well in Iran but now lived abroad. None of them intended to return to Iran, so talking to a reporter would not put them in danger.

Michelle's article appeared in the *Sunday Star* on January 30, 2005. Even though I had hardly slept the night before and was wide awake at 5:00 a.m., I didn't jump out of bed and run to the door to get the paper. The previous night, Andre had arrived home from a business trip, and he was still fast asleep. I waited. At 8:00 a.m., I couldn't bear waiting any longer and edged out of bed. When I opened the front door, the frosty January air poured into the house like ice water. I grabbed the newspaper, ran back to our bedroom, and spread the paper on the bed. Andre squirmed.

Michelle had written a two-page article about me that included a photo of me the *Star* photographer had taken in the Swiss Chalet kitchen. I was in my uniform. I remembered the surprise on my boss's face when I asked him if it was okay for a reporter to come to the restaurant to interview me and for a photographer to take photos.

"Reporter? What's going on, Marina?" he wanted to know.

I told him about the book. He had always been very good to me, and he said he didn't have any problem as long as the newspaper people showed up in the afternoon when the restaurant wasn't busy and they didn't get in anyone's way.

The title of the article was "The Woman without a Past." I truly *had* been a woman without a past. I had been stripped of my identity in Evin—at least, this was what the prison authorities had tried to do to me, and for a long time, they seemed to have succeeded. For close to twenty years, I had floated in the world like a shadow, meaningless and without a destination. Now everything was different. I had taken charge. I had stood up.

Within a few hours, my inbox was full of supportive emails from friends and acquaintances. One of the messages was from Flavia, my book-club friend:

> Dear Marina,
>
> Are you moved? In a stupor? I imagine your feelings are very mixed today.

*Thank you for allowing some of your heart to be placed on the
page. I know there will be many people who will be touched—all
for different reasons. You did the right thing.*

People were indeed touched. Telling my story had become
such a desperate need for me that I had not thought much about
reactions. My neighbours now looked at me as if they had never
seen me before. When we ran into one another after the article
appeared, they stopped and shook my hand and said they had
no idea I had had such a difficult past. They said, as well, that
they didn't know Iran had so many political prisoners and treated
them so badly. When I told them that the majority of the prisoners
had been teenagers, they wanted to know why, and I explained to
them that if you wanted to control a country, you had to control
its young generation. If you tortured and executed teenagers, not
only would the rest of them get the message, but their parents, too,
would refrain from criticizing the government, realizing the high
price of dissidence.

I took a copy of the *Sunday Star* to my father. I had told him
I was writing a memoir. I explained that the article in the paper
was a summary of what had happened to me in Evin. He put the
paper on his kitchen table and began telling me about one of his
neighbours who was moving to a nursing home because she had
become too weak to care for herself. My father was not ready to
acknowledge my past. I had to give him time.

About two weeks later, I phoned my father and asked him if he
had read the article. He said he had not and changed the subject.
I had expected Alik to call me, but I didn't hear a word from him.
They were both still intent on ignoring my past. I decided not to
bring up the topic again unless they mentioned it themselves. It
was now their turn to take a step forward. Except, they didn't. I was

my family's dirty laundry, and to their horror, I had hung myself out to dry in public.

After the article appeared, I felt awkward at Swiss Chalet. My co-workers and customers wanted to know more. I told them I was writing a book. "When will it be published?" they asked. I replied that I had no idea; it wasn't ready yet. Where did I find the time to write a book while working at a restaurant and raising a family? they wanted to know. "You do what you have to do," I said. It was astounding that my customers were more interested in my story than my own family was.

Helen came to the restaurant without Mark one day. My heart sank. I ran to the hostess stand.

"Where's Mark?" I asked.

"I had to send him to a home," she said. "I couldn't manage anymore."

She looked lonely and out of place. As fragile as a china figurine.

"You have to care for yourself now, Helen. You did all you could for Mark."

"I saw a story about you in the paper. Boy, was I ever surprised! You never talked about yourself."

"Some things are hard to say."

"I know, but I'm glad you did when there was still time. Life takes opportunities away in a blink."

# Rachel's Letter

The first publishing house I submitted my manuscript to rejected it. I was devastated. The editor told me I had too many characters in the book; as a result, the reader didn't have a chance to feel for them. He had a point. I had to make it possible for the reader to feel for the prisoners, and in order to feel for them, the reader needed to get to know them. Too many characters made that impossible.

The only solution that came to my mind was to merge my cellmates' lives. I would recount events as I remembered them, but instead of connecting them to fifteen individuals, I would connect them to four or five. My own story would be told exactly as I recalled it.

The editor's concern wasn't my only issue. I had to protect the privacy of my cellmates. I was not in touch with them to ask for permission to tell about their experiences, so I had to find a way to protect their privacy without compromising the integrity of the story. Merging my friends' lives would solve that problem, as well.

Being rejected was painful, but I remembered what Lee Gowan had told our class about rejections. Every writer, he said, even the most successful, has been rejected, in some cases not only once or twice but tens of times. I couldn't give up.

I allowed myself to feel devastated for only a day or two—after all, being upset was normal. But I knew I had to move on, rewrite, and try again. Not every publisher is the right match for every writer. I believed that the right publishing house for me was out there, and I had to persevere and find it.

Altogether, I took seven creative writing courses to obtain the Certificate in Creative Writing from the School of Continuing Studies at the University of Toronto. My manuscript became my Final Project—the last step before graduation. For the Final Project Tutorial, I had to submit eighty pages of my work to an instructor who would work with me to improve it. Then I had to defend my work in front of the Final Project Panel, which consisted of Lee Gowan, my Final Project Tutorial instructor, and one other instructor from the school or a prominent member of the literary community.

From the available instructors for the Final Project, I chose Rachel Manley. Lee Gowan had recommended her, and I had read her wonderful memoir, *Drumblair*, winner of the Governor General's Award in 1997.

Rachel Manley is the daughter of Michael Manley, who was the prime minister of Jamaica from 1972 to 1980 and then again from 1989 to 1992. Initially, I had resisted reading her memoir. Unlike me, Rachel came from a privileged family. I believed that we couldn't possibly have anything in common. I was nobody and she was the daughter of a prime minister. She had probably lived a very comfortable life and had always had everything she had ever dreamed of. What would a woman like her write about?

I read Rachel Manley's book, hoping to learn from it, and I felt ashamed for the judgment I had placed on her. Yes, she was privileged, but she had had her own trials, and she had beautifully put them into words. She had transported me to Jamaica, a country I knew almost nothing about. Through her words, I felt her love for her country, as if I had been there and had seen its beauty through her eyes, the eyes of a curious little girl raised by her grandparents, trying to find her place in the world. In an odd way, maybe my life had been easier than Rachel's, because I had had no legend to live up to.

I decided to give Rachel my entire manuscript, even though I was only supposed to send her eighty pages. How could I take my life apart? That would be like dissecting a body and offering only an arm or leg to explain the person.

She asked me to deliver the manuscript to her house so we could meet and chat. I got off the subway a few stops too early and decided to walk the rest of the way even though her home was quite a distance. It was just before 10:00 a.m. Most stores were still closed and office workers were already at work, so the street was quiet. Every few minutes a red streetcar glided by. It was the end of summer, and the sun had already grown weaker. In Tehran, the weather had never been an important factor in my life because the weather was usually good. With the Alborz Mountains north of the city, Tehran does not have a desert climate and enjoys mild springs and falls, hot dry summers, and relatively cold winters, including some snowfall. Shortly after we arrived in Toronto, the obsession Canadians have with weather surprised me. Didn't they have anything better to talk about? I gradually discovered the reason for their fixation. Anyone who has waited for a bus at −28°C with a wind chill of −37°C understands what I mean. In most parts of Canada, good weather is a novelty, something to be savoured and cherished. Once summer ends, I try to feel the warmth of the sun on my skin as often as I can, because I know that the mercilessly long winter is just around the corner. How fortunate I am to live in a country where bad weather ranks as one of its people's biggest problems!

My mind went back to Rachel. She could hate my manuscript. She might not be the Rachel I had come to know from *Drumblair*.

After all, *Drumblair* was a book and Rachel was a person. Was Jane Austen truly the person I came to know through her writings? Even though she wrote fiction, now that I wrote, I understood that a writer cannot hide behind her words, because the writing will be superficial. Jane Austen was magical in making her readers feel the emotions of her characters, and to do this in such a masterful manner, she had to be honest. So in the end, I decided to trust Rachel Manley.

Rachel lived in a little brick townhouse on a clean, quiet street. As she welcomed me, her musical Jamaican accent made me think of the gentle waves of the Caribbean Sea. I followed her as she quickly climbed the flight of stairs that led to her living room. She was packing to move to another house, and boxes lay scattered everywhere. She apologized for the mess and explained that she was moving because her current home was too tiny for her many visitors from Jamaica.

That I was in the house of a great writer who was the daughter of a prime minister was hard for me to believe, yet Rachel seemed as frazzled by life's little challenges as anyone. Would I have felt the same visiting Jane Austen at her house, nervously waiting for her to read my book? *My book?* Yes, my book. But what if it never got published? What if no one ever read it? What if my memories died with me? No, I wouldn't allow that. I would fight to have my story remembered.

I sat at Rachel's dining table, and she inquired about my manuscript, tucking her straight brown hair behind her ears.

"So tell me about your book," she said with a reserved expression on her face. I told her the same thing I had told Lee Gowan— and I watched her eyes change. Before sharing my story, I had been unaware of the powerful effect it would have on people. To me, it was simply the story of my life, which I was still trying to understand. I didn't see it as extraordinary. I wasn't looking for pity or even sympathy. All I wanted was for people to know, remember, and never let what had happened to me and others in Iran happen again.

I left my manuscript with Rachel, feeling as if I had reached inside my chest, pulled out my heart, and put it on her dining-room table.

Now I had to wait.

A few weeks later, I received this email from her:

> *Dear Marina,*
>
> *I have lived with your book, and therefore with your spirit, for the last month. I cannot say how profoundly it has affected me. It is quite exquisite. It slowly moved into my mind like a plant growing, and I am full of its leaves and musings. It even made me cry, which I haven't done reading a book in a long time … It has such depth and beauty and human forgiveness, that at the end we are left more with your calm than with the horror of what was done to you …*
>
> *Rachel*

She liked it. Really liked it! She had called it "exquisite"! I said the word and it made me smile. For some reason, I had never considered that writing could be exquisite. For me, *exquisite* was an adjective to describe a soufflé or a creampuff. I read her email again and again, until I had almost memorized it: "… at the end we are left more with your calm than with the horror of what was done to you …"

My *calm*? Yes, maybe that was the right word for it.

Or was it? Two or three people who had read my manuscript told me they had felt a "lack of emotion" in my writing. Of course it had a lack of emotion. What did they expect? That I would allow myself to feel? *I had been in a state of shock.* Writing about what had happened to me in Iran meant living it again. Was this so hard for "normal" people to understand? The truth is that a tortured sixteen-year-old girl removes herself from the horror surrounding her, because if she doesn't, she will lose her mind. When raped, she feels ashamed, so she shifts her focus from herself and tries to find normalcy, kindness, and humanity in a world that has slipped into madness. How else could I have felt?

*Calm.*

Rachel was very kind and generous, but she was wrong about my "calm." What she had called calm was a state of shock that refused to let go.

Still, she had liked the manuscript. This was what mattered.

# A Sound Recorder and a Microphone

By putting my story on paper and sharing it with others, in a way I marched back inside Evin and reclaimed myself. I am finally free, because I have faced the past and accepted that I cannot alter it. Yes, Evin changed me, but the girl I once was is still inside the experienced woman I have become. I still have faith in the same God. I still despise hatred and cherish compassion and forgiveness. I still respect others and their values and want them to respect me and mine. I still believe we are human beings first and our religion comes after that. The Islamic Republic of Iran tried to win me over through torture and intimidation. I accept none of their beliefs.

In January 2006, Beverley Slopen, a well-known and respected literary agent in Toronto, took me on and submitted my manuscript to a few Canadian publishers, and in February 2006, I signed a contract with Penguin Canada. They scheduled the release of *Prisoner of Tehran* for April 2007.

Signing the contract with Penguin was a milestone in my life. For four years, writing the book had been my purpose and my destination. With every cell of my body, I believed that I had lived to write that book. I had never thought of what I would do next. I wasn't even sure what *next* meant exactly. I somehow believed I was supposed to die the day I signed a contract. Yet I was still alive. It was as if I had survived Evin again and had to keep on going.

I gradually became accustomed to talking about Evin. My trembling diminished, and I hardly ever came close to tears. I had seen people cry while speaking about their traumatic experiences, and I didn't know why I was in control. Friends had told me that I was strong, but I wasn't trying not to cry; I just didn't feel like it. My only emotional outbursts, aside from the episode at my mother's funeral, had occurred while I was working on my book. While writing about the past, I sometimes felt so terribly overwhelmed that I locked myself in the bathroom and screamed for a few minutes until I felt better. I even turned on the shower to muffle the awful noise I made. If Andre and the boys were home when this happened, I would find them standing at the bathroom door, terrified. Every time, I smiled and told them that I was upset for no good reason and that I needed to vent. They would nod, looking helpless and confused.

By the time my manuscript landed on my editors' desks in Canada, the United Kingdom, and the United States, it was well chiselled, so the editorial process did not take long. Once the editing, copy-editing, proofreading, and production work were done, I had to let the book face the world. To me, writing it had been like giving birth, only more so because my book came from my DNA alone. I was my book's mother *and* father. Expectant mothers don't always bestow a name on their unborn child, but my manuscript needed a working title since I couldn't just call the manuscript "it." I chose *Echoes of an Angel* because of the dream I had had about the Angel of Death when I was a child. As the publishing date drew closer, though, I had to give the work a final title. I was thinking about the key words in the manuscript one day on the subway, when *prisoner* and *Tehran* came to mind and connected: *Prisoner of Tehran*.

As I waited for the actual publication date, I began to work on a project for CBC Radio. I had sent in a proposal for a documentary about my prison experience to the producers of *Outfront*, a program devoted to listeners' stories. Carma Jolly, one of the producers, explained that I could make a documentary about something that had happened twenty years ago only if I could relate it to the present. I had told her that my father and mother had refused to talk to me about my past, and she knew that my mother had passed away and that my father lived not too far from me.

"Why don't you interview your dad?" she asked casually, as if this were as simple as my dropping in to say hello to my father. "I'll give you recording equipment, and you can go to his place, ask him questions, and record what he says."

I felt like running out of the room. Was she serious? My father and I spoke briefly on the phone once a month, but after my mother's funeral, we had avoided each other. Even though he was in good health, he *was* eighty-five years old. How could I bring up such a difficult issue with a man his age? And if I decided to do it, where would I start?

Carma handed me recording equipment stored in a small black pouch. She even checked the batteries and gave me extra ones. I accepted the equipment without a word and walked out.

On the subway train home, I stared into the blackness outside the window. The reflections of passengers floated like phantoms in the underworld. I had a microphone and a recorder. I was not just Marina anymore. I was a reporter, a journalist. I could do this. I had to do this. For twenty years, I had had questions I needed to ask. My father could die without me getting another chance. By writing about the past, I had faced myself. Now I had to face my father.

Gathering the courage to go to my father's apartment took me two days. He lived in a seniors building a twenty-minute drive from my house. I had always called him before visiting, but this time I did not. He was surprised to see me. We gave each other a ceremonial hug. He had always been organized, and his apartment was clean and tidy. A black-and-white photo of my mother, taken when she was in her thirties, stared at me from a coffee table. I sat at the dining table and put the recording equipment on it.

"What's this?" my father asked.

"A sound recorder and a microphone," I said in a small voice.

"What for?"

"I'm interviewing you, Papa."

"Interviewing *me?*"

I nodded and reminded myself I had every right to go ahead. "For CBC Radio. I'm making a documentary."

My father looked as if I had just told him I was an alien from another galaxy and could prove it. He offered me some tea and went to make it. As soon as he sat down, I held the microphone close to my mouth and said, "What do you remember about the day I was released and came home from Evin?"

"We were very happy to see you," he said in a tone that fathers use to avoid explaining difficult matters to their young children.

*We were very happy to see you.* His sentence was a dam so desperately struggling to hold back a flood. Was this all he had to say after twenty years of silence? He was still hiding. This was his way of telling me I had better stop.

Except, I couldn't.

"I remember we talked about the weather and normal things. I was shocked that nobody asked me about the prison," I continued.

"The weather?"

"Yes, the weather."

He couldn't have forgotten. His memory was still sharp. He just had a habit of remembering only what he wanted to.

"It wasn't suitable to talk about it. Everything was behind us," he said decisively.

Suitable? Wasn't *suitable*?

"As time went by, I was hurt that no one ever asked me anything," I said. I could see the discomfort in his eyes, but I couldn't back off now.

He collected himself. "Well, jail is jail, and we knew that it was not correct to remind you. I didn't want to hurt you by making you think about the past. We knew that terrible things had happened to you, but we didn't know what they were. And we were glad we didn't know, because if we had known, it would have hurt us, and why would we have wanted that? So we decided to stay away from it."

*We were glad we didn't know ...*

My heart constricted as if shrinking to the size of a pea. What are you supposed to do when something so terrible happens to you that even your mother and father don't want to hear about it? My early numbness had turned into anger, and my anger had spilled out in screams, but my ordeal was no easier to bear. A poisonous sadness flowed yet in my veins. I couldn't remain still, or it would slowly and painfully kill me.

Forgive.

I remembered my father's tears on the night of my arrest. He looked so devastated and helpless. As my father, he was supposed to protect me, but he couldn't. Two members of the Revolutionary Guard had stood in our house with guns, threatening us all. He had to let them take me. Now that I am a mother, I know how difficult this must have been for him. I wondered exactly what to forgive my father for. I had been angry with him, but for so long I didn't exactly know why. Suddenly, it was obvious: I had to forgive him for trying to forget. I'd needed guidance to understand the horrible things that had happened to me and the person I had become. When my family refused to help me, I'd had no one else to rely on. Then, like everyone around me, I tried to forget. I continued to live in an emotional coma, unable to love, hate, feel anger, find peace, or forgive.

I had many people to forgive, including myself. I had started with Ali, because if not, I would have gone mad in Evin after he died. What do I mean when I say I forgave him? For one thing, that I am not angry with him anymore. When he forced himself upon me, I felt ashamed and I wanted to die. Because I was so young, I blamed myself even more than I blamed him. Even though I had sympathy for him, a victim who became a torturer, what he did to people in Evin was terribly wrong. His anger, which was the result of the torture he had endured in Evin during the time of the shah, had turned into hatred, and then he had sought revenge as an interrogator in an evil regime. I had seen some humanity in him, but this could not, and would not, justify his actions.

Yes, I forgave Ali, but forgiving and forgetting are two different things. Forgiving lets you count all the wrongs done to you, remember how terrible you felt when you experienced them, and still wish the perpetrator no ill. With all my heart, I asked God to forgive Ali and help him understand how he had made me feel. I asked Him to give Ali peace. Yet if Ali were alive today, I would want him to stand trial, not for what he did to me but for what he did to others. I would want him, though, to have a fair trial according to the law, not one based on revenge. Revenge destroys any humanity. It has nothing to do with justice, and it always perpetuates the awful cycle of violence.

I forgave Ali. Now I had to forgive my father, and do it before he died.

MY TWO-PART DOCUMENTARY, titled "Walls Like Snakes," aired on CBC Radio One's *Outfront* on April 4 and 5, 2006, and those who heard it told me that what my father had *not* said spoke much louder than what he had. They were right. He said he was happy to see me after two years, but he never said a word about disowning me when he heard I had converted to Islam. My mother told me about it after my release as she and I had tea a few days before I married Andre. I don't know why she brought it up. It was almost as if she wanted me to hate my father. I was shocked to hear it. But it didn't matter; I was getting married and was about to begin a new life, and I didn't care if they approved of me or not. I told my mother that my father could think as he wished, and I left the room. Why didn't my father himself tell me about this? Why didn't he ask me the reason for my conversion? Would it have made any difference to him to know that I converted to protect him and my mother? He had placed judgment on me without having all the facts. And the most hurtful part was that he had never cared about religion and didn't even believe in God.

In the *Outfront* interview, my father said that he didn't want to know about what happened to me in the prison because "it wasn't suitable to talk about it." This meant that he did have an idea, if only a vague one, of what had gone on in Evin. He didn't want to know about the torture and rape of his daughter. I understood quite well that he had suffered and that it was very difficult to bring up such a painful issue, but hiding the truth doesn't erase it. I felt that I deserved my father's acknowledgment; yet he wasn't ready to give it. I was not angry with him any longer; still, I felt sad and lonely and wished he had the courage to face the past and to support me.

As time went by, my relationship with my father gradually improved. We have not become best friends, but the great stone wall of silence and secrets that had stood between us has crumbled.

After my mother's death, my father became quite depressed. My parents had been married for about fifty-eight years, and it was normal for my father to struggle to cope with the loss. He had to start a new life at the age of seventy-nine. After about a year his mood began to improve, and he started making friends with his neighbours, many of whom were Russian and Persian. Following the *Outfront* interview I began visiting him once a week, and during my visits he told me about his youth. My father and I had never had meaningful conversations, and our talks introduced me to his world.

My father's mother, Xena, had opened a boarding house after her husband was robbed and murdered shortly after their arrival in Tehran. This much I knew. I asked my father if he had any idea where *Bahboo* got the money from to start a business, but he said he didn't know. All he could tell me was that she began small and then expanded. I was surprised that he didn't have more information about that period in *Bahboo*'s life, but then I remembered that after trauma, silence sets in. *Bahboo* had written a few pages about her life in Russia, and she gave me her manuscript just before she died, but there was no mention of her life in Iran in it. Maybe she was trying to forget her husband's tragic death. My father told me that seventeen years after his father was killed, the man who had murdered him was released from prison, and *Bahboo* did her best to make sure that my father wouldn't hear about this because she was afraid that he might seek revenge. My father discovered the truth many years later.

My father told me that all the boarders at *Bahboo*'s house were Russian, and this surprised me.

"Were there many Russians in Tehran back then?" I asked.

"Yes. Some were immigrants like us, but many of them were in Iran temporarily and worked for different companies. We're talking the 1930s here. I had gone to two of those companies myself. One of them was Persaz Neft, which had to do with the oil industry, and the other was Shark."

"But that's an English name."

"That's what it was called."

Until the end of the fifth grade, my father had attended the Soviet School in Tehran, which was for Russian-speaking children. Then the minister of culture announced that Iranian citizens could not go to foreign schools. My father had been born in Iran shortly after his parents arrived there, so he had to go to a Persian school. But in the Soviet School they had studied everything in Russian, and he couldn't read or write in Persian. He could only speak it.

"So what did you do?" I asked.

"My mother got me a tutor that summer. At the beginning of the school year, I went for an exam at a Persian school named Tadayyon and was accepted into the fourth grade. It wasn't easy at the beginning. The kids and the teachers were mean to me because I was different. They didn't call me by my name. They called me *'Roosi'*—Russian. I got my high-school diploma at a school named College, which had an American principal. They later changed the name of the school to Alborz."

From 1925 to 1941, Reza Shah Pahlavi was the king of Iran. Reza Shah didn't trust Great Britain and the Soviet Union, so Iran's relations with both countries deteriorated. To counterbalance their influence in Iran, Reza Shah turned to Germany, and before the Second World War, Germany became Iran's largest trading partner. Reza Shah's foreign policy of playing the Soviets against the British failed when those two countries joined in 1941 to fight the Germans. Reza Shah declared neutrality in the war and refused to allow Iranian territory to become a transport corridor. Shortly afterward, the two Allies occupied Iran to deliver ammunition and food to the Russian front. Supplies were shipped to southern Iran through the Oman Sea and the Persian Gulf. Then they were put on northbound trains and, using the Trans-Iranian Railway, travelled across the country to reach the Soviet Union from behind the European front. The Allies forced Reza Shah into exile, and Reza Shah's son, Mohammad Reza Pahlavi, replaced his father on the throne on September 16, 1941.

My father's official name on his Iranian identification papers is Gholamreza Moradi-Bakht—a decidedly Muslim name. When my grandmother arrived in Iran in 1921 and applied for Iranian identification papers,* she was not allowed to keep her foreign name. So, at the government office where they issued the papers, the clerk who handled her case chose first and last names for her that were considered "appropriate." Her real first name was Xena, but the clerk entered it as Zeenat, which sounds relatively similar but is Persian; for her last name, he gave her Moradi, which sounds close to Morateva, her real last name. But because Moradi was a common name in Iran, the clerk added the suffix Bakht to it, which means "luck." My father's name on his baptism papers from the Russian Orthodox Church in Tehran is Nicolai; however, for the reasons I just explained, on his official government-issued papers, his name was changed to Gholamreza.

After getting his high-school diploma, my father began working at a bank. In 1942, at the age of twenty-one, he married my mother. They rented an apartment on Shah Avenue, where I was born twenty-three years later. *Bahboo* moved in with them soon after the marriage, because she had grown too tired to run her boarding house. Back then, my father's salary was 300 *tomans* a month. Rent was 265 *tomans* a month, so he needed a second job. Since he had been a teenager, my father had regularly attended dance parties at the homes of other immigrants and foreigners in Tehran, and people always told him that he was a great dancer and would ask him to teach them. Because he was not making enough money at his day job, he decided to open a dance studio at our apartment. Before long, his dance studio became such a success that he quit his job at the bank and dedicated all his time to his business. Modern,

---

*She probably did not apply for the papers immediately after her arrival but did so a few years later.

fashionable cabarets and hotels such as the Astoria and Palace had opened in Tehran, and members of the upper class who frequented them to dine and dance signed up for my father's class to learn new moves and show off to their friends. My father was even invited to the shah's court to teach the courtiers.

After my mother's death, loneliness pushed my father to try to find his sister, Tamara, who was four years older than he. My father had not heard from her since 1966. In 1934, when Tamara was seventeen, she fell in love with a Russian who was staying at *Bahboo*'s boarding house. They married, and she returned to Moscow with him. Not long before *Bahboo* died, she told me that for years she had sent care packages filled with soap, toothpaste, and clothes to Tamara because these items were scarce where Tamara lived. Apparently, Tamara had divorced her husband after she discovered he was a KGB agent. She remarried and somehow ended up in the city of Simferopol in Ukraine. In 1966, a year after I was born, the shah's secret police, SAVAK, summoned my father to their offices and asked him why he was communicating with someone in the Soviet Union. He told them that this person was his sister. The SAVAK official who interviewed my father knew he could read and write in Russian and invited him to work for them, but my father politely refused, saying that he had always avoided politics and wasn't suitable for the job. They told him that he was no longer allowed to communicate with anyone in the Soviet Union. Tamara's last letter came in 1966. After that, we never heard from her again.

When members of the Revolutionary Guard arrested me in January 1982, they took a few of my books—all Western novels—as evidence of my activities against the Islamic government. My mother was so terrified that after they left she destroyed all the literature in the house, including *Bahboo*'s manuscript and Tamara's letters. We lived in an apartment with no yard or fireplace, so she couldn't burn them, and throwing them into the garbage could attract attention. So she came up with a painfully brilliant idea: she washed the books in our wringer washer, turned them into a paste, and gradually mixed the paste with everyday garbage. However, my father saved Tamara's last letter, which was in a bluish white envelope with a blue-and-red border and the hammer-and-sickle Soviet logo on its top left corner. All my father had left from his sister was that letter.

A few months after my mother's death, my father wrote to Tamara's last known address, explaining that he was looking for his sister who had lived there forty years earlier. Even though he had little hope of hearing back, to his surprise, he received a letter from a different address in Simferopol. The letter was from a woman named Natasha, and she was Tamara's granddaughter. Tamara's neighbours had opened my father's letter and had contacted Natasha to let her know that her great-uncle was searching for his sister and her family. Shocked, Natasha immediately wrote back to my father. Tamara had died six years earlier. She had had only one son, Victor, who had passed away a short time before she did. My father was saddened to hear about Tamara's death and Victor's, but he was overjoyed to have found family.

This was a new beginning for my father. He was suddenly much happier and more optimistic. He began spending hours writing to Natasha every week. He learned that she had a sister named Svetlana and three daughters and a son.

When I was growing up, my father's family had been a mystery to me. We regularly saw my mother's three sisters, one brother, and their spouses and children, but a thick fog covered my father's side. Tamara's story had always intrigued me, and I became even more interested after *Bahboo* told me that I looked very much like her. What else did Tamara and I have in common?

In 2004, my father announced that he was going to Ukraine for a one-month visit. Even though he was in relatively good health and was quite active, I was worried for him; after all, he was eighty-three years old. However, he insisted that he had to go. He made all the arrangements and bought his tickets. His enthusiasm astonished me, but once I thought about it, I understood it. My father had never been close to Alik and me. He had been a severe, cold figure who had hovered over our lives at a distance. As children, we heard his voice only when he was displeased. After my release from Evin when I desperately needed money to pay thirty-five hundred dollars to the government of Iran for a passport, he refused to lend it to me, even though he had just sold our cottage at the Caspian Sea and had enough money. He said he didn't think that Andre and I would be able to succeed abroad. I was devastated. I got angry and called my father a selfish man who cared only about money. He knew I could be arrested again for returning to my church and marrying Andre. My life was in danger, yet he refused to help me.

Andre's father had worked at a furniture factory during the last few years of his life. With the help of the factory owner, he and a few other workers had invested in a piece of land to build a small condominium building. When Andre's father passed away, this project hadn't started yet, but Andre made more payments toward it. Shortly after my father refused to lend me money for a passport, Andre received a phone call from a lady who worked at his father's factory, and she informed us that work on the building had begun. We told her we were planning to leave the country but had run into some financial problems. She offered to buy our share in the building and pay us five hundred thousand *tomans* more than what we had already invested. Strangely, we needed that exact amount. When I put the money in a briefcase to deliver it to Evin prison, my father told me I was an idiot, that they would take the money but would not let me leave. I ignored him.

Now, fourteen years later, my father, who had never shown much interest in his children, was enthusiastic about going to

Ukraine to see relatives he barely knew. Gradually, I realized that this was probably because he could start his relationship with them from scratch and become a more loving person. There was no history between them, no painful memories to face. That my father wanted to better himself and be good to others mattered to me. He began sending money to Ukraine, and I was proud of him for it. Even though Natasha was a head nurse, she made just sixty dollars a month. My father was not wealthy and his only income was the small pension he received from the Canadian government, but during his visit to Ukraine, he realized that compared with our relatives in Simferopol, he was truly a rich man. This made him appreciate Canada more.

My father's trip was a success. Our relatives were happy to see him. They were very kind to him and took him around the city. He went to Tamara's grave and Victor's, and this meant a lot to him. My father had connected to his history and had found himself. Once he returned to Toronto, he was noticeably happier. He kept telling me about Maria, Natasha's youngest daughter, who was fourteen years old. Maria began writing to my father regularly and called him "Great-grandfather." When I saw her photo, I was surprised to notice that she bore a slight physical resemblance to me. Like me, she was a very good student and wanted to go to medical school. She was artistic and drew sketches of all of us from the photos my father had sent her. One of my hobbies when I was a teenager had been drawing sketches from photos. My father proudly showed me Maria's work, telling me how lovely and talented she was. As I watched my father, I realized that he was trying to do for Maria what he had never done for me. Goodness and love were spreading in my father's life, bringing light to his world. Even though our relationship had improved after my mother's death, I knew that I would always be a reminder of pain and suffering to him. Maria was everything I might have been, and I was grateful to her for making my father happy.

After *Prisoner of Tehran* was published I gave a copy to my father. Although it took him a while to start reading it, he eventually read it twice and told me he was proud of me. I never thought I would hear him speak those words. He left his copy of my book on a coffee table in his apartment to make sure that all his visitors saw it. He told friends, acquaintances, sometimes strangers that his daughter was a famous author. He had blamed me for my imprisonment and everything that followed. He had been ashamed of me because of my conversion to Islam and my relationship with Ali. Even though we had never talked about Ali, I was sure that my father had read about him in the *Toronto Star* article, but my father didn't say a word about Ali to me. Then, after my book came out, my father saw how well it was received, and he admitted that maybe he had been too severe. The book was much more detailed than the article, and it enabled him to see the situation from my perspective.

When in December 2007 my photo appeared on the cover of the Canadian book-publishing magazine *Quill & Quire*, he left the magazine on his dining table and never moved it. Whenever I go to his place, I still see it there. I look like Cinderella in that photo. They had called me from the magazine and had asked if I owned a nice dress. I only had pant and skirt suits. So they borrowed a dress for me from Holt Renfrew. I gasped when I saw it. It was red, very red, and although I would never have worn it in the real world, I decided to play dress-up and indulge myself, if only for a few minutes. At the photo shoot, I remembered that thirty-eight years earlier, my family and I had gone to a professional photographer for a family portrait. I could see that photo in my mind. My mother and father were young and elegant. I wore a blue satin dress with a white belt and shiny black shoes. Alik looked quite handsome in his very-sixties shirt, which had a ruffled collar and cuffs. My mother had sewn it for him. The photo was black-and-white, but I clearly remember the colour of that shirt. Its mustard-yellow fabric was covered with light- and dark-brown polka dots each the size of a dime.

Soon after the publication of *Prisoner of Tehran*, Alik wrote to me in an email:

> *Your life took a very difficult path and now it is great to*
> *see you getting some redemption for all your suffering. My*
> *congratulations for all the recognition and awards you will be*
> *receiving.*
>
> *I quote Emily Dickinson: "Not knowing when the dawn will*
> *come, I open every door."*
>
> *Your dawn has come. Enjoy it.*

I was stunned.

For a few years after my arrival in Canada, Alik and I had seen each other regularly at family functions, but we'd had a falling-out over my deteriorating relationship with my parents. I had told my parents frankly that I could not live up to their expectations of life in Canada. They wanted me to buy new furniture and move to a bigger house because most of our friends and relatives had a more expensive lifestyle. In Iran, we call this way of thinking *cheshm-o hamcheshmi*, which more or less means "living to other people's standards." I literally couldn't afford to satisfy my parents, and I refused to go into debt to please them or anyone else. My husband and children were my priority and I had to focus my energy on them. My parents didn't like that, and their unhappiness affected my relationship with Alik. Maybe if we had been closer in age, things would have been different, but we didn't have much in common.

Not long after *Prisoner of Tehran* appeared, Alik and I went out for lunch. I realized I could not remember a time when we had been alone together. He visited my father every Sunday and me every Friday. We had not been trying to avoid each other, but our lives had been separate for twenty-eight years. Unlike Alik, who had grown up during the time of the shah, I had come of age during the time of the Islamic Republic, and my reality was quite different from his. I was sure that every time he saw me, the shadow of Evin and what I had gone through got in his way of connecting to me. Maybe he felt guilty for not being able to help me. He had never talked to me about guilt, but I had wondered about it. A friend of mine who was never in Evin had told me about blaming himself for not saving me from the prison. I laughed and told him not to be silly. There wasn't anything he or anyone else could have done. I have never blamed anyone for my time in Evin. Only the Islamic Republic is responsible for that.

I told Alik that I had been shocked to see him quote Emily Dickinson; I had no idea that he read poetry. He said that he had always loved literature and was an avid reader. It seemed I knew more about my neighbours than I did about my brother. To my surprise, he said he had always wanted to become a writer. We talked about my book, and he revealed that even though he was aware that Evin was a horrible place, he had no idea how awful it truly was until he read my book.

I sat quietly, looking at him.

I had finally found my brother and father in the rubble of the silence and secrets of our past.

A few days later, Alik and my father came to the launch of *Prisoner of Tehran*, a reception held at the Faculty Club of the University of Toronto. They had told me they would be coming, but I didn't see them in the audience. However, when I stood at the podium, I spotted them in the front row. As I spoke, I noticed that my editor at Penguin Canada, Diane Turbide, put her arm around my father's shoulder. They were both crying. I had to look the other way not to lose control.

# The List of Names

A few days after "Walls Like Snakes" aired on CBC Radio One, I received a phone call from an Iranian-Canadian university professor who had heard it and been impressed. I will call her Professor M. here. When we met for lunch a few days later, she told me she was beginning a project that would study the memoirs of Iran's political prisoners. Eventually, she would create a website that would be a resource centre for those who wanted to learn more about the experiences of these prisoners. She needed someone fluent in both English and Persian to translate excerpts of prison memoirs from Persian into English and to summarize them. She also wanted to create a haven where former women political prisoners from the Middle East could express themselves by telling their stories through visual arts, dance, music, and creative writing. I agreed to help her, hoping that we would be finished translating by April 2007; my book would be released then and I would have to go on a book tour.

In early October 2006, I signed a six-month contract and began reading and translating prison memoirs. The task was emotionally exhausting—I was reading and writing about torture four to five hours a day. But I pressed on because I believed the work was important.

I had a few meetings with Professor M. and an ex–political prisoner from Iran who was working on the same project, and the project was going well. However, within two months it became clear that we would have to continue our work after I came back from my book tour: the amount of material to read was simply too large.

Shortly before I left on my book tour, Professor M. asked me if I could transcribe the names of about twenty-five-hundred women political prisoners executed in Iran's prisons. This list was by no means a complete one. The names of many who lost their lives in Evin and other Iranian prisons have never been recorded. I hesitated a little before taking on this task. Twenty-five-hundred names ... twenty-five-hundred lost lives. How many of those women did I know? How many were my friends?

Before every name, I paused and took a deep breath. After transcribing an unfamiliar name, I would stop a few moments and try to imagine what her owner had looked like. What colour were her eyes, her hair? Was her hair long or short? Did she have any brothers or sisters? Was she married? Did she have children or was she a teenager? What were her hopes and dreams?

Eventually, I came to a name I knew. Shahnoosh Behzadi. I read her name over and over. Up to that instant, I had somehow hoped that the news I'd heard in 1981 about her death had been false, that she had somehow survived and was living a happy life in a quiet, safe corner of the world. But those little black letters printed on a sheet of paper confirmed, with terrible finality, that she had died a horrible death at fifteen. Tears blinded me.

Shahnoosh Behzadi had been my classmate from the fourth grade on. We met when I transferred to Giv Elementary School, a Zoroastrian school for girls that accepted students of every faith.

On my first day at Giv just before the morning bell, I stood in the middle of the schoolyard and glanced around, desperate to find a familiar face. I knew that a few of my friends from my former school were supposed to come to Giv, but I had yet to spot one. A loud, moving sea of children surrounded me, and I felt overwhelmed. My heart pounded and sweat dripped down my forehead.

Suddenly, I found myself squeezed tight. I had no idea who was embracing me. All I could see was grey fabric and strands of curly, dark-brown hair.

"She's so tiny and cute!" the girl said.

I tried to break free from her arms. Finally, she released me and I had a look at her. She was tall and thin. I later discovered that she was a Zoroastrian. With a motherly smile, she stroked my hair.

"You're new here! What's your name?"

"Marina," I said breathlessly.

"What a pretty name!" she exclaimed, and turned to the friend standing behind her. "Fariba, her name is Marina. Isn't that cute?"

Fariba nodded, smiled, and tucked her straight brown hair behind her ears. She was taller than I was but shorter than her friend.

"What grade are you in?" Fariba asked me.

"Four," I responded proudly.

"Us, too!" said the girl who had hugged me. "We'll help you with everything! Follow us!"

The bell rang, and when I gazed around me, I didn't feel like a stranger anymore. I had friends: Fariba and—

The two girls had begun to walk away from me.

"Hey, wait! What's your name?" I called after them.

The tall girl looked back and said, "Shahnoosh. Hurry up!"

I ran.

Shahnoosh was goodness. This is the best way I can describe her. She simply didn't know how to be mean. She wasn't what would be considered pretty, but she had so much love in her heart that it created beauty. I suspect she had a learning disability, because she struggled to keep up in class. Later, in high school, she asked me to help her with science and math. Tutoring her was fun, because she made me feel special and always told me that I was very smart. We never became best friends, but when I think of my school days, I realize that her presence made those days much happier. She always had a hug for everyone who needed it and befriended those who were the loneliest.

Revolutions take societies apart. When the Islamic Revolution succeeded, it changed everything, especially school. My generation had grown up with the old regime's laws, which all of a sudden no longer applied. However, the new regime needed time to establish itself and write new laws. This short transition period lasted only a few months. During it, Marxist and Marxist-Islamist groups, which had been illegal during the time of the shah and had operated underground, surfaced and became popular in high schools and universities. I was in the eighth grade then and far too young to understand political groups, but many eleventh- and twelfth-grade students suddenly announced they were followers. Despite ideological differences, many of those groups had supported the Islamic Revolution, and had played a large role in its success. Their plan was to take over the country once the shah was deposed, but they failed. Marxist and Marxist-Islamist students organized political discussion meetings during recess, but I rarely saw Shahnoosh at any of them. She was probably the only person in school who remained more or less unchanged by the Islamic Republic. After a while I grew tired of those meetings. Even though I wanted and tried to fit in, I couldn't. I was a devout Catholic and could get along with neither Marxists nor Islamists. Soon, I drifted away from all my friends and became so depressed that when the academic year of 1981–82 began, I refused to go back to school. Seeing my fragile emotional state, my parents decided to let me take a year off school.

In early fall of 1981 I heard from a young man at my church that Shahnoosh had been arrested and then executed. I simply could not believe it. This was impossible. Why arrest Shahnoosh? She was not politically active. Executed? It had to be a mistake.

Now, twenty-five years later, I sat with a list of the names of the executed on my desk. The list included Shahnoosh Behzadi. My beautiful friend.

IN 2009, another beautiful young woman, Neda Agha-Soltan, was killed in Iran. Unlike Shahnoosh's death, hers was captured on a cell-phone camera and broadcast on YouTube. Mahmoud Ahmadinejad had just become the president of Iran for a second term. The Supreme Leader, Ayatollah Khamenei, and the Council of Guardians, which oversees elections in Iran, obviously favoured him. There had been many signs of irregularities and fraud during the election. Supporters of Mir-Hossein Mousavi and Ayatollah Karroubi, two reformist presidential candidates, filled the streets of Tehran and other large cities to protest. Such crowds had not been seen since 1979 and the days of the rallies against the shah. The people were shouting "Death to the dictator!" and "Where is our vote?" Basij (a civilian militia), Revolutionary Guard, and the police attacked the crowds and killed, injured, and arrested many. YouTube filled with images of violence. The clip of Neda Agha-Soltan's death spread across the Internet and millions saw it.

A bullet hit Neda in the chest just below her neck, and she lost her balance and fell. In vain, people rushed to help her. A doctor present at the scene applied pressure to her wound and tried to slow the bleeding, but suddenly, blood spilled from her nose and mouth, her eyes rolled back, and she died on the sidewalk. Another innocent life lost. I watched the video only once, but it burned itself into my soul. I can play it over and over from memory, rewind, pause, or fast-forward it. She is wearing a knee-length black coat, a black head scarf, blue jeans, and running shoes. She has beautiful hands with long fingers. Perfect eyebrows. Gorgeous eyes. The shock on her face when the bullet hits her is unbearable. It is as if she wants to scream "Why?" but can't.

MY MEMORIES OF SHAHNOOSH and all the friends I lost seethed in me as I travelled the world to speak about *Prisoner of Tehran* and the horrors of Evin. In strange hotels, when and if I fell asleep, I dreamed of going for walks on the shores of the Caspian with my prison friends. We cried and laughed, grieved and danced. In one of my dreams, Shahnoosh and I held hands and spun until we collapsed, laughing. Once we caught our breath, she turned to me, smiled, and said, "Happiness is our only revenge."

Shortly after I returned from my book tour, I received a phone call from Professor M. I thought she might want to talk about my book—I had given her an advance copy to read. Or maybe she was going to ask me to sign another contract to continue the work we had started a few months earlier. But I was wrong.

"I can't work with you anymore," she said in a measured tone.

"Why?" I asked, puzzled.

She explained that her political friends, who were supporters of far-left Iranian political groups operating in exile, believed that I was a traitor, a *tavvab,* because I had broken under torture and married Ali. They were angry that I had shown no sign of remorse.

*Remorse?* For what? For being tortured and raped?

All the muscles in my body tightened. She had known my story when she had first approached me. My eyes filled with tears, but I held them back. I tried to say something, but words were swirling in my head.

"I see …" I managed to mumble.

"I have to insist that you do not mention in interviews that you have worked with me," she said.

"Why?"

"Because some people say that I helped you write your book ..."

"This is ridiculous! Why would anyone say that?"

"Well, some people think I helped you."

"I helped *you* with your work—you didn't help me with mine."

"I just called to let you know this, okay?" She hung up.

I stood there in my kitchen, struggling to understand what had just happened. But I couldn't get my mind around it. I had considered her a friend.

A few weeks later, I read a letter she had put on a website she had created. In it, she explained that she had come to know me after I was interviewed by CBC Radio and TV and a story about me was published in the *Toronto Star*. She also mentioned that after seeing and hearing the interviews, she had hired another Iranian-Canadian ex-prisoner and me for six months. This was exactly what had happened. I read on.

"During this process," she wrote,* "I became more familiar with Marina Nemat's political views, and it was obvious to me that her story of the prison was different from other published memoirs. In her interview with the *Toronto Star* (January 30, 2005), she had mentioned her 'marriage' with her interrogator and was not hiding it, and she had said that she would publish her memoir. To understand the difference between Marina's experience in the prison and the ones of other women political prisoners, from the beginning [of the project] to the time that her book was published, I asked a few women political prisoners about her, but no one knew anything, and no one accused her of being a *tavvab* ..."

Then she noted that after the publication of *Prisoner of Tehran*, a few ex–political prisoners said that I was a traitor. She added, "According to the criticisms [of a few ex–political prisoners] of

---

*Translated from the Persian.

*Prisoner of Tehran*, today, I have no doubt that Marina Nemat is a *tavvab ...*"

I stared at my computer screen, unable to read any further. In Evin when interrogating me, Hamehd had called me a "dirty infidel." He had told me that I deserved to die, that the world had forgotten about me, and that my execution would make it a better place. Now individuals who claimed to believe in freedom and democracy called me names and condemned me. But I would not become disheartened. I knew Shahnoosh was watching over me.

# Shaadi's Card

M y story was now in book form, yet a terrible urge impelled me to tell it again and again. A friend warned me that survivor's guilt was driving me and it would eventually take over my life: I was running like a marathon runner with no finish line in sight, and in the end, I would die of exhaustion. Maybe she was right, but I was supposed to have died at sixteen; now I was overdue.

My publishers sent me around the world, and at almost every book signing, a few Iranians would ask me to sign my book for them in Persian. Some were ex–political prisoners themselves, and some had had a loved one imprisoned in Iran. After one event, a young Iranian woman broke into tears, telling me her mother had been a prisoner in Evin but had never talked about it. Another woman recounted that her brother had been severely tortured in Evin but had survived. He, too, was mostly silent about the experience. Amid the hugs and tears, I was always on the lookout for a familiar face, hoping to find my prison friends in the crowd, but this didn't happen. It took a while for my friends from Iran to contact me, and the first contact came in an unexpected way after Voice of America's Persian News Network did a TV interview with me in Persian in Los Angeles, California. It was broadcast worldwide, and phone calls and emails were accepted during the show. The kindness and support of Iranians from around the globe overwhelmed me. There were even messages from Iran sent by those who had satellite dishes and been able to watch it.

A few months after the interview, I received a large envelope from my publisher in the United States. I shook it over a table in my living room, and a small white envelope fell out. I looked at the sender's name and froze: Shaadi Golzari. I read the name again and again, my heart beating faster. I ripped open the envelope to find a card from one of my best friends from elementary and high school in Tehran. She had never been arrested, but she had watched her friends disappear one by one. Now she lived in Los Angeles.

After Evin, I didn't try to contact any of my classmates for many years, and I saw only one of the girls who had been in prison with me: Shahnaz. Her release had come a few months before mine. We had not known each other prior to Evin, but I had given her my phone number. She called me one day in Tehran and then stopped by for a brief visit. She had been on the verge of a nervous breakdown in Evin, and I had been very worried about her. I was amazed at how "normal" we both now looked. We chatted in my bedroom, its large windows looking out on a backyard that overflowed with roses of every colour. While I was in prison, my parents had moved in with a friend who had a large house, and my new bedroom was overwhelmingly pink. We sat in pink armchairs and sipped Earl Grey tea from gold-rimmed china teacups with pink roses on them. Shahnaz must have come directly from the salon. Every strand of her long straight black hair was perfectly in place. She was elegantly dressed in a tight black skirt and a blue silk blouse. Like me, she wore high heels, and I wondered if, after all the lashings she had endured, her shoes hurt her feet as much as my shoes did mine. We didn't talk about Evin. She had a perpetual smile on her face that concealed the fear and worry I had always seen in her large, sad brown eyes. We each said "those days" maybe once or twice with a smile and a shrug. We were not ready to talk about the horrors we had witnessed. Our experience lived in us, and we were both aware of it, but we had decided to ignore it. However, her presence in my house spoke louder than any words ever could. She had come despite the fact that every second she spent with me transported her back to the trauma she wanted to forget. She had come to show me that what we shared and the friendship that had carried us through so much pain would remain a part of her, even though neither she nor I could find the courage to express our feelings. Before leaving, she hugged me, and I felt the same tremble in her body that I had felt as we embraced each other in Evin, listening to gunshots. She put on her black *chador* just before she walked onto the street through my front door. I never saw her again.

After Shahnaz's visit, I went to the home of only one prison friend. She was still in Evin at the time. Before my release, she had asked me to tell her parents something she had been unable to tell them herself: that she had been sentenced to twenty years.

I don't have a clear memory of the hour I spent with her family. I just remember looking down all the time. I wanted to tell her parents the truth, but I didn't have the strength. How could I gaze into their eyes and say that their daughter would remain in prison for such a long time when I had been released? Except, I had made a promise to her, so I told her brother-in-law as he drove me home. Devastated, he nodded and said he would break the news to the family.

Now a voice from the past was calling to me. Shaadi had written her telephone number on the card she had sent me. I phoned her immediately. The phone rang three times—an eternity—before she answered.

"Shaadi?" I mumbled. "It's me, Marina."

"Oh, my God! Wait … I might kill someone … God … I'm driving … on the highway … I'm pulling … over … hang on … is this really you, Marina?"

"It's me … How are you?"

"I thought you'd never call! I thought you didn't want to speak to me."

"What are you talking about? Why wouldn't I want to speak to you? I just got your card. I phoned immediately."

She told me she had sent the card to my publisher a few months earlier. It had taken my publisher a while to send readers' letters to me.

She said she had read my book and was thrilled to find bits and pieces of herself in it. She remembered my room, my books, my balcony, the pencil case I sold Sarah, and my father's blue Oldsmobile. To talk to someone I shared so many memories with was comforting. She was in touch with a few of our friends who had been in prison. Most of them still lived in Iran; after their release, they had managed to continue their studies, and then they had gotten married. I was relieved to hear they had survived. Shaadi had visited with some of them on a recent trip back to Iran. Not surprisingly, they hadn't wanted to talk about Evin.

Shaadi's mother, who lived in Iran, had told her about my book when she had seen me on Voice of America's Persian News Network. She immediately phoned her daughter in L.A.

"Marina is on TV!" her mother said to her excitedly.

"Marina? Which Marina?"

"How many Marinas do you know?"

"But *Madar joon*, I'm in the States and you're in Iran!"

"The broadcast is live. On satellite. It's happening at the Borders bookstore close to your house."

Shaadi ran to the store, only to find that the interview had not been live after all but had taken place a few days earlier. One of the employees who noticed her distress told her to write to my publisher.

Shaadi told me that she soon had to attend a family function in New York City—an hour's plane ride from me in Toronto. I couldn't miss the opportunity to see my long-lost friend, so I bought an airline ticket to New York.

On the plane, I went through my memories of Shaadi. In a way, it felt as though I'd known her in another lifetime, but somehow, it also felt like only the other day that we had sat on her bed, our knees crossed and our heads bent toward each other, as we'd talked about boys and gossiped about friends. She had always been carefree, and her joyful laughter bubbled up from deep inside her. She seemed to walk on a cloud. Before the revolution, we'd had no secrets between us. We'd played silly little games as young girls do and lived in a world half real and half make-believe where every wonderful thing could happen.

When the revolution came and things grew more complicated by the day, I slowly withdrew from her and all my friends. What was left of that joyful young girl? Was I at all the Marina she remembered?

We had decided to meet at the entrance of my publisher's building on Avenue of the Americas in New York. People flowed around me like an enormous school of fish. They appeared full of purpose and determination. I wondered if any of them could imagine how it felt to find a friend after so many years and so much pain. I wanted to stop them and tell them about the friends I had lost and the one I had finally found.

I recognized Shaadi as soon as she turned the corner. She was wearing a red top and a black skirt. At first glance, she looked almost exactly as I remembered her. Even her hairstyle was more or less the same, her long hair falling on her shoulders. As I held her in my arms, tears gathered in my eyes, the world moved backward in time—and I was home.

We took the subway to the apartment of the relative she was staying with, and we were so busy talking we missed our stop. She told me that after many of her friends, including me, were arrested in the early eighties, she became terribly depressed. Nevertheless, she finished high school and entered university to train as a nurse. After getting a degree, she worked in Iran for a while, but the conditions were so difficult that she at last decided she couldn't bear the pressure any longer. She was tired of always worrying about the Revolutionary Guard arresting her because a few strands of her hair were showing or because she might have said something "wrong." She found a job in a hospital in Dubai. The pay was relatively good, and in the beginning, she was happy. Her new home, with its amazing skyscrapers and architectural wonders, truly impressed her. Many Iranians had gone to Dubai for work, so she didn't feel too out of place. She was happy that even though local women had to wear the *hejab*, foreign women didn't have to cover their hair.

Shaadi worked in the emergency department of the hospital, and she noticed that most nights, at least one badly beaten foreign woman was brought in. The vast majority of these women were from Pakistan, India, and the Philippines, and served as nannies or maids. At the outset, she didn't make much of the beaten foreign women, because she thought that the attacks were isolated incidents. But one night she had to attend to a woman who had been so badly beaten her skull had cracked. When Shaadi asked the head nurse if the woman's injuries had been reported to the police, she was told that because the woman worked for a well-known and powerful local family, no report would be sent in. Shaadi was shocked and disgusted. Life in Dubai became unbearable for her when she realized that the authorities did nothing to help the women who had moved there in search of a better life. She went to the U.S. Embassy and applied for a visa.

When Shaadi and I arrived at the apartment, her parents, who were visiting from Iran, warmly greeted me. Her mother was as beautiful as ever, with her round face and big smile, and her father was as hospitable and wise as I remembered him. They had arrived from Tehran only days earlier. They told me that the apartment I had grown up in was still there, and so was the little convenience store where I used to buy chocolate milk on my way to school. I asked them if the owner, *Aghayeh* Rostami, still ran the store, and they said he did. I wondered if he remembered me. Speaking to people who had seen the same sights, heard the same sounds, and felt the same joys and fears as I had was heartwarming. These people were a reminder that my memories were not only mine. Shaadi mentioned that when we were kids, her sister, who was a few years younger, loved coming to my house because I let her borrow my books. I owned quite a few titles of a Persian series named *Ketabha-yeh Talayi,* which she'd loved. I had forgotten all about that.

Going to Evin was like falling from the sky. It shattered my life, and I spent the eighteen years that followed pretending nothing was broken. Only after I began to write *Prisoner of Tehran* did I start to put myself back together. My book became a candle that I lit and placed in the window of my life, a light that helped me find myself. My book also made it possible for my friends to find me. Shaadi was the first of many.

I closed my eyes for a moment and saw Rahzi Avenue, with its dusty sidewalks, small shops, and old houses. I could even smell the crisp scent of freshly ironed linen coming from the dry cleaners close to *Aghayeh* Rostami's store. I could see *Aghayeh* Rostami smiling at me from over the counter. If, from my house, I walked east on Shah Avenue instead of walking north on Rahzi, I would soon arrive at Albert's second-hand bookstore. He would give me a pat on the back and hand me a new book, sometimes also offering me a Mishka chocolate or a bottle of Coke. We would talk about the last book I had read. One day, Albert asked me if I wanted to become a writer, and I laughed.

"Why do you laugh, Marina?" he asked.

"Writers are smart," I said.

"You're smart."

I shook my head and said, "No."

"Imagine people going to bookstores to buy your books one day! Wouldn't that be wonderful?"

"Writers are not like me, Albert. They're special. I think they might even be fairies or something like that."

Even after *Prisoner of Tehran* was published and became a bestseller, I didn't see myself as a writer. A part of me still believed that writers were another breed, and I was simply not one of them. I'd written a book because I had had to. Yet I knew that Albert would be proud of me. He immigrated to the United States when I was twelve to join his son. I have no doubt Albert passed away— because if he were alive, he would have found me and reminded me that he had been right.

# A Persian Poem
## in the Russian Alphabet

As I was writing *Prisoner of Tehran*, even though I knew that the Iranian government would accuse me of lying and deny that it had ever abused prisoners, I could never have predicted the venomous personal attacks that would be unleashed against me.

In May 2007 Radio Zamaneh, an independent Persian-language radio station based in Amsterdam that broadcasts via short wave, satellite, and the Internet, asked me for an interview, and I agreed to do it while I was in London.

I waited for one of the station's producers, Dariush Rajabian, in the foyer of my hotel. We had never met but had spoken briefly by phone. Soon, a Russian-looking young man with short light-brown hair and blue eyes entered the hotel. I was sure he couldn't be Dariush. However, the young man approached me and in perfect Persian said, *"Ba dorood bar shoma, Khanoomeh Nemat"*—which means, "Greetings to you, Mrs. Nemat." Most Iranians greet each other with *"Salam,"* an Arabic word that has entered the Persian language. *Ba dorood* is old-fashioned and a little unusual. Still, I didn't make much of it. Many Iranians in exile prefer to call themselves Persians in an effort to separate themselves from the Islamic Republic. They see the Islamic Revolution as the second Arab invasion of Iran, and refrain from using Arabic words that have entered the Persian language—though this is not an easy task.

In 1935, Reza Shah Pahlavi, who was then the king of Iran, declared *Iran* the official name of Persia (what the country had been known as in the Western world for a very long time). *Iran* is a cognate of *Aryan* and means "Land of the Aryans." A few Persian scholars protested this decision on the ground that it broke with the history of the country and seemed influenced by Nazi propaganda. But Reza Shah argued that the people of Persia had called their country *Iran* for hundreds of years, and that *Persia* derived from *Pars* or *Fars*, the name of a province in central Iran. He hoped that officially calling the country *Iran* would give it a modern image. In 1953, Mohammad Reza Shah Pahlavi (Reza Shah's son) decreed that both *Iran* and *Persia* could be used.

To have a very Russian-looking man greet me in an old-fashioned Persian manner was jarring, but I reminded myself that even though I wasn't blue-eyed, I was part Russian myself. Dariush and I sat down in a quiet corner of the foyer, and I told him that I had to ask him a question before he began the interview.

"You don't look Persian. Where're you from?"

"Tajikistan," he said.

This explained his perfect Persian.

I had never met anyone from Tajikistan, but I knew that it had once been part of the Persian Empire and that Tajiks, like all Persian peoples, traced their origins to the ancient Aryan nomads who settled in central Asia as early as four thousand years ago.

When Dariush and I first started talking, *I* seemed to be interviewing *him*. I learned that he was born in 1974 in Dushanbe, Tajikistan, and came from a large family. Persian language and literature had fascinated him from a young age. Under the Soviet regime, Persian literature had been taught in Tajikistan schools, but the Persian was written using the Russian alphabet. I found this bizarre, until it occurred to me that in a way a Persian poem written using the Russian alphabet and I could be compared.

Even though I was born in Tehran, my first language was Russian. At the age of five when I first went to kindergarten, I discovered that none of my classmates spoke Russian, and this confused me. However, they accepted me, and I soon made friends. When *Bahboo* picked me up at school at the end of the day, she spoke Russian to me. I used to feel embarrassed and responded in Persian. I even tried to make *Bahboo* speak Persian, but she refused, telling me that Russian was a better language, *our* language. After *Bahboo* died, I realized that I wanted to be both Russian *and* Persian. I taught myself the Russian alphabet and began, with great difficulty, to read the few books of Russian poetry we had at home. I ultimately grew to adore Pushkin as much as Rumi.

Dariush told me that he had taught himself the Persian alphabet and had eventually learned to read and write properly. He and I had more in common than he knew. As a teenager, he had worked for various radio stations. Then, in 1992, not too long after the breakup of the Soviet Union, Tajikistan became independent and fell into a five-year civil war. Soon after the turmoil began, Dariush left Tajikistan and went into exile. He travelled in Russia and then lived in Iran for some time. From 1995 to 1997, he was the acting editor of Tehran Radio's Russian Service, worked as a German translator for *Graphic* magazine, and served as a Russian interpreter and translator for the Iranian Ministry of Foreign Affairs. From 1997 to 1999, he was a member of the Aga Khan Humanities Project for Central Asia. He began working as a reporter for the BBC World Service in 1999, and then he became the producer of the BBC World Service's Persian program in London.

When I finally had asked Dariush all my questions, he had a chance to ask me his.

"Why did you decide to write your book in English, considering that you speak Persian very well and most of the events of the book took place in Iran?"

Many other journalists had asked me the same thing.

"When I was nine," I said, "I discovered a second-hand bookstore that sold only English-language books. The owner, Albert, was a kind Armenian Iranian. I didn't have much money to buy books, but Albert was generous, and he let me borrow books from him. I loved reading, and now I had no choice but to read in English. Eventually, English became the language of literature for me."

Dariush wanted to know if we spoke Persian at home when I was growing up, and I explained that my parents spoke Russian to each other.

"How interesting!" he said, surprised. "They were Russian?"

I explained their background, and added that after *Bahboo's* death, I refused to speak Russian with my parents because I felt that Russian was something special *Bahboo* and I had shared.

Many fellow Persians are probably disappointed that I have chosen to write in English, but the truth is that by sheer happenstance, English has become the language in which I can express myself best. When talking about everyday matters with Iranian friends, I am very comfortable speaking Persian, but when expressing my feelings and thoughts, English comes to me more easily. I have not used my Russian in many years, and it has become quite rusty.

Dariush asked me why I had finally decided to write *Prisoner of Tehran*, and as I had told tens of other journalists, I said that I didn't rationally decide to write it, but that I desperately needed to. I would have gone mad if I had not put my story down on paper.

"When you left Iran and before writing the book, did you tell your story to officials at the Canadian Embassy so they would accept you as a refugee? Some people think you made up the whole thing to be accepted into Canada," he said.

The idea was so absurd it made me laugh.

I explained that we didn't come to Canada as refugees. From Tehran we went to Madrid, and there we went straight to a Catholic refugee agency that knew our story through reliable sources. At the agency they told us that we *would be* accepted as refugees, but because of the heavy backlog, it could take us three years to arrive in Canada. However, Canada was where we wanted to go because my brother had moved there and we had heard that it was a wonderful place to live. The agency suggested that we should go to the Canadian Embassy and apply as immigrants, because they were processed much more quickly than refugees. And this is what we did. At the Canadian Embassy, I didn't emphasize my imprisonment. Instead, we asked to have Andre's degree evaluated in Ottawa. Andre was an electrical engineer with a master's degree from the University of Tehran and had published papers in well-known international magazines in his field. In the end, Canada accepted us as independent immigrants because of Andre's qualifications. That we were both fluent in English also helped. From Madrid, Andre and I went to Budapest and arrived in Canada ten months later as independent immigrants.

When we left Iran in 1990, just being an Iranian Christian was reason enough to claim refugee status. I had a few Iranian Christian friends who had gone to the United States as refugees, even though they themselves had never been persecuted. I didn't need to make up a story. Was the government of Iran trying to discredit me by accusing me of lying, or were the comments about me making up my story those of narrow-minded individuals? Negative reactions shouldn't have surprised me. Of course they would say that I had lied about my imprisonment and torture in Evin to gain refugee status. The government of Iran had never admitted that it had political prisoners, let alone that it had tortured and executed teenagers. I had most certainly hit a nerve, and now they were doing damage control. Naïve individuals who had not even read my book might fall for their lies. I had to continue what I was doing. As a witness, I had to testify.

Dariush said that my life story was so interesting it would make a great Hollywood movie.

"It's so unusual for one person to have experienced all the strange events that you have recounted in your book," he added, "so some of our listeners have asked how much of your book was really the truth and how much of it was the result of your imagination?"

Some people thought that the torture, rape, and execution of political prisoners in Iran were figments of my imagination? I felt sick to my stomach. So if "strange" and "unusual" things happened to someone, it automatically meant that those events never happened? This was not just about me; it was about thousands of teenagers who had suffered in silence. Knowingly or unknowingly, some individuals were trying to turn the terrible crime of torture into a political game. I couldn't allow this to happen. I collected myself and responded to the question. I explained that nothing in my book was the result of my imagination. I had changed some details and most names. As I had stated in my author's note, I had also merged the stories of my friends to protect their privacy. But this had not affected the reality of events. I had been imprisoned, tortured, and forced to marry my interrogator, and I had witnessed the suffering of my friends in Evin. I had in no way made up what happened.*

A battle had begun, and I was on its front line. I was its flag holder. Was I standing alone? No, many people supported me and stood with me. This was about us, my young girlfriends and me in Evin; about the ones who were not politically active but were caught in the madness that engulfed Iran in the 1980s.

---

*The complete Persian text of Dariush's interview with me is available at www.radiozamaneh.org/special/2007/05/post_230html.

After the interview, Dariush and I had dinner together and talked for two more hours. He had come to me with bias, but in the end, I felt that he had put it aside.

That night in my hotel room, I Googled myself out of curiosity and found a handful of comments that called me a liar, a traitor, and a whore. It was easy for people to say anything they wanted on the Internet without being held accountable. They didn't even have to reveal their real names. No one had ever confronted me at any of my public events around the world. Hiding in cyberspace was the coward's way out. I hoped that my children didn't see those comments online. I shut down my computer and went to bed.

The next day was Saturday. I had decided to stay in London for the weekend to explore the city and visit an old family friend, Hooshang *Khan*,* whom I had not seen in seventeen years. I had been exhausted the previous night, so I didn't set my alarm. I woke with the pale orange glow of the sun spreading in my room and was shocked to find Andre lying next to me in my twin-size bed, fast asleep. I touched his hair, and he opened his eyes a little.

"What are you doing here?" I said. "You're supposed to be at home in Canada. When did you get here? How did you get into the room? How did you fit in this bed? How—"

"Don't ask so many questions. I just wanted to be with you," he interrupted me, smiling.

I put my arms around him and closed my eyes. When I opened them a moment later, he wasn't there. It had been a dream. I got out of bed and started my day. I had to rush. I was supposed to be at Hooshang *Khan*'s apartment at noon.

In the evening when I got back to the hotel, my cell phone rang. It was Andre.

*Like *agha*, *khan* means "mister" in Persian. However, *agha* usually (not always) comes before a name, whereas *khan* almost always comes after it.

"How was Hooshang *Khan?*" he asked.

"He was well. He's older, of course, but he hasn't changed much. He was so happy to see me. He ordered in some food, and we had *chelokabab*\* for lunch. It felt like home. I finally apologized to him for yelling at him when he told me I shouldn't marry you. He said he understood my reaction and had never been angry at me."

"So … tell me, what's happening in London?"

"Nothing remarkable. Same stuff. Interviews and events. They all went well."

"You sure?"

"Yeah. Why?"

"They say if you want to know what your wife is up to, Google her!"

"What do you mean?"

"Some people are attacking you online."

"I know."

"And you didn't bother to tell me?"

I said I didn't want to upset him. Andre had every right to be worried for me, but regardless of the cost, I had to continue what I had started. I understood the risk I was taking.

---

\*Rice with beef kebabs.

# A Persian Song Named *Soltan-eh Ghalbha* (King of Hearts)

Hooshang *Khan* gave me a bouquet of nineteen pink roses on my nineteenth birthday, only days after my release from Evin. I put them in a vase, sat in a chair, and stared at them for a long time. I had spent my two previous birthdays in prison.

When I announced that I was going to marry Andre, Hooshang *Khan* tried to change my mind. He said it was suicide. I had been forced to convert to Islam in the prison, and in the eyes of the Iranian regime, I was now a Muslim woman. A Muslim woman is not allowed to marry a Christian man. If I announced that I had returned to Christianity, I could be arrested, even executed. Hooshang *Khan* insisted that I could have a relationship with Andre, but we should leave marriage for when we left Iran. I yelled at him, saying that I would do as I pleased, that neither he nor anyone else had the right to tell me whom I should or should not marry. Colour left his face, but he didn't say a word and walked out of my room.

Before my time in the prison, Andre and I had both been very shy and had never even kissed. After my release, Andre didn't seem to have changed much. He was a perfect gentleman and as shy as ever. He didn't know it at the time, but after marrying Ali, I spent two or three nights a week with him in a solitary cell, and Ali made it clear to me that I had to satisfy his sexual appetite. Sometimes, he would even walk into my cell in the middle of the day and tell me to take off my clothes. I resisted him in the beginning, and kicked and screamed. I even managed to hurt him a few times, but he never backed off. He told me that screaming wouldn't get me anywhere but would only scare the other prisoners. He was right. If I didn't resist, it would be over more quickly, and I would suffer less.

The day after my arrest, my mother called Andre at seven in the morning and told him that I had been taken to Evin. Even though Andre knew there was a good chance I would not survive, he never lost hope of seeing me again. He was twenty-three years old and a university student. However, all Iranian universities had been closed. They were to be restructured and de-Westernized under the Iranian Cultural Revolution (1980–1983), which purged thousands of faculty, staff, and students, the majority of whom were followers or members of leftist groups. While the universities were shut down, Andre taught English at an Armenian school in Tehran and coached the school's various sports teams; he had been a track-and-field champion in Iran at the national level and had won many medals. He also attended Italian-language classes at the Italian Institute of Culture in Tehran and continued playing the organ at our church and Armenian Catholic churches. While I was in prison, a few young women pursued Andre, but after my release, he told me he had never been interested in them.

Before I married Ali, I asked him to let me say goodbye to Andre. He promised he would and he kept his word. Andre was permitted to visit me in Evin only once. It was so brave of him to come—for all he knew, prison authorities could have kept him there. At the time, they only let close family members—mother, father, husband, wife, and children—visit prisoners. Allowing a friend to come was unheard of. Andre and I stood on either side of the glass barrier in the visiting room and stared at each other for a while. Phones had been installed and we could talk, but we knew we were being watched. He asked me how I was doing, and I said I was okay. I wanted to tell him about my marriage to Ali, yet I couldn't. Instead, I told him to forget about me and move on, but he said he would wait for me.

When I returned home from Evin, Andre told me he somehow knew he had to take care of me. We spent a lot of time together in my parents' backyard and in my room, since he was helping me with my studies. I never went back to school after Evin. I went for the necessary exams and eventually got my high-school diploma. To keep myself busy, I, too, signed up for Italian lessons at the Italian Institute of Culture in Tehran.

When all was in place for our wedding, which took place on July 18, 1985, Andre and I realized that we needed someone to pick up our wedding cake at the bakery and deliver it to the church, where we were having a small reception after the ceremony. At the time, many middle- and upper-class families rented banquet halls for weddings, but we had decided to keep ours as quiet as possible and have a simple party at the church hall, serving only fruits, soft drinks, and cake. There would be no music or dancing—we couldn't risk being heard from the street. What if someone reported us to the Revolutionary Guard? Hooshang *Khan* volunteered to bring the cake. He found someone to drive him to the bakery, and he held the large cake on his lap all the way to the church. It was a very hot day, so by the time he arrived, the two-tiered pink cake had slightly melted and become lopsided. The cake would never have survived a trip in the car trunk. Hooshang *Khan* had saved the day.

My father walked me down the aisle. One of my mother's sisters, Aunt Latif, had made my simple white dress. The church was full. Andre's father had passed away while I was in prison, and his aunt who had raised him had returned to Hungary shortly before the wedding. She had become old and frail, and had wanted to be back home with her sister and the rest of her relatives. I had never met Andre's father. Just before my arrest, Andre wanted to invite me to his house to meet his father and aunt, but we never got the chance. I was saddened that no one from Andre's family was present at our wedding, but none of his relatives, including his sister, was in Iran. Two of my mother's sisters and their families came to the church, but my mother's eldest sister, Zenia, and my mother's brother, Ismael, did not. Aunt Zenia had had a fight with my father over money. She had not been herself lately and had been behaving strangely. I was hugely disappointed not to see her and Uncle Ismael in the crowd, but I had fought hard to get to that day, and nothing short of being arrested could spoil it for me.

IN 1938, at the age of twenty-eight, Andre's father, Mihaly, a Hungarian carpenter, arrived in Iran to work on a new palace named Kakh-eh Marmar. It was being built for the crown prince of Iran, Mohammad Reza Pahlavi, who was soon to marry the beautiful Princess Fawzieh of Egypt. Mihaly had heard about the job from a friend who worked at the Hungarian Ministry of Foreign Affairs in Budapest. The promised pay was good and the prospect of travelling to Iran was exciting, so Mihaly applied and was hired. He left his fiancée, Juliana, in Budapest in the hope of returning home immediately after completion of the palace, but the Second World War prevented that. While the war raged in Europe and Hungary stood by Germany, the Allies entered Iran to deliver supplies to Russia from the south, and Mihaly, along with other Italian, Hungarian, and German nationals working in Iran, was expelled and sent to a special camp in India. After the war, he returned to Iran instead of his native Hungary because Hungary had become Communist. He hoped that the Communist regime would soon topple and he could go back home, but years went by and this did not happen. Hungarians weren't allowed to leave their country at that time, and Juliana was unable to join Mihaly. She was forced to remain in Hungary until the anti-Communist revolution of 1956, which opened the Hungarian borders for a brief time and permitted her to enter Austria as a refugee. She later joined her long-lost love in Iran after eighteen years of separation. They married immediately and had two children: Andre and, fifteen months later, his sister. Juliana passed away when Andre was only four and his sister two and a half. After her death, one of Mihaly's sisters, an unmarried woman of about sixty, travelled to Iran to help her brother raise his children. In time, she proved to be a wonderful substitute for the mother taken from them.

EVENTUALLY *Prisoner of Tehran* was translated into Italian, and at a dinner party in a restaurant in the city of Cosenza in southern Italy, I saw Princess India, the granddaughter of Mohammed Zahir Shah, the last king of Afghanistan. She lived in Italy and had just received an award for her aid and charity work in her country. She was a handsome woman, and appeared to be in her sixties. I had been introduced to her the morning of the dinner party. We had talked briefly in Farsi, the official language of Afghanistan. Even though the Farsi of Afghanistan (called Farsi-yeh Dari) is considered a dialect of the Persian language, Iranian Farsi and Afghan Farsi are similar. The princess had smiled as I spoke Farsi to her, eyeing me with undisguised intensity. At dinner we had more time to talk, and she told me about her family. I was surprised to hear that when she had been very young, she had married an Iranian and had lived in both Tehran and the city of Mashad in northeastern Iran. We talked about poetry and recited to each other a few lines from the works of famous Persian poets. She asked me about my family and I told her about my parents, and Andre and his parents.

The princess's eyes widened with surprise. "What was Andre's father's name?" she asked.

"Mihaly Nemat," I said, wondering why she wanted to know.

"This is so strange! How is this even possible? Mihaly Nemat made all my furniture in Iran. He was a very skilled carpenter, and he did an amazing job for me!"

I didn't know what to say.

"He had a wife, but no children back then."

"They had two children. Andre and his sister. Andre's mother died when he was four."

The coincidence astounded me. I couldn't wait to tell Andre I had met someone who had known his father.

The princess and I also spoke of Iran and its beauty, and then she asked me if I knew any Persian songs. She wanted me to sing one to her. I cannot sing well, but my unexpected connection to her had stirred so many emotions I somehow didn't mind. The restaurant was noisy; people had finished their food and were chatting, so I gathered my courage and sang her an old song named *Soltan-eh Ghalbha* (King of the Hearts) from a Persian movie that first came out in 1968. I wasn't quite sure why I had chosen that song. I listen to a great deal of Persian music and have many favourites, but I have loved *Soltan-eh Ghalbha* since I was a young child. I often hummed it when I was in solitary confinement in Evin, thinking of Andre. For the princess, I sang the words to the song:

> *My heart sometimes tells me to leave, and it sometimes tells me to stay, but I cannot bear this. How can I live without you? When one is so deeply in love, the world seems so small. You are always in my heart, and I will never leave you. Only you are the Soltan of my heart. You are my beloved, and we are one. Now that I am far away from you, I will not give my heart to anyone else. I long for you, my beautiful lover.*

As I sang, the princess's eyes filled with tears. The song resurrected memories for her of all she had witnessed and all she had lost. We were very different; she was an Afghan princess and I was an ordinary Persian woman. But we had both suffered—and now our paths had crossed in Cosenza, where I sang a Persian love song for her. She held my hand in hers as I sang, and it was as if the words of the song brought us into one body, one existence.

# Fatelessness and
## The Diary of Anne Frank

After a speaking engagement of mine in a Toronto suburb, a woman in the audience asked me why I showed almost no anger in *Prisoner of Tehran*. This was one of the most insightful questions I had been asked. I told her that in prison I had usually blamed myself for all that had gone on and felt guilty about everything. Years later when I thought of the cruelties I had witnessed in Evin, of the torture and death of my friends, I felt a leaden sadness—thick and dark and desperate for goodness. Anger does not have the ability to carry the weight of what I feel. Maybe nothing does. Maybe a new emotion needs to be created for it. In prison, numbness overtook me. After about sixteen years, it started to diminish. I finally began to feel. I got angry at my father when, at my mother's funeral, he told me that she had forgiven me before her death. However, my anger quickly turned into grief—a flood threatening to drown me from within. Then came a terrible sense of frustration that melted into helplessness, followed by an overwhelming need to make amends and find humanity and forgiveness. Anger cannot fix; it destroys. I have already had enough death and destruction in my life.

I clearly remember the L-shaped hallway of block 246 in Evin. The cells. The girls. My first night there. My feet were terribly swollen and I could hardly walk. I had not had much to eat or drink in days. Even though I felt safer in 246 than I had in the interrogation building, the strangeness of the environment made me think I was suffocating. The cell I was put in was about seventeen by twenty-five feet, its floor covered with a worn brown carpet. Just above my eye level, a metal shelf ran across the wall; plastic bags filled with clothes sat on top of it and smaller bags hung from hooks beneath it. The beige paint covering the walls and the metal doors was thin and dirty. In one corner of the cell stood a bunk bed. Jars and containers of different shapes and sizes covered the lower bunk, and plastic bags stuffed with clothes sat piled on the upper. In another corner, next to a barred window, grey military blankets lay stacked almost to the ceiling. There were teenage girls everywhere. Most of them sat talking on the floor in groups of two or three. The barred window looked out over a small, empty, paved courtyard. I was in a world I didn't understand at all. Tears gathered in my eyes and a terrible pain exploded in my chest. Only when Sarah suddenly appeared beside me did I feel better. She had been in Evin longer than I had. I could rely on her. And time proved that she could rely on me. How do teenage girls survive hell? They do it by being who they are, by remembering that they are human beings and have families who love them. In Evin, the present was so horrible we rarely talked about it, and the future didn't exist, so all we had was the past. We survived by talking about our homes, moms, dads, brothers, sisters, aunts, uncles, cousins, birthday parties, weddings, New Year's celebrations, our favourite books, poems, films, and music. These long conversations somehow created a collective memory that became our beacon of hope. The more we shared, the brighter the light of hope glowed. We wanted to go home, and we helped one another believe that we would indeed be released one day. Every minute, we risked facing torture, even execution, but amid all the horror, there was some happiness. Human beings have a miraculous ability to create hope out of nothing.

MY CELLMATES AND I were not the only ones in the world able to find light in seemingly absolute darkness. In 2007, I read a book titled *Fatelessness*, a novel written in 1975 by Imre Kertész, a Hungarian writer imprisoned in concentration camps as a youth. In the last two pages of the book, sixteen-year-old Georg Koves is finally going home from a concentration camp at the end of the Second World War. He is on his way to find his mother, who has also survived the Holocaust, when he pauses to rest and think:

> But one shouldn't exaggerate, as this is precisely the crux of it: I am here, and I am well aware that I shall accept any rationale as the price for being able to live. Yes, as I looked around this placid, twilit square, this street, weather–beaten yet full of a thousand promises, I was already feeling a growing readiness to continue my uncontinuable life. My mother was waiting, and would no doubt greatly rejoice over me. I recollect that she had once conceived a plan that I should become an engineer, a doctor, or something like that. No doubt that is how it will be, just as she wished; there is nothing impossible that we do not live through naturally, and keeping a watch on me on my journey, like some inescapable trap, I already know there will be happiness. For even there, next to the chimneys, in the intervals between the torments, there was something that resembled happiness. Everyone asks only about the hardships and the "atrocities," whereas for me perhaps it is that experience which will remain the most memorable. Yes, the next time I am asked, I

*ought to speak about that, the happiness of the concentration
camps.*

*If indeed I am asked. And provided I myself don't forget.**

IT WAS RAINING when I was released from Evin. I had to walk to
Luna Park, an amusement park located about a mile and a half
south of the prison. The government had taken over a part of it
to use as a base for shuttle buses for visitors to the prison. When
prisoners were released, families had to wait for their loved one in
the park. A gust of wind heavy with cold droplets of rain whipped
against me. Adjusting my black *chador*, I carefully made my way
down the few steps that led to the quiet, narrow street. I paused,
looked up, and watched the clouds move with the strong wind.
For a moment, a breathtaking small patch of blue sky appeared.
Although pale, it was still lively against the shades of grey. My eyes
followed the road. A white car turned the corner. The driver, a
middle-aged man, slowed and stared at me but continued on his
path. My socks were soaked inside my rubber slippers, and my feet
were freezing. I walked quickly, with steady steps. It was 1984, and
I had waited for this day for two years, two months, and twelve
days. I wanted to go home and restart my life where I had left off.
Unlike Georg Koves, I didn't pause. But like him, I thought about
my moments of happiness in the hell I was leaving. As I walked
home, I didn't think of the horror I had been drowning in for more
than two years. There had been times when, briefly, I had been able
to surface and breathe. Without those little breaths, I would have
died. My cellmates were my air—or, as Kertész put it, "the intervals
between the torment." It was only when I was released and went
home that I realized life would never be the same. I had changed.

---

*Imre Kertész, *Fatelessness, A Novel,* translated from Hungarian by Tim Wilkinson. (New
York: Random House, 2004), 261–262.

Everything had changed. I didn't belong anywhere. During my first nights home, I closed my eyes and listened to the stillness of the night. I missed my friends, the girls with whom I had developed irreplaceable relationships. Without their friendship, which was the warmth that sustained me in a perpetually frozen realm of darkness, I felt a terrible gap in my life. I had wanted to come home, but it was as if my home had been wiped out of existence and the place where I now lived was only a clumsy replica. I wanted to be with Sarah. Would they ever let her go? We had been through life and death together, through madness and hope, through love and despair. We understood each other. I had returned to my family, but they were all strangers to me. Sarah knew what it meant to look straight into the eyes of death and watch it leave you behind and take the people you loved. As Kertész had said, I had to live an "uncontinuable life."

I have recurring images of my last month of Ramadan in Evin, when we had to fast and refrain from eating and drinking from dawn until dusk. We received larger and better rations to break our fast at the end of each day. The guards sometimes even gave each cell a watermelon. Most of us had not seen one in months or years. During the day we would put the watermelons in large buckets of cold tap water so that they would cool, and we would break them immediately after saying our Namaz at sunset. I remember running my hands over their cold, smooth skin. My friends and I sat together to break our fast, passing pieces of watermelon to one another. The sun had set, but the air was heavy with heat. First, we closed our eyes and let the scent of the fruit fill us, and then we bit into it, allowing its sweet, cold juice to tingle our chapped lips and wash away the bitter dryness of our mouths and throats. We giggled as young girls do. Yes, there was happiness in Evin, and it lived in the sisterhood that connected us to one another.

I READ *The Diary of Anne Frank* after coming to Canada, so it was relatively fresh in my mind when I went to Amsterdam in May 2007. Even though our circumstances had been very different, I felt a special closeness to Anne, as if she were a friend I had lost. The first place I visited in Amsterdam was the Anne Frank House, where Anne and her parents and sister, another family, and a dentist had hidden from the Nazis. In 1960, the house became a museum open to the public. To welcome visitors, the front part of the building—the former business premises—was rebuilt as a reception and exhibition space. Only the back of the house, also known as the Secret Annex, remained in its original state. I cried my way through it. I wished Anne were here to see that a million people visited the Secret Annex every year and that her book was read and cherished by millions more. I felt her presence as I stopped at every corner and remembered parts of her diary—but her presence was not a sad one; it was full of life and energy.

In large font, sentences from her diary are written on walls throughout the house, magnifying the suffering of not only one young girl but of a people. One sentence reads, "We're very afraid the neighbours might hear or see us."

Fear, silence, and horror. I knew them well.

Silence has a persistent presence; once it enters, it refuses to leave. After the Holocaust, victims found it difficult to talk about their experiences, and those listening found the experiences too painful to hear—so silence endured. However, Anne's voice finally triumphed. Those who put her and millions of others in concentration camps and tried to wipe them from memory failed. Anne's vivid presence in the house became stronger with every passing moment.

Anne's bedroom in the Secret Annex reminded me of mine in Tehran, but my room had only one twin-size bed, when Anne's room had two. At first, Anne shared her room with her sister,

Margot. Then a dentist named Fritz Pfeffer arrived; he, too, was hiding from the Nazis. Like me, Anne had a small wooden desk in a corner. However, my room had a glass door that opened onto a balcony, when her room was cut off from the outside world. Both Anne and I had put a few posters on our bedroom walls: hers were of film stars such as Greta Garbo, or Dutch royalty and nature; mine were of Donny and Marie Osmond. How nice it would have been to have posters to decorate my cell when I was in solitary confinement in Evin. Anne and I had a great deal in common, including our love for literature, and I am sure that had we known each other, we would have become good friends. I was astounded to learn that her cat's name had been Mouschi—the nickname I gave Andre after my release from prison. Anne couldn't take her cat to the Secret Annex and she missed him terribly.

Of the eight people who had hidden in the Secret Annex for two years, seven died in concentration camps. Only Anne's father, Otto Frank, survived. In Anne Frank House, I watched an interview with Mr. Frank, done after his release from Auschwitz and the publication of Anne's diary.

He said, "To build a future, you have to know the past ..."

There is much wisdom in this small sentence.

A few weeks after visiting the house, I watched a documentary about a man who had suffered brain damage and had forgotten everything about his past. He had also lost the ability to form any new long-term memories. As a result, he was incapable of planning. He awoke every day forgetting all about yesterday, unable to understand the concept of tomorrow. Because he never remembered the past, the future had no meaning for him. If this can happen to an individual, it can also happen to a people.

The people of Iran have to shake off their collective amnesia, face their past, and then plan for a better future. Facing the past means facing mistakes. We have to accept responsibility. We made decisions and took steps that led to a revolution. It went terribly wrong and gave birth to a dictatorship that claimed the lives of thousands of young Iranians and left thousands of others broken. Facing the past is not about pointing fingers; it's about acknowledgment. Each one of us could probably have made different choices that could have saved lives, but we didn't. We have to remember that it's never too late to take a stand. In 2009, Iranians rose up and did just that: demanded justice and democracy. As a survivor of Evin, it is my duty to remind Iranians that revolutions and movements can go astray. Violence leads to violence. Torture and murder are wrong and never lead to justice. The end, no matter how sacred it is, can never justify the means. As long as there is a Supreme Leader in Iran who can veto the decisions of the people, democracy cannot root and grow.

In Anne Frank House, I also watched an interview with Hannah Goslar, Anne's neighbour, friend, and classmate. Like Anne, Hannah was sent to Bergen-Belsen concentration camp, and she was one of the last people to see Anne alive. A barbed-wire fence had separated the two girls, and Anne had cried and told Hannah that she had nobody, which wasn't true—but Anne wasn't aware her father had survived. Hannah believed that if Anne had known her father was alive, she would have lived. I agree with her. Hope has miraculous powers. Anne died only days before the liberation. With a great deal of sadness in her eyes, Hannah said that Anne's death and her own survival were "cruel accidents." Yes, maybe both our survivals are cruel accidents, or maybe they are the will of God; either way, life is precious.

On Thursday morning, March 25, 2010, a beautiful sunny day, I stood in Auschwitz and looked down a narrow road sandwiched between two rows of red-brick, two-storey buildings. Unlike the flimsy wooden barracks I had seen in other concentration camps, these were well built and appeared sturdy. Many tour buses sat parked in the parking lot, and tourists of all ages and nationalities walked everywhere. I was on a trip organized by the Friends of Simon Wiesenthal Centre for Holocaust Studies. Birds sang in the pale sun, and the clear voice of our young tour guide, Anna, who was knowledgeable and professional, streamed through my headset. But I wasn't listening. The bricks of Auschwitz were almost identical in colour to those at Evin. I reached out and touched them, and tears blinded me. We had just seen piles of the thousands of shoes taken from the victims of Auschwitz, and I remembered that in Evin, guards had taken my white-and-red Puma running shoes and had given me rubber slippers, instead. Where were my shoes and those of my prison friends? Had they been destroyed? We entered a barrack, and I peered into the bright, average-size room on my right. A wooden table stood in the middle of the room, with a few chairs around it. Anna explained that this room was used for arbitrary trials and that most of the prisoners tried here were sentenced to death and executed in the courtyard behind the building. In Evin prison, the Sharia judge who had condemned me to death probably sat in a similar room and drank tea as he passed on verdicts.

I followed my group down the hall and into the basement. A friend turned around, looked at me, and asked, "You okay?" I nodded, but I could hardly breathe.

On my left was a dark cell with a small barred window. This was where Father Maximilian Kolbe, canonized by Pope John Paul II in 1982, was killed in August 1941. During the Second World War, he had provided shelter to Polish refugees, including two thousand Jews. In February 1941, the Gestapo arrested him. He was transferred to Auschwitz about three months later. In July 1941, a man from Kolbe's barrack vanished, and the deputy camp commander picked ten men to starve to death in order to discourage further escapes. One of the selected men begged not to be killed, saying that he had family waiting for him. Kolbe volunteered to go in his place. I wished I had been as brave as Kolbe, but I was not.

After three weeks of dehydration and starvation, only Kolbe and three others were still alive. Each time the guards checked on him, Kolbe was standing or kneeling in the middle of the cell and looking calmly at those who entered. When his remaining cellmates had died, Kolbe was killed with an injection of carbolic acid.

I gazed at the small barred window of Kolbe's cell. It was as if I were back in my cell at Evin. Even though Auschwitz was now a museum and a place of remembrance, I knew that Evin was still operational: innocents were still being tortured and executed there. I searched my heart for something more I could do for them. My legs somehow carried me out of the barrack and back into the spring sun. I sat on the steps and covered my face with my hands. I couldn't stop crying. Maximilian Kolbe is the patron saint of political prisoners. I begged him to show me the way to help bring about real change in Iran without endangering more lives.

As in the concentration camps, life in the public cellblocks at Evin revolved around routines that, even though tedious, carried us through the days. The constant religious-education programs broadcast for hours every day on the closed-circuit television of the prison were designed to brainwash us, but after a while, even as I sat in front of the TV, I didn't hear a word of them. I either whispered poems to a friend sitting next to me or I daydreamed about going home. I heard from one of my cellmates who had been in Evin during the time of the shah that back then, each cell in 246 held five or six prisoners. In my time, we numbered sixty to seventy. When so many people have to live in a small space, simple tasks become challenging. Finding a place to sleep, dividing food, tidying up, washing dishes, cleaning the bathrooms, and taking showers were all major issues that required a great deal of organization. We chose girls to do different jobs, and the duties usually changed hands weekly. One week, for example, I would be the "sleeping-spot authority." This meant I had to make sure everyone had a place to sleep. This might sound simple, but it was not. There were so many of us that we had to sleep not only on the floor in the cells but also in the hallway. There was absolutely no room to spare. The lights were turned off in the cells at night, but they remained on in the hallway, so sleeping in the cells was more comfortable. In addition, your chances of getting stepped on while asleep increased dramatically in the hallway, because you would be in the way of the people who needed to use the bathroom. In the cells, some girls preferred to sleep close to the windows because we usually left them open even in winter. However, others preferred to be far from them so that they wouldn't be cold. And we all always wanted to sleep next to our friends.

Dividing the food, which typically consisted of bread with dates, rice, or soup, was a challenge, as well. We didn't get much food in Evin, and making sure that everyone had an equal share was not easy.

Cleaning was another problem. Imagine cleaning a bathroom used by three hundred and fifty to four hundred people. We had warm water once every two or three weeks for two to three hours each time. Water customarily warmed up in the middle of the night. When you were your cell's shower worker, you had to send sixty to seventy sleepy girls to use four or five shower stalls in a matter of minutes. The shower worker had to stand at the door of the shower room and rush girls in and out. Shower nights were always loud.

"Afsaneh, Fereshteh, Nahid! Get out! You've been in there forever! I told you that you had four minutes!" the shower worker would yell.

"I've been here for only two minutes! I still have soap in my hair!" the girl inside would shout back.

"Doesn't matter! Out! People are waiting! Do you want them to have to wash up with cold water? Out!"

And if the worker had been too hard on someone and the next day that person was called for interrogation and was tortured, the worker would feel horrible for days. The injured always received longer turns and help in the shower. My first evening in 246 was shower night. I couldn't stand on my feet well because of the lashing, so Sarah helped me, and the girl in charge gave us extra time.

I have faith that one day Evin, like the Secret Annex and Auschwitz, will become a museum where people will honour those who suffered and died. One day, young and old will walk its hallways, look inside its cells and torture rooms, and learn about a dark time in Iran's history when the torture of teenagers was considered a good deed, done to please God and protect the country from evil.

# My Dragonfly Brooch

In August 2007, while I was in Edinburgh, I gave a short phone interview to Radio Hambastegi, a Persian-language radio station based in Stockholm. Soon after returning home to Toronto I received an email from the interviewer, Nasser Yousefi, with the link* to the program they had had on my book. Only when I clicked on the link and began listening did I realize that the program was about three hours long. The first interviews were with three of my critics, who had been prisoners in Evin and members of Communist or Marxist-Islamist groups. Two of them had written their own memoirs of Evin. They believed that my book shouldn't have been published because my experience of Evin was different from theirs. They said that I had not properly conveyed the horrors of Evin and that I had not told the story of the heroes of the prison who had suffered and died for their ideology and beliefs.

Before the interviews, Nasser had given a brief introduction on memory and memoir writing, and had quoted from a Persian-language publication named *Baran*. He said that events happened in a place and time, and the exact retelling of them was impossible, because when events become memories they exist only in our

---

*http://biphome.spray.se/radiohambastegi/2007/marina070811.ram.

mind, and how we view them depends on our perspective. Even immediately after we see a photo, remembering its details clearly is impossible since human memory is, simply, imperfect. He compared writing a memoir to making a movie: two directors making a film from one book might end up with two very different accounts. Some scenes we fast-forward and some we put in slow motion because of the way we feel about them. He concluded that we therefore had to respect memory and memoirs and never consider them completely accurate, because all humans look at the world through a lens, and there is nothing we can do about that.

I had hoped that my critics would deliver a rational review of my book—which is how a literary review should be. But what I heard on the radio show was an extreme personal attack. My critics called me a liar, a *tavvab,* and a traitor, and claimed that I had written *Prisoner of Tehran* for money. One woman openly admitted that she had not read my book; she had only read *about* it. She said, "I first criticized Marina's book, but then when I saw that some people had turned this [criticism] into a personal attack on her, I pulled myself aside from that ... This [book] is not the truth of the pain of those who suffered in prison and were tortured. It is important for every publisher to sell books. This [book] is not the description of the pains Marina endured. It has been twisted and turned into something that would sell ... This book is the result of the work of a group of people [and not only Marina] ..."

To me, these attacks were very much like the intolerance of the Islamic Republic: if you're not with us and like us, if you don't share the same religion or ideology with us, then we're against you.

I have experienced how a victim can become a torturer—Ali, the guard I was forced to marry, had been tortured in Evin during the time of the shah. Torture creates a vicious cycle that repeats itself as long as victims give in to hatred and let it blind them. If my critics ever have authority over me, they will probably ban my book. They call me a *tavvab,* but if I have betrayed anyone, I have betrayed myself and my religion, not them or their ideology. I was coerced into converting to Islam and marrying my interrogator, but my humanity and who I am have remained intact, even after the pressure and brainwashing that I was subjected to in Evin. The Islamic Republic of Iran tried to turn me into an angry, illogical, and dysfunctional individual, but it failed. What do my critics see when they look at themselves in a mirror? Heroes? Maybe. But all the heroes I know, including my close friends in Evin, are open-minded individuals. Even though they had to pretend that they had "repented," they always preserved their goodness and humanity.

Those who have spoken against me in chat rooms or on air are a small group of twenty-five or thirty men and women. They were adults when they were arrested and had been active members of various opposition political groups. Their ideology was everything to them, and they bravely fought for it, which I respect. But they know nothing of how a helpless sixteen-year-old feels under torture, of how she would be willing to confess to anything or share any information with prison authorities to stop the vicious beatings.

I personally know only one of my critics: Soudabeh Ardavan. Online and in the interview with Radio Hambastegi, she accused me of being a traitor. I had seen her at two events during the winter of 2006 in Toronto. Then I attended a dinner party where I saw her again and where I also met a few other ex-prisoners from Iran. Even though *Prisoner of Tehran* had not yet appeared in print, my story was not a secret. Michelle Shephard's article "The Woman without a Past" had come out in the *Toronto Star* a year earlier, and my interview with my father on CBC Radio (during which I explained the details of my experience, including my marriage to Ali) had been broadcast; both were available on the Internet.

Ms. Ardavan admitted in her interview with Nasser that before my book came out, she had never mentioned that she had known me in Evin. But after the success of the book, she remembered that she had. She said that from Qezel Hessar prison, she had been moved to Bandeh yek in Evin, which she said was the cellblock for *tavvabs* and traitors. I was never in Bandeh yek, also known as 240, but I vaguely remember someone who bore a resemblance to Ms. Ardavan in 246, where I spent most of my time while in Evin. Ms. Ardavan said that in Bandeh yek, she had heard that I had married my interrogator, and she had been appalled and disgusted by it. In an online article, she has written (translated from Persian):*

> ... *One day I asked my friend, whom in my book,* Memoirs of the Prison, *I have called Mother Maryam: "Who are these two girls who, from morning till night, stand in front of the wall, wearing chadors and headscarves, and [they pray] not like all the others, but they hold a [copy of]* Mafateeh *[a book of prayers] in their hands above their heads?" She told me: "They were both Christians but have converted to Islam and are* tavvabs. *The one on the left is Marina, and she has married her interrogator."*
> ... *She [Marina] had wrapped her head in a white headscarf and her body in a white* chador, *and all I could see was her face, not even her chin. She was pale and her eyes were devoid of emotion. She never looked at us and was busy with her own things ...*

Ms. Ardavan said that I slept in the same bed in my cell with someone who had tortured innocent people because of their way of thinking. She asked if I ever thought about the heroes who gave their lives for freedom, the ones who never cooperated with the regime.

---

*http://asre-nou.net/1386/tir/8/m-marina.html.

"If Zahra Kazemi died under torture and rape in prison," she added, "what does this have to do with Marina, who turned her time in Evin into a honeymoon ..."

*Honeymoon?* Was she in my cell as I screamed when Ali forced himself on me?

In Evin, then for many years after, I had believed that most of my friends were unaware of my marriage to Ali: after all, they never mentioned it to me. But now I realize that they did not say anything because they loved me and in no way doubted I had been forced into the marriage. I never used my status as Ali's wife as a tool of power, and this proved that I was ashamed of the marriage— so they respected my privacy. The handful of prisoners who did consider me a traitor didn't dare say anything to me out of fear for their safety. They didn't know me well enough to understand I would not have used my influence against them. Even though I had converted to Islam and married Ali, I had consciously chosen never to hurt anyone in any way.

Ms. Ardavan said that one of the reasons she had criticized me and the publication of my book was that I had claimed Ali and his family had some goodness in them, whereas she believed that all Evin interrogators, including Ali, were completely evil.

"Even though we [Marina Nemat's critics] have told our own personal accounts of the prison," she said in the radio interview, "none of us has ever said that ... Ali Moosavi, the torturer, threw himself in front of bullets to save us. How can Marina portray him as a human being ..."

I have every right to tell what happened to me, and my accusers have the right to their accounts of Evin.

During the radio program, another woman who had been in prison for a few years claimed that the "atmosphere" in *Prisoner of Tehran* was "made up." She argued that it would have been impossible for a nine-year-old like me going to school in Tehran to have such good command of the English language that she could read books in English.* In elementary school, my English was by no means perfect, but I could—with difficulty and the help of a dictionary—understand the words of C.S. Lewis in the *Chronicles of Narnia*. And I became better and better at English with practice and perseverance, not to mention my love for English literature. I was a lonely child with an unhappy family life, and books became my refuge. I was not the only elementary-school student in Tehran who knew English. Even though private schools did not exist in Iran when I was growing up, a few schools had strong English programs, among them my elementary schools, Payk-eh Danesh and Giv. But there were others, as well. Students at Soheil and Andisheh had a facility in English that was probably even greater than mine.

The woman also said that it would have been impossible for an interrogator like Ali to take a prisoner out of Evin on leaves of absence. Maybe she had forgotten, but interrogators had extreme powers, and they did sometimes take inmates out for different reasons. Here in the West we have the rule of law. Not only in prisons but everywhere, we must follow the law and the law is protected. If we break the law, we have to face consequences defined by the law. In Iran and many other Third World countries, however, money and connections sometimes count above all else. In Iran, even if you want to follow the law to, for example, get a building permit, in many cases you have to know an official, bribe someone, or both. In the 1980s, almost anything could happen in Iranian prisons. Even if a prisoner died under torture, the interrogator would not be held accountable. At the same time, if an interrogator wanted, he could grant "favours" to a prisoner.

---

*In *Prisoner of Tehran*, I explained that I began reading English books when I was nine.

In the last part of the radio program, three Iranian writers spoke in support of me. One of them, Nasrin Parvaz, had been a political prisoner for eight years and had written a memoir in Persian. She commended me for keeping my head up despite all that I had endured in Evin, and expressed her extreme disappointment in the way my accusers had attacked me, which she called "psychological stoning."

Ms. Parvaz was outraged that a few people had called my forced marriage to Ali a "honeymoon," when it was nothing but rape. She explained that in the eighties, the Islamic government imprisoned and tortured thousands of teenagers and tried to destroy them by turning them into *tavvab*s. Only a few prisoners managed to stand up for their beliefs, and they were by no means a majority. The young *tavvab*s were like springs that would bend but not break under pressure, bouncing right back at the first opportunity. She believed that one of the reasons the regime massacred thousands of political prisoners in the summer of 1988 was that prison authorities had finally realized the *tavvab* phenomenon was a sign of the failure of the regime's brutal policies in prisons. *Tavvab*s had not truly repented, and they would stab the Islamic government in the back at the first opportunity.

In Evin while I was in solitary confinement, I kneaded a piece of stale bread with a little water and used it to make a two-inch dragonfly. I had always loved dragonflies and had spent hours watching them at my parents' cottage by the Caspian Sea. Just before my release, I gave my dragonfly to one of my cellmates named Nahid. A few days earlier, she had told me a story she had made up, in which the main characters were my dragonfly and a three-inch horse she had constructed herself. One of the legs of her horse and one of the wings of my dragonfly had broken off. Nahid was an amazing storyteller and could change her voice to represent each character.

She said that one day a stallion and a dragonfly decided to have a race. All the animals in the jungle bet on the stallion, but the wise owl said that the dragonfly would win. Early in the race, the stallion was far ahead. Except, he arrived at a lake and decided not to swim across it but to go around. The dragonfly, however, flew over the lake and almost caught up with her opponent. Then it began to rain heavily. As the dragonfly squeezed herself into a crack in a rock, one of her wings broke off. Still, she had faith that she could continue the race. The skies cleared before long, but the ground had become terribly muddy. As the dragonfly crossed the finish line, panting and struggling, she heard cries from behind her. The stallion had slipped in the mud and broken a leg.

I forgot Nahid's story until years later when I saw a beautiful silver dragonfly brooch in a shop window. It had blue wings. Tears filled my eyes. I rarely buy jewellery, but I had to have it. It made me think of my young cellmates and their terrifying race for survival. I hoped that their delicate strength had led them home.

# Photos of
# My Children

When *Prisoner of Tehran* came out, my sons were eighteen and fourteen years old. I took them to a couple of my speaking engagements. Even though they were curious, they felt uncomfortable hearing about my prison experiences and rarely asked questions. However, they were excited to see me on *The Hour*—a popular television news show on CBC—because they think that the host, George Stroumboulopoulos, is totally cool. George asked me about my children's reactions to the book, and after the interview, he suggested I bring my boys to the studio so they could be part of the audience in future segments. At first, the boys seemed excited, but the smiles on their faces soon faded into thoughtful expressions, and they declined George's offer. They want to be independent and not seen just as their mother's sons or in relation to her experiences.

My becoming a public figure has been very hard on my children. I only hope they will fully understand my motives one day. I know that they are proud of me—I am a successful writer. But I'm sure they would prefer that I wrote fiction. In a way, I became two different people when I decided to tell my story: one is the quiet, dedicated wife and mother who does laundry, chauffeurs the children, cooks, cleans, and fusses over insignificant things; the other is the ex–political prisoner, the writer, and the activist, who travels, gives interviews, and speaks at events around the world. At the beginning of my journey as a writer, my family lived with the former and the world knew the latter, but gradually, the two women merged.

After I gave a Canadian company the stage rights to *Prisoner of Tehran*, I told my son Thomas, who was sixteen at the time, that I expected him to attend the opening of the play. Andre was present when I mentioned this, and he said he wasn't sure it would be suitable for Thomas to be there. I was bewildered. Not only did Thomas know my story quite well, he was the same age I had been when arrested and imprisoned. Our children deserved to know the unfiltered truth. Adult children of Holocaust survivors and those of former Iranian political prisoners had come up to me after my speaking engagements, broken down in my arms, and told me how they had suffered because of their parents' refusal to share their experiences. With time, my sons have become more and more comfortable with my past. However, there is no doubt that it is difficult for children, teenagers, even adults to deal with the suffering of their parents, especially when this suffering stems from violent acts. Nevertheless, I believe that knowing the truth is always better than remaining in ignorance.

One day Thomas and I ran into a friend of mine who works with autistic children. She told me that the government had cut some of her funding. I knew what a dedicated teacher she was, so I offered to help with her fundraising efforts. Thomas listened silently to our conversation. When we got home, he looked at me as we were taking off our coats and said, "Mom, you are *not* going to write anything against the government of Canada, are you? I don't want you to go to prison here."

I was shocked. He knows full well that Canada is a democratic country and Canadians don't go to prison for criticizing the government. Fear had gotten the best of him, causing him to put logic aside. I assured him that I would not be arrested in Canada; I had no intention of breaking the law. But this was not enough for him. I had to promise him that I would not write an article criticizing the cutting of funds for programs targeting autistic children.

I have always wondered how much my elder son, Michael, remembers from his first few years of life. Sometimes when I ask him if he recalls this or that from Iran or Hungary, he says he doesn't. I have memories from when I was four years old, but Michael was not even three when we came to Canada, so there is a good chance that he doesn't remember anything from his days in Tehran and Budapest. But some of those days were so traumatic for him and for all of us that I have no doubt he has stored them somewhere in his subconscious. Maybe they come to him as nightmares and he has no idea that they truly happened.

Michael was born in December 1988, four months after the end of the Iran–Iraq War that had raged for eight years. Andre and I lived in the city of Zahedan at the time, which is in the province of Sistan and Baluchistan and close to Iran's border with Pakistan and Afghanistan. We had moved to Zahedan in March 1987. Because Andre had a master's degree, he was permitted to teach at a university in a remote city in Iran for three years instead of fighting in the war against Iraq. I would have done anything to save Andre from going to war, and spending three years in Zahedan, which is about sixteen hundred kilometres southeast of Tehran, seemed a tiny price to pay for his safety. The university allowed professors and their families to live in well-built houses on its grounds, so we settled into a small one-bedroom house on campus.

I had never lived in the desert. Tehran is located at the foot of the Alborz Mountains and is relatively green. But Zahedan is surrounded by sand—a hot, moving, golden sea that drowns all sound and colour. At night, the sky becomes a black ocean full of silver stars, threatening to swallow everything it touches. Before the rise of Reza Shah Pahlavi in 1925, Zahedan was only a small village called Dozz-aap, from the Persian *Dozd-aab*, meaning "water thief." This name is given to a sandy land formation that quickly swallows any water that falls on it.

The first time we arrived at Zahedan Airport, I was separated from Andre at security check. I made it to the public concourse before him and waited in a corner, trying to spot the professor from the university who was to pick us up there. As I glanced around, I noticed a member of the Revolutionary Guard staring at me. I looked the other way. The man walked toward me.

"Where are you coming from?" he asked me, his tone intimidating.

My heart began to race.

"Tehran," I said.

"Are you travelling alone?"

"No. I'm with my husband. He should be here any moment."

"Your *husband*?" he said mockingly.

Suddenly, Andre and the professor from the university appeared next to me.

"Is there a problem?" the professor inquired of the guard angrily. "Why are you harassing this young woman?"

"Are you her husband?" the guard wanted to know.

"*I* am her husband," Andre responded.

"We teach at the university," the professor said. "Can we help you?"

"No. Move along."

As we walked away, Andre wanted to know why the Guard member had picked on me. I said I didn't know. I had been minding my own business.

We drove along city streets, and I noticed that the Revolutionary Guard had almost no presence here. Most of the locals wore the traditional clothing of the region—long shirts and baggy pants for men; colourful long dresses and not-so-covering head scarves for women. I soon learned that drug dealers had a great deal of influence in the city. They were armed, and they disliked the Revolutionary Guard and anyone with strong ties to the government. The professor assured me that members of the Revolutionary Guard would not bother me on city streets. Indeed, the drug dealers had attacked many government convoys on the mountainous part of the road leading to the city.

Andre and I decided to explore the market shortly after our arrival in Zahedan. We had heard that we could buy fine china for a fraction of the regular price; we also needed food to fill our fridge. As we walked down one of the dusty streets of the bazaar, with its small shops and street vendors, a man wearing the traditional local clothing approached us and greeted us in English. We were shocked. Andre is blue-eyed and blond and looks very Western, so the man had probably assumed that we were foreigners. In Persian, Andre explained that we were Iranian and he was in Zahedan to teach at the university.

"We like professors," the man said. "So good of you to come here to teach our children. Zahedan is a nice place. You're safe here."

We thanked him and walked away. I was beginning to like Zahedan. It seemed that the only places in the city where the Revolutionary Guard had influence were the airport and government buildings.

Andre loved teaching and was soon working long hours. He was either in class, preparing for it, or correcting papers. I, on the other hand, didn't have much to do. I spent my days cooking, cleaning, or staring out the window at the pale sky. I didn't drive. The university was outside the city, twenty minutes by car, so I couldn't get out much. It was usually extremely hot in Zahedan—

between 35 and 45°C—so I couldn't even go for long walks. Most of the other professors' wives were a few years older than I was, and most of them had children and were busy with their daily lives. Every weekend, we would get together with a few university families for dinner, but during the week, I was mostly on my own. I was extraordinarily careful not to ever mention that I had been in prison, since that could have cost Andre his job.

During the height of the Iran–Iraq War, Tehran came under regular Scud-missile attacks, so I appreciated the peace and quiet of Zahedan then more than ever before. Because of the distance between Zahedan and the Iran–Iraq border, the war had not touched the city, and its remoteness gave it a sleepy, easy calm.

Yet the truth was that even though at the beginning I was glad to be so far away from Tehran and my memories, within a few months I began to feel terribly bored. I didn't even have any books to read, because after my ordeal I was afraid to buy books considered illegal, which included Western novels. I envied women who worked outside the home, but with my political record, I didn't have any hope of finding a job: most good positions available to women in Zahedan were government related.

Every day was the same as the one before it. I was grateful for my safety, but I craved human interaction and some culture. Andre seemed to live in a universe that was busy, fulfilling, and exciting. However, my world had frozen in time. I found it ironic that I had been lonely most of my life: locked out on the balcony during my childhood, put away in solitary confinement during my teenage years, and now safely concealed in Zahedan.

Andre's life literally depended on his job, because if the university was not happy with his performance, he could be sent to the front. On top of that, he is a perfectionist, the kind of person who always gives his very best to his job. The silence that surrounded my past lived between us, and we talked only about daily matters. Andre had been raised by his aunt; she'd been a meticulous housekeeper and a fantastic cook, and he expected me to be likewise. He didn't cook and didn't like helping in the kitchen. I didn't mind it—there was nothing else to do. What annoyed me was that he expected me to always do as I was told. I knew that he was better and smarter than I was, but I still wanted him to respect my ways, even if they were imperfect. As a good wife, I believed I had to be supportive and understanding and to remember that life was a give-and-take. I loved Andre and I had chosen to marry him, and I would do all I could to make our marriage work. Even though the shadow of my past hung over my life and small things like a smell or a word sometimes evoked painful memories, I managed to push them back, keep them at bay, and look ahead. But I felt isolated. A distance lay between us that even love could not bridge. I knew this, but I chose to ignore it, hoping that time would fix everything.

In the spring of 1988, I discovered that I was expecting. My pregnancy brought a new light into my life. Sometime during my eighth month, I went to the local hospital for an ultrasound. Zahedan was a small city and my gynecologist happened to be at the hospital that day. The ultrasound showed that the baby's head was too big for the baby's age. The gynecologist believed that the baby was hydrocephalic, a serious condition in which water accumulates in the brain. The radiologist who performed the ultrasound, however, believed that the large size of the head wasn't enough to assume hydrocephalus, that there should have been other signs, which were absent. I lay on the bed, listening to the two doctors arguing about my baby.

"We should just drill a hole in its head and pull the baby out with forceps. It's not worth a Caesarean section," the gynecologist said.

Andre and I had had enough. I immediately got on a plane and flew to Tehran. There I saw another doctor, who told me that the baby—whom we later named Michael—was fine; he just had a big head. Five weeks later, Michael was born healthy. The new doctor turned out to be right!

SOON AFTER MY RELEASE from Evin, I realized that I was now in a larger prison the size of Iran: no one wanted to know what had happened to me, I couldn't go back to school, and I couldn't get a job. I was suffocating, and everyone seemed to think everything was well. All this made me yearn to leave the country. Andre and I had talked about immigrating, but we couldn't until I got a passport and he finished his three years of teaching in Zahedan. After Michael's birth, our leaving Iran became more urgent. Neither Andre nor I wanted our son to go to school in the Islamic Republic and have to yell "Death to America," "Death to Israel," and *"Allaho Akbar"* before going to class.

Finally, in October 1990, Andre, Michael, and I left Iran for Madrid, Spain, and a few days later, we went to Budapest, Hungary, where Andre had many relatives. This was only a year after the fall of Communism there.

We were greatly on edge in Madrid, with no idea what would happen to us. We had little money and we didn't speak Spanish. Andre and I ate only one meal a day to reduce our expenses, but we made sure that Michael was happy and comfortable. Even though the unfamiliar surroundings intimidated us, the beauty of the city, with its wide streets, magnificent fountains, glorious historical buildings, beautiful parks, and splendid shops, captivated us. Madrid was full of colour and energy. When we arrived at the airport in Budapest, though, we were surprised to find it even gloomier than the airport in Tehran. We were overjoyed at reuniting with Andre's sister, aunts, uncles, and cousins, but we both immediately noticed that the city was predominantly grey and that a sadness hung over it. Most passersby trudged along, clad in drab clothes. Most buildings were in poor repair and had not been painted in a long time. The stultifying effects of Communism were still evident. That it was November and the sun rarely shone didn't help. After only a week in Budapest, I began feeling depressed.

For our first few days, we stayed with Andre's sister. She was single and lived in a small fourth-floor apartment. The Communists had divided large houses into tiny apartments, and even though Andre's sister had a good job, her home consisted of one average-size room, with a tiny kitchen and a bathroom. Andre, Michael, and I eventually moved to another apartment across the city. It was older but a little bigger. Andre, who spoke Hungarian, found a job as an engineer in a large Hungarian company, but his salary was not even enough to cover our rent. After the fall of Communism, prices had soared. During the Communist regime the government had allowed people to live in state-owned apartments for a low rent. Once the political system changed, the new government announced that the ownership of properties the previous regime had rented out would be transferred to the tenants. So Andre's sister now owned her apartment, but because we were new in the country, we had to pay rent.

My sister-in-law and all Andre's relatives were extremely kind and generous to us. They invited us to their homes for traditional Hungarian meals and assisted us in any way they could. His sister even helped us with our expenses. I spent my days cooking and cleaning and doing things with Michael. I took him to the park every day and I read to him from English books. I was shocked that sometimes on the street, the tram, the subway, or at the park, people swore at me, calling me a Gypsy. They had probably never seen an Iranian, and because I had long dark hair and large dark eyes, they assumed I was Roma. This made me feel very sympathetic toward that minority.

At the beginning of our stay in Budapest, I tried to communicate with people at the grocery store and other public places in English or Russian, but I soon learned that almost no one spoke English and everyone pretended not to understand Russian. Russian had been taught in schools under Communism, but because Hungarians hated the Soviets, they hated their language, as well. I felt completely isolated in Hungary, but we had applied to go to Canada as independent immigrants, and I had faith that Canada would accept us.

One late-spring day I noticed a Roma woman at a street corner in Budapest. She was sitting behind a dirty cardboard box with something written on it in Hungarian. She had large dark eyes like mine, and her curly dark-brown hair reached her waist; her clothes were worn. I had been hunting for an address and, unable to find it, I needed to ask someone for directions. But I was wary of approaching passersby: I didn't want them to think that I was begging—I had no desire to be sworn at. The woman looked like a nice person, so I went up to her and, in broken Hungarian, tried to ask her which way to go. I had put some effort into learning Hungarian, but my progress had been painfully slow. The woman eyed me with an amused expression and shrugged. I repeated what I had said but in Russian this time, and she laughed.

"Where are you from?" she asked in Russian. "You have a strange accent."

"Iran," I said.

She was shocked. "What are you doing here? Begging?"

"No. It's a long story. I need to find an address."

"I'll help you if you tell me what you're doing here."

It sounded fair.

"I've escaped Iran. My husband's parents were Hungarian, so we're staying with his relatives here. We want to go to Canada, where I have a brother. I was a political prisoner in Iran."

"Political prisoner? That's not good! And I thought *I* had bad fortune ... They hurt you?"

I nodded. That a complete stranger, a woman some people considered a second-class citizen, had asked me a question that my family never had astounded me. But then I realized that because we did not know each other, she had allowed herself to be curious, not worrying about hurting my feelings or getting hurt herself. She wanted to know if I had been tortured, and I told her a little about Evin.

"Do people speak Russian in Iran?" she asked.

"No. Both my grandmothers were Russian. They escaped to Iran after the 1917 revolution."

"You look like us and you don't have a real home, so you're a Gypsy," she announced.

"I guess I am."

"The address you want is not far. Go straight and take the third right."

"Thanks."

"Would you like me to read your palm?"

"I don't have much money."

"For you, my strange, tortured sister, I'll do it free."

I extended my hand; she took it and studied my palm for a minute.

"You'll make it to Canada ... Aha! I see your time in prison right here in your lifeline. As if your life ended and then started again."

"It was exactly like that."

"Your son is ill." She looked at Michael. My child *had* been very ill, but he didn't show it.

"He is. He has a serious illness," I said.

"Yes, but he will live and become a strong man."

I wanted to believe her.

"I wouldn't lie to you. It's written. And you will do important things and travel to many countries."

"Just Canada will do."

"You'll get there."

I tried to give her some money, but she wouldn't accept any. I thanked her again and walked away. How on earth had she known about Michael's illness? I glanced back. She waved at me. I felt much better than I had in a long, long time. Maybe this was God's way of telling me that things would turn out all right.

In January 1991, two months after our arrival in Budapest, we had noticed that something was wrong with Michael. He was as happy and energetic as ever, but his eyes were swollen every morning when he awoke. I guessed that this was the result of an allergy of some sort and didn't worry, but I asked Andre's sister to get us a doctor's appointment. At the time, Hungarian doctors made house calls, and a young doctor came to our house. Like me, he believed that Michael was suffering from allergies, and he asked me to watch Michael to see if the swelling got worse after he ate certain things. I monitored Michael. No matter what he ate or did, his eyes were swollen every morning. Finally, the doctor sent us to the children's hospital to have a urine test done. Because Andre was extremely busy at work, his sister accompanied us. At the hospital, the doctor told us that Michael had a high level of protein in his urine.

He had to be admitted.

I was shocked. I had thought they would give us a few pills and send us home, but the doctor said Michael's condition was serious. I agreed to let Michael stay in the hospital, but then I was told I could not stay with him and could see him only a couple of hours every day at visiting time. My sister-in-law was translating for me, and I asked her to say that this was unacceptable. I understood that hospital rules didn't allow parents to remain with their young children, but our case was not ordinary. Michael did not speak Hungarian and couldn't communicate with the hospital staff. He would be terrified. Not that I spoke much Hungarian, but I was an adult and could somehow manage the situation, even if I had to use sign language. The doctor in charge said, "No," and I became angry. I was tired of not being understood.

"Why don't you people speak English or Russian?" I snapped in broken Russian, switching to English when I couldn't find the words quickly enough. "You're doctors, for heaven's sake! You're educated people! Only Hungarian? This is ridiculous! I come from Iran and I have just a high-school diploma, but I speak four languages—Persian, Russian, English, and Italian. What's wrong with you? Communism is over! The walls have collapsed! Get out of your shells! It's cruel not to let a parent stay with a small child! It's medieval! It's Communist!"

I was crying.

Andre's sister tried to calm me. At this point, the doctor and the head nurse were crying, too, but I wasn't done with them. One of the nurses called Andre, and he came. Finally, they agreed to let me stay with Michael during the day, but I had to go home at night. It was better than nothing.

Michael's condition was deteriorating rapidly. His whole body had become extremely swollen. A biopsy of his kidneys showed that something was wrong, but the doctors couldn't pinpoint the cause. All they knew was that he had a form of nephrosis. They speculated that because we had emigrated from the Middle East, his condition stemmed from a viral or bacterial infection they were not familiar with. And because they didn't know the exact cause, they decided not to put Michael on steroids, the only medication that usually helps the condition.

Michael was very brave. He never complained and remained cheerful. I played with him all day, held him, and read to him.

At night, Andre or I helped him brush his teeth and read him a bedtime story. Then we both kissed him good night, and I told him that I'd be right back first thing in the morning and Andre would come immediately after work. Michael never cried when we left but waved and blew us kisses, but we wept as we went down the stairs. Michael was in a room with a few other children, and his window faced the hospital yard. Andre and I always paused in the yard before we left, looked up at his window, and prayed, wondering if he would be alive the next day.

Since the moment Michael was born, I had protected him. I fully understood that this world was a difficult place, but I had vowed to do everything in my power to make sure he was safe and had a good life. Now, on our way to a better life, an illness was taking him from us. We knew we would fight his illness to the last ounce of our strength, but as I prayed, I was well aware that I was not in control. For reasons I could not understand, God had decided that Michael should fall ill. As every cell of my body screamed with the agony of a mother terrified of losing her child, I realized that I had learned a painful but valuable lesson: I could not keep the people I loved in this world if God decided to take them. I cried and I felt devastated, but in the end, I bowed to God. Michael was His child before he was mine, and if He decided to take him back, I had to trust that He would take good care of him.

Michael fought not only that terrible disease but also the awful infections that plagued him in the hospital. The blood-pressure medication that was prescribed lessened his symptoms, reducing the amount of protein that his kidneys filtered out. His condition stabilized, and at least he didn't get worse. In time, the doctors let us take him home, but we knew that if something else wasn't done, his kidneys would fail. It was now even more important for us to get to Canada. We hoped that Canadian doctors would be better than Hungarian ones.

Shortly after our arrival in Toronto we opened the phone book and found a children's clinic in Richmond Hill. The pediatrician there sent us to the Hospital for Sick Children. Compared with the children's hospital in Budapest, Sick Kids was heaven. The doctors spoke English, and they patiently listened to us. The hospital was bright and modern and had a cheerful staff. In Hungary, every time lab technicians needed to test Michael's blood they took vial after vial of blood. The process went on forever and was painful. Michael suffered, and we suffered with him. In Canada, they extracted only a tiny amount of blood each time, in only a few seconds.

At Sick Kids, Michael's doctor put him on steroids. She was not sure if the medication would work, but nothing else could be done. Michael didn't need to be admitted, but we had to keep a close eye on him. Steroids cause a great number of side effects, and the road ahead wouldn't be easy. After starting the medication, Michael threw up for days. Then he became tired and irritable. We had been told that steroids would cause behavioural problems that would go away as soon as he stopped taking the drug.

Michael was on steroids for three years, and his illness gradually disappeared. He had regular checkups at Sick Kids until he turned eighteen. He has never had a relapse.

# My Canadian Passport

Andre, Michael, and I took our Canadian citizenship oath and received our citizenship certificates on May 29, 1995. We didn't have a ceremony with other new Canadians because we had decided we could not wait until July 1—Canada Day. We wanted to vote in the upcoming general election in Ontario in June, so we contacted the authorities and they gave us a private appointment before the public ceremony. For the first time in his life, Michael wore a suit and a tie, and Andre and I dressed in our best outfits. We had passed the citizenship test, which deals with Canadian history and geography. Andre applied for his Canadian passport as soon as we became citizens because he needed to travel for work, but I had no travel plans and didn't get mine until *Prisoner of Tehran* came out in 2007. After leaving Iran, Andre and I never renewed our Iranian passports.

Once I began to travel abroad, I always looked at the passports of other travellers as I lined up in strange airports to have my passport stamped, trying to discover where the travellers were from. After September 11, 2001, individuals from the Middle East could be harassed at security checks, especially in the United States, but in Canada and Europe as well. I always presented my Canadian passport with pride and a smile. Whenever I went to the United

States, the American customs officer would ask me when I had last been to Iran. I would reply that I hadn't returned since leaving in 1990. Once Iran is free from dictatorship and tyranny, I will apply for an Iranian passport, but I will never forget that Canada gave us a home when we were in desperate need.

Establishing ourselves in Canada took us years, and only after *Prisoner of Tehran* appeared did I truly feel at home here. Canada has made it possible for me to recover my voice and become an advocate for those who cannot speak out. This does not mean that I believe Canada is perfect; it is not. However, in Canada we have the opportunity to speak and be heard.

When I received an email from the Royal Canadian Mounted Police inviting me to address a seminar on torture in September 2007, I was pleasantly surprised. The email explained that the seminar aimed to inform RCMP members about the illegality and odiousness of torture. It noted that victims were the most important persons in a criminal investigation, but their voices were usually not heard. The RCMP wanted a survivor to talk about her experience to reveal torture's inhumanity.

That a Canadian institution was inviting me to address such a crucial issue meant a great deal to me. If someone had told me when I was in Evin that I would one day speak at a conference on torture, I would not have believed it. Back then, the world had forgotten about my friends and me. So many years later, the situation in Iran had not improved much, but at last, I had the opportunity to talk to the world about it. I accepted the RCMP invitation. I believe that many organizations like the RCMP that sometimes do wrong are composed of good men and women. I have faith that they can learn from their mistakes and make sure that things change for the better. They were willing to give me a chance to bear witness, so I had to take it. My testimony could potentially help many. Having been a victim of torture has affected and defined me. Head held high, I have to use all I have learned and try to stop torture in any shape or form.

As a child, I never imagined that I would one day put "victim of torture" on my résumé. I had wanted to become a medical doctor, and I was hard-working enough to do it, but after prison I abhorred the thought of going back to school in the Islamic Republic. I knew authorities would watch my every move and continue their relentless efforts to brainwash me and turn me into an obedient citizen.

RCMP headquarters sat on the outskirts of Ottawa in a large and impressive modern building that belonged to one of the high-tech giants of the dot-com bubble. Before the seminar began, I met the other speakers: assistant Crown attorney Don Macdougall; Department of Justice lawyer John McManus; Concordia history professor, author, and director of the Montreal Institute for Genocide and Human Rights Studies Dr. Frank Chalk; and former CIA agent, author, and subject of the movie *Syriana* Robert Baer. They were to speak about state torture and its history; I was the victim who would help the audience understand how it felt to be tortured. I was to put a human face on the faceless victim, who is usually only a number, a vague and insignificant entity.

The seminar took place in a state-of-the art auditorium. Approximately two hundred members of the RCMP attended. Don Macdougall began his talk by explaining what torture is under the law. I had never thought much about how the law describes it—I had always assumed that the nature of torture was obvious. But apparently, the need for a legal description existed. Mr. Macdougall said that torture was pain or suffering inflicted on a person. The pain needs to be severe and there needs to be a purpose for it: to obtain information, a statement, or for any reason based on discrimination.

*Severe pain?* Did they have a pain meter? I wondered, a machine that measured suffering? Where was the line between "severe" and "not severe?" Maybe anything 10 and over was severe and your pain was the result of torture, but at 9.5 your pain wasn't severe and not the result of torture. Many victims of torture have visible injuries. If people had looked at my feet the first few days after I was lashed, they would have been horrified, but I gradually healed, and before long, no one could see the marks unless he or she knew what to look for. Still, if someone carefully touches the soles of my feet, especially my left foot, even now he or she will feel little bumps of scar tissue. But some methods of torture don't leave visible scars: sleep deprivation, hot and cold shocks, water boarding, psychological intimidation, rape, long periods of solitary confinement, mock executions, to name a few. What about the victims of those horrible acts?

"Torture always has to have been inflicted by an official or officer," Mr. Macdougall said. "And an official or officer can be liable for torture as a party even when he or she has not directly taken part in it. According to Canadian law, if an official has a real suspicion that torture is taking place and ignores it, he or she can be as guilty as the perpetrator. Canadian soldiers were accused of torture in Somalia in 1993 and were court-martialled. One of them was charged with murder and three others with torture. According to Canadian law, a Canadian can be charged for torture even if the crime is committed outside Canada."

My mind drifted back to Evin and my visits to the Hosseinieh, a gym-size room on the prison grounds where hundreds could gather. The guards took us there to listen to propaganda speeches, attend group prayers, and hear the "confessions" of other prisoners. One day, prison authorities recited a list of recent executions. I knew a few of the girls whose names were on the list, but none was a close friend of mine. Prison authorities had never announced names in this manner, and no one knew why they were doing it this time. The names I recognized belonged to prisoners who had cooperated with authorities and "repented" of their anti-revolutionary actions. Was this the authorities' way of showing us that even those who had "repented" were not immune from capital punishment? A sense of shock filled the Hosseinieh as the names were read. It was as if no one was breathing. Silence was an ocean that had drowned us all.

During another of our visits to the Hosseinieh, the guards told us that a few members of a human-rights organization (perhaps the Red Cross) had come to talk to us and see with their own eyes that we were all fine and thriving in Evin! One of the visitors, a middle-aged woman who wore a head scarf, not a *chador,* sat next to me. In English, she asked me how the girls in the prison were doing, and I silently looked at her. She repeated her question, and I said, "Fine." A part of me wanted to scream, *How do you think we're doing? They're torturing us, raping us, and killing us, and you sit there smiling and ask how we're doing? You'll go back to your nice life, and we'll stay here. What do you honestly expect us to tell you? Do you really think we can tell you the truth? They will shoot us right behind those doors if we say a word about what really happens here.*

Back then, the thought of going to conferences and talking about torture and what could be done about it would have frustrated me. I wanted out of Evin immediately, and I wanted torture and executions to stop at once. I wanted the people of Iran to march into the prison and free us before another innocent life was lost. But this didn't happen. I did not understand what use it was for people to talk about torture while we suffered. Twenty-five years later, I came to see that my only way to fight the terrible things that had happened—and were still happening in Iran and in other countries around the world—was to attend conferences, write books and articles, and speak at events.

John McManus, another speaker at the RCMP seminar, recounted his experience as a clerk at the Federal Court of Canada when he first became a lawyer. He had worked for Justice William McKeown, and they had done many judicial reviews of the applications of refugee claimants. When Justice McKeown, who was unfailingly thorough, found a legal problem in a case, he would send the case back to the review board for reconsideration. Mr. McManus remembered one case in particular. A woman from Chile had been a political prisoner during the reign of General Augusto Pinochet and had been tortured. After her ordeal, she slowly tried to reintegrate herself into society. In the beginning, she was afraid to even step out of her house. Then she began going out with friends and was making progress. One day at the market, she saw one of her torturers. He came up to her and said that just because General Pinochet was no longer president, it didn't mean that she was safe. His supporters knew exactly where she lived, and they could find her easily. She fled the country the next day and claimed refugee status in Canada, but she was denied. Canadian authorities said that since Pinochet was no longer president, she would not be in danger if she returned to Chile. However, Justice McKeown decided that she was suffering from post-traumatic stress disorder (PTSD), which was the result of the torture she had endured. The incident at the market had brought her extreme fear to the surface once more. As far as Mr. McManus could remember, this was probably the only time Justice McKeown sent back a file to the review board not for reconsideration but to order refugee status for the claimant.

I was impressed with Justice McKeown's decision.

In the summer of 2009, a friend of mine—also an ex–political prisoner from Iran—told me that in 2001 or 2002, at a protest rally against the Iranian regime taking place in front of a federal building in Los Angeles, California, she saw her interrogator. She couldn't believe her eyes and felt paralyzed. I asked her if she went to the authorities, did anything to expose him. She said she did not. She couldn't move and had to look away. When she finally looked back, the man was walking off. He disappeared into the crowd. My friend had already been in the United States for a few years and had had plans to visit her family in Iran. She cancelled her ticket and has never been back.

What would I do if I were to run into one of my interrogators? Ali is dead, but what about Hamehd? I have heard that he was killed, but I am not sure how reliable that information is. If he were alive, would I even recognize him after all these years? If I did spot him in a crowd, what would I do? I don't know. There is a good possibility that—just like my friend—I, too, would be paralyzed.

During one of my talks in Toronto, I made it clear that I was against torture in any shape or form, and for any reason, and a man in the audience said that in order for us Westerners to save our way of life from Islamism and terrorists, we had to do whatever it took. I asked him how far he was willing to go to save his way of life.

"As far as it takes," he said.

"That is what Hitler said," I responded. "You can get so consumed with saving your way of life that in the process, as you get really busy torturing people, you forget what your way of life was in the first place. When we talk about our way of life, don't we mean the way of a society that is not only democratic but also shows unconditional respect for the rights of all human beings? Don't we mean a society that has a clear understanding of right and wrong and knows that wrong can never lead to right? All horrors in history have happened when we have begun justifying things."

In Evin, they believed I knew the whereabouts of a girl named Shahrzad, and they kept on asking me about her. She was a member of a Marxist group and was a friend of a friend of mine. We met after school one day, and she walked home with me. She invited me to join her group, but I refused. I explained to her that I respected her beliefs, but I was a devout Catholic and could never get along with Marxists. She went her way, and I never saw her again. Apparently, she was being watched at the time, and this was how my interrogators had discovered that I had met with her. She went into hiding, but I was arrested. However, I wasn't arrested only because of her. My high-school principal, who was a member of the Revolutionary Guard, had given my name, along with the names of many students from my school, to the Courts of Islamic Justice.

Under torture, I told my interrogators the truth, but they didn't believe me. I was a naïve girl who thought that if she told the truth, she would be saved. What I failed to see was that my interrogators' main purpose in torturing me was not to find Shahrzad but to destroy me. Of course, it would have been a bonus had I told them where she was.

After *Prisoner of Tehran* appeared in print, I met some ex–political prisoners from different countries of South America who had been active members of various political groups. They had been trained to withhold information and tell lies for the first twenty-four hours of their interrogation. After twenty-four hours, they were allowed to share some of what they knew with the authorities. This gave their comrades some time to escape. I was sixteen when arrested, I was not a member of any political group, and I had never been taught what to do under torture.

At the RCMP seminar, Dr. Frank Chalk talked at length about the history of torture and said that in medieval times strict rules governed the torture chamber. The instruments of torture were shown to the potential victim. That often did the trick and the accused would recant—the prospect of having parts of one's flesh torn from one's body was, to say the least, intimidating. The judge accompanied the accused into the torture chamber, and notaries documented the proceedings. A doctor's presence was usually required, even though the job of the doctor was only to throw a bucket of water on the accused. And no defence lawyer was present in the chamber.

I was amazed at how procedures in the prisons of the Islamic Republic of Iran were similar to those of the prisons in medieval Europe. In Evin before they took me into the torture room, my interrogators first made me sit in the hallway and listen to a victim undergoing torture. It was a man, and he was being lashed. I heard the sound of the lash cutting the air. Then the man screamed. It went on and on. Never-ending agony. They finally took me into the same room and tied me up. Not only were there no defence lawyers present, but there were also no notaries or doctors.

I would have told them where Shahrzad was had I known. But I didn't, and I thanked God for it. The interrogators gave me papers to sign, and I signed them all without reading a word.

In early summer 2009, a friend sent me a very short—less than two minutes—video clip. Where it was filmed is not clear, but it seems to have been a European city. A group of Iranian protesters have gathered in front of an Iranian Embassy and are yelling slogans against the Islamic regime. Embassy staff are watching the crowd. A female protester's voice rises above everyone else's: "We'll kill you all! We'll execute you all! We'll make you suffer!"

I can understand her anger, but don't we protest against the Iranian regime *because* it kills, executes, and tortures? When the regime finally collapses and power changes hands, if the new authorities behave the same way as the ones who came before them, we will not be much better off than we are today. Is this the kind of justice we seek? Iran will not become a better place until we accept that killing and torture are wrong under any circumstances.

I witnessed how the Revolutionary Guard and the Courts of Islamic Justice took over the work of SAVAK, the shah's secret police, after the 1979 Islamic Revolution in Iran. In the name of protecting the revolution and national security, they committed countless atrocities. During the time of the shah, Evin perhaps held a few hundred prisoners, but in the eighties, there were thousands, the vast majority of whom were teenagers. After the lashings and beatings, prisoners were sent to different cells, many of which were solitary. Solitary confinement is a form of torture designed to break the human spirit. The loneliness and the lack of communication with others can make one mad.

When I was in solitary confinement in the 209 section of Evin prison, prisoners could shower once a week. In the beginning, a female guard who was probably in her late fifties would escort me to the shower stalls. She never said much and was not mean. She never rushed me or called me names. After a while, a young woman took her place. The first time she came to walk me to the showers, she flung open the door of my cell without any warning, so I didn't have a chance to put on my *chador* and blindfold. She screamed at me for not having them on. When I protested, she said that I was a dirty Christian, an unclean infidel, and I didn't deserve to be treated like a human being.

"I've heard all about you," she said. "They say you've converted to Islam. Yeah, right! You might have fooled some people. Not me. I know what you're made of. You're a dirty whore! Married your interrogator. Whatever. He'll get tired of you, you know. Then you'll get what you deserve."

I didn't say a word and ignored her.

On our way to the showers, she stopped at the cell next to mine and kicked the door open. A woman screamed.

"Get up, you dirty infidel!" the guard yelled. "Just like the Christian, you have no shame! Where's your *chador*? Put it on! Baha'i, Christian—what's the difference? The two of you can shower together. They must shoot you both. I don't even know why I have to take you to wash up. No amount of washing will make you clean."

I heard a rustle of fabric and then footsteps, and a hand hung on to my *chador* from the back. It was the woman from the other cell. Like me, she was blindfolded. I grabbed the end of the stick the guard placed in my hand, and we followed her.

The woman who was following me to the showers was the only Baha'i I met in the prison, even though there were many others.

At the door of the shower room, the guard made sure we understood that we had only five minutes.

"If you take longer, I'll drag you out naked!" she barked.

The other prisoner and I stepped in and closed the door behind us. Hastily, we both started to undress. Once we had removed our *chador*s, we turned our backs to each other to give us each some privacy.

"My name is Marina," I said, pulling off my shirt and putting it in the bottom of the plastic bag that contained my towel.

"Minoo," she said.

"You Baha'i?" I asked.

"Yeah. You Christian?"

"Yeah." I slid off my pants and put them in my bag.

"I heard what she said to you," Minoo told me.

I didn't react.

I took off my bra and panties and stepped into a shower stall. Minoo did the same. The cement floor was rough under my feet, but it seemed relatively clean. The water was lukewarm. At least it was not freezing cold.

"The guard said … you … you married your interrogator … Is it true?" Minoo asked.

I soaped my hair and body as quickly as I could.

"I heard a woman scream last night. Was it you?" Minoo wanted to know.

I rinsed off the soap, stepped out of the stall, and wrapped myself in my towel.

"You might want to hurry up," I advised. "I don't think the guard was kidding when she said she would drag us out of here naked."

Water was dripping from my hair as I donned my clothes. Minoo was now drying herself. She was in her late twenties.

"I wasn't screaming," I said. "I don't anymore."

"I haven't been able to sleep," Minoo said. "All night, I think someone will rape me." Tears were falling down her cheeks.

"Are you married?" I asked her.

"Yes."

"Don't worry. They won't touch you."

"Is this how it works?"

"People don't talk about these things … but I think you're safe."

"Is anyone else from your family here?" she asked.

"No."

"Lucky you. My parents and my husband are here, too."

"Sorry to hear that."

"How old are you?"

"Seventeen."

"Dear God! A child!"

"How long have you been here?" I asked. She must have been arrested recently if she was surprised to see a seventeen-year-old in Evin.

"Three days."

"I hope they let you go soon."

The shower-room door was kicked open, and the woman guard barged in.

"Didn't I tell you not to talk to each other? Move!"

When the guard let Minoo into her cell, I heard some strange noises. Minoo moaned. I guessed that the guard had pushed and hit her.

"You didn't have to do that," I said when the guard closed the door of Minoo's cell.

"I do what I want! I'll beat you to death!"

She didn't, probably because she was afraid of Ali. She just locked me up and left. I never saw Minoo again.

Even though *Ahl al-Ketab* (People of the Book: Christians, Jews, and Zoroastrians) are recognized religious minorities in Iran, according to some—but not all—Shia religious leaders, they are considered *kafar* and as a result are categorized as *najess,* or "unclean." A *kafar* is a person who has denied God and the prophethood of Muhammad. Ayatollah Khomeini discussed the *nejasat*—"uncleanliness"—issue in detail. When asked what the status of *Ahl al-Ketab* was in relation to purity, he said, "Non-Muslims of any religion or creed are *najess.*"*

Most of my friends are Muslim, and they do not at all consider those who follow other religions unclean. Even Ali didn't believe that I was *najess* and did not agree with Khomeini on this matter.

According to the Islamic law that governs Iran, *Ahl al-Ketab* are supposed to be protected and have the right to practise their religion. However, the Baha'i, who are the largest religious minority in Iran, remain "non-recognized" and do not have legal status. The authorities have declared them "unprotected infidels." According to the laws of the Islamic Republic, everyone must belong to one of the four officially recognized religions. For example, in order to apply for the general examination to enter any university in Iran or to apply for any job in the government, the applicant has to answer a multiple-choice question about his or her religion. This question has four possible answers: Muslim, Zoroastrian, Jewish, or Christian.**

---

*Eliz Sanasarian, *Religious Minorities in Iran,* (Cambridge: Cambridge University Press, 2000), 85.

**Page 6 of "Discrimination against Religious Minorities in Iran," a report presented by the FIDH (Fédération Internationale des Ligues des Droits de l'Homme) and the Ligue de Défense des Droits de l'Homme en Iran, 63rd Session of the Committee on the Elimination of Racial Discrimination, August 2003 (www.fidh.org/IMG/pdf/ir0108a.pdf).

As I walked to the podium of the RCMP seminar in Ottawa in 2007, I did not feel nervous. Since the publication of *Prisoner of Tehran*, I had had a great deal of practice in public speaking, and I was used to the anticipating silence of the audience. They had their mindsets, perspectives, and expectations, but I didn't think about that as I looked at the crowd. I had learned to take myself out of the space I was in physically. I entered a state of mind where I was alone with only one other person, an imaginary friend who had finally asked me the question I had long yearned to hear: "What happened to you?" I always started at the beginning. I spoke about my childhood, our apartment in downtown Tehran, our neighbourhood, and our cottage by the Caspian Sea ... I painted a vivid picture, and as I went on, I could see the colours, smell the scents, and hear the sounds of my homeland. So many years had gone by since Evin, and this gap had made it possible for me to feel safe enough to enter the world that had caused me great suffering. But the passage of time had not made me immune to pain. My talks were always a balancing act over an abyss of devastating sadness. However, as I felt the dark heavy grief rise toward me like a huge wave, I also felt a sense of peace, which became a life jacket keeping me afloat. I was finally bearing witness.

I am always in control when I talk about how they tortured me. As I speak about the lash landing on the bare soles of my feet, I never flinch. My heartbeat always quickens and my hands become icy, but that is all. I always admit that I would have sold my soul to escape the torture. Even though I felt abandoned, frightened, alone, forgotten, and ashamed as they were beating me, and I wondered what I had done to deserve it, now I know that my torturers were afraid of me. I had threatened them in such a manner that they wanted me to die in a horribly painful way. They wanted to wipe me out of existence. Now I understand that I shouldn't have felt ashamed under torture even when I felt broken, because there was a part of me that they never managed to destroy.

What always makes me emotional and brings tears to my eyes is talking about my prison friends. They know how it feels to be in prison instead of high school. They know what it means to be like a piece of glass that has fallen from a tremendous height and, upon impact, has turned not into shards but dust. They know the pain of trying to put oneself back together.

I HAVE THOUGHT a great deal about what I heard during the RCMP seminar in Ottawa, and I have tried to connect it to dilemmas of the post–9/11 world. We know that the RCMP shared unreliable information with American authorities and played a role in events that led to the torture of four Canadian citizens: Maher Arar, Abdullah al-Maliki, Ahmad el-Maati, and Muayyed Nureddin. They were arrested and tortured in countries where torture is common practice. In Arar's case, this false information led to his arrest while he was in transit in New York's JFK Airport when returning home from a vacation. U.S. officials detained him and interrogated him about alleged links to al Qaeda. Then they sent him to Syria, where he was tortured and beaten and sentenced to months in a grave-like cell. He was finally released and returned to Canada in October 2003. On January 28, 2004, under pressure from Canadian human-rights organizations and a growing number of citizens, the Canadian government announced a Commission of Inquiry into the Actions of Canadian Officials in Relation to Maher Arar. In September 2006, the commissioner of the inquiry, Justice Dennis O'Connor, cleared Mr. Arar of all terrorism allegations, stating that he was able to say categorically that there was no evidence that Mr. Arar had committed any offence or that his activities constituted a threat to the security of Canada.

In October 2008, former Supreme Court of Canada justice Frank Iacobucci, who had conducted a closed-door inquiry into the events leading to the detentions of Abdullah al-Maliki, Ahmad el-Maati, and Muayyed Nureddin, released a public version of a confidential report. It concluded that all three men were detained and suffered mistreatment that amounted to torture as defined in the United Nations convention banning torture. In all three cases, Mr. Iacobucci stipulated that the initial detentions were not directly the result of the actions of Canadian officials. However, Canadian officials indirectly contributed to the detentions and mistreatment of Mr. el-Maati and Mr. Nureddin. In Mr. al-Maliki's case, Mr. Iacobucci said he was unable to determine on the record available to him, whether the actions of Canadian officials likely contributed to Mr. al-Maliki's detention in Syria.

I am very proud to be Canadian, and I believe that even though not perfect, Canada is a democratic country with the potential of leading the world in the fight against human-rights violations. However, after 9/11, we fell prey to the fear-mongering policies of the Bush administration. In the name of fighting terror, basic human rights became a casualty, and we forgot that our laws, which are the result of a democratic process and are supposed to protect *all* Canadian citizens against injustice, are the heart of who we are. These laws define our way of life—a way of life the U.S. government declared was in danger because of terrorists. What we failed to see is that a few fanatic men with bombs are less dangerous to us than the violation of the laws that have made Canada a democratic and free country.

There is no doubt that the RCMP has made terrible mistakes and those responsible must be held accountable. But accountability is not synonymous with revenge. Justice isn't only about forcing a few officials to resign; it is about making sure that what happened to Maher Arar never happens to anyone again. The real issue isn't whether Arar had connections to terrorist organizations. It is that he should not have been sent to Syria, where undoubtedly he would be tortured.

But *how* can we make sure that things like that never happen again? The first step is for the Canadian government to apologize to all those who, as a result of the sharing of false and/or unreliable information by CISIS or the RCMP, were tortured and/or imprisoned.

The second step is for the Canadian government to compensate the victims for their ordeals. As a Canadian taxpayer, I feel responsible for what happened to those men, and I have to take a stand. I was tortured in Iran and I know I will never receive an apology from the Iranian government; they refuse even to acknowledge that they have ever tortured anybody. Not only have I never been compensated for my ordeal, but when I decided to leave Iran, I had to pay a large sum of money to get a passport and guarantee my return. I have a receipt for the money, yet I do not imagine, not even for a moment, that I will get the money back. However, when I heard on the radio that Maher Arar had received an apology and ten million dollars, it felt like a victory to me. Even though money can never make up for the agony victims of torture endure, it helps them put their lives back together and take care of their families.

The third step is for the Canadian government to conduct an independent and impartial criminal investigation of the Canadian officials responsible.

The fourth step is for the RCMP to make sure that all its officers are properly trained and understand that torture is wrong not only in Canada but anywhere in the world. They need to be aware that sharing information with countries that use torture can have serious consequences.

A fifth step is necessary: dialogue between the victims and the RCMP and the Canadian government. Victims need to be heard and their experiences have to be shared and understood in a human, personal way. This step might prove to be the most difficult one, since victims are not likely to trust the RCMP or the government enough to sit at a table with them. Yes, there are many obstacles along the way. However, dialogue needs to begin, and if I can do anything to help create awareness about torture and what it does to people, I will do it to the best of my abilities. The RCMP, CISIS, and the Canadian government must all understand that under any circumstances, the rule of law, itself the result of a democratic process, has to come before everything else. Because of the possibility of a terrorist attack on American or Canadian soil, we cannot deport people to countries that use torture; we have to deal with the threat according to our own laws. Once we begin to ignore our values, we risk sliding down a slippery slope that will lead to nothing but disaster.

The last—but not the least—step is to lay charges against the officials who have tortured Canadians in Syria, Egypt, or any other country. Torture will continue to exist as long as governments and individuals can get away with it.

I have given many talks in high schools, and I sometimes speak to students about the Holocaust, a well-documented example of how countries can go completely mad. I sometimes read short passages from books about the Holocaust, including *Fatelessness*. I love speaking to young people. They are always open-minded and inquisitive and pose wonderfully unfiltered questions. At different schools, students have asked me exactly the same questions: "But, Miss, how is it possible that the police go to your neighbours, people you have been friends with forever, and take them away to kill them for no good reason? How is it possible not to protest something like that and not do anything about it? How can it happen?"

I have told these young people that if I had not lived through the Iranian revolution, I would not have had an answer for their question. "In history," I have explained, "horror doesn't usually happen overnight, but it unfolds little by little. We see danger signs popping up around us, but because we notice only one sign here and one there, we dismiss it as insignificant, and by the time we realize that something terrible has happened, it's too late. If we speak out at this point, we will be arrested, tortured, even killed. To give your life for your friend or neighbour is noble, but it's not easy, and even though a few people are willing to risk their lives for others, the majority of us usually remain silent."

After 9/11, I watched danger signs appear in Canada and the United States. The invasion of Iraq based on lies and deceit was the biggest of them, and of course there was the deportation of a few Muslims to countries like Syria and Egypt to be interrogated under torture. Paranoia and fear took over the world. The Guantanamo Bay detainment camp emblemizes that fear. And I find it terribly disturbing that in many ways Guantanamo is very much like Evin: a black hole into which people disappear, many without real evidence against them; a place where there is no access to due process, and prisoners can be terribly mistreated and humiliated and kept indefinitely for reasons that supposedly have to do with national security. The government of Iran imprisoned me because it thought I was a danger to Iran's national security. I was sixteen, but this didn't mean anything to Iranian officials.

As I write these lines, a young Canadian languishes in the Guantanamo Bay prison camp. His name is Omar Khadr. He was shot and captured in Afghanistan at the age of fifteen. For three months, he was held at the U.S. prison in Bagram. Sedated and shackled, he was taken to his first interrogation hours after being discharged from a military hospital. In October 2002, he was transferred to Guantanamo Bay prison camp, and he has been rotting in that horrible place for more than eight years. Unlike him, I have never participated in an armed conflict and have never touched a gun in my life, but this doesn't mean that it is okay to imprison a fifteen-year-old boy, who, like everyone else, is supposed to be assumed innocent until proven guilty. In fact, international law demands that because he was a child soldier, he should not be prosecuted but that every effort be made to rehabilitate him. Omar needs help and compassion, not intimidation and punishment. He was in Afghanistan because his family had taken him there, where, allegedly, he killed an American medic. He needs a fair trial, not a military tribunal. Injustice is injustice, no matter if it is committed in the East or the West. The Canadian government has refused to ask that Omar be returned to this country, even though he is a Canadian citizen. To me, this is a disgrace—and another warning sign that human rights are being ignored even in Canada.

# My Rosary

In December 2007, when I was leaving home to go to Italy to receive the Human Dignity Prize from the European Parliament, Andre warned me—as he did each time that I went on a trip—to be careful. I couldn't understand how he had found the courage to let me continue what I had begun. Writing a memoir is one thing; travelling the world and constantly testifying against the Islamic Republic of Iran is another. Had our positions been reversed, I probably would have done everything in my power to stop him. He had married a quiet, shy young woman who just wanted to live a normal life with him and raise a family. This was the person I had been for the first seventeen years of our marriage. I seemed to have forgotten my two years in Evin. But then they resurfaced—and completely redefined me. The real Marina who had been buried somewhere inside me was a stranger to Andre. He had never truly known her, because even though Andre and I had met before my incarceration, the arrest of my friends had already affected me and I had withdrawn from the world. Living with me after *Prisoner of Tehran* was like living with someone who had recovered from extreme amnesia.

Despite all this, Andre stood by me. We did sometimes argue and disagree. He listened to my interviews and criticized me for being too direct and politically incorrect. He warned me not to use the word *Islamist*. I disagreed. I have nothing against Islam—many of my friends are Muslim. I have great respect for every religion. To me, Islamism is an ideology that has used Islam and twisted it into a dangerous, bloodthirsty, and rigid way of thought that has no respect for life. Today's Islamists are like the Christians of the Middle Ages who branded those who were different as "witches" and burned them. The Inquisition had nothing to do with Christ, and it caused great damage to Christianity.

Shortly after the spring 2009 unrest in Iran, the School of Continuing Studies at the University of Toronto invited me to present a creative-writing award. Andre accompanied me to the ceremony. I gave a little talk, and at the end, I asked for a moment of silence for all the innocents killed in Iran during the previous weeks. Following the event, as we were walking to the car, Andre told me that I had been wrong to ask for the moment of silence, because the gathering was a non-political event and not everyone in the audience might have agreed with me.

"You must be kidding!" I exploded. "Innocent people have died. This is a fact, okay? I can do nothing about that except ask for one moment—one measly moment—to remember the dead! It's about human rights ... right and wrong! We can't just shut up!"

Andre didn't respond. He knew I would never take a step back on such issues. He was probably asking himself who this woman walking next to him was. The Marina he had married twenty-four years earlier would never have reacted this way and would have apologized for stepping out of line.

I RECEIVED the Human Dignity Prize in Milan at Palazzo delle Stelline, which was built in the sixteenth century and had been an orphanage for many years. In the late 1980s, it was beautifully renovated, restored, and transformed into a centre for conferences and meetings. Activity buzzed around me as I waited in a room for the event to begin. Reporters came and went. The assistants of one of the vice-presidents of the European parliament, Mr. Mario Mauro, who had nominated me for the award, rushed in and out to make sure everything was in place. I sat at a window and filled my eyes with the surreal view it offered: a cloudless deep-blue sky resting above the terracotta roof and the orange-yellow walls of the Palazzo, which surrounded a courtyard carpeted with a green lawn.

Why did I feel so calm? Why was I so poised? Where was my excitement? I was about to receive the first Human Dignity Prize. Many people had told me that they could only guess how excited I was. Well, I was mildly excited, but I didn't tell them that. I didn't want anyone to think I was ungrateful. Actually, I was very grateful. But this gratitude translated into a calm sense of awe, which in turn caused me to feel guilty for not being excited enough. The problem was that I somehow still expected myself to be normal. Yet it was as if I had been in a huge explosion and my body was full of hundreds of pieces of shrapnel. With my own fingers, I had pulled out a few large pieces from my flesh, but many pieces remained. I was still avoiding both sadness and happiness. I couldn't help it. Numbness protected me. It had become a custom-made organ in my body, a special kidney that filtered feelings and didn't allow in too much pain if things went wrong. I didn't trust the world and knew full well that even the happiest moment could disappear in just a blink.

Over the red roof of the Palazzo, the Milanese-style dome of the Church of Santa Maria delle Grazie was directly in my view. Saint Mary of the Graces. I am sure she didn't quite feel "full of grace" when her son was crucified like a common thief. She must have been devastated. I am a mother; I know. She would have willingly volunteered to be crucified instead of Jesus. But He had to suffer. He had to die a horrible death. And she had to watch it unfold. Full of grace. How did she deal with the pain? Did she ever succumb to numbness to survive? I wish I could ask her what grace consists of. Is it solely a divine gift, or does it have to be earned, or is it both? I assume it's both. A gift from God that needs to mature through hardship. Its worst enemies are anger, fear, and hatred; its best friends are love and forgiveness.

"Dear Mary, please ask God to forgive me for everything," I whispered. The guilt I felt was as heavy as ever. But could she hear me? Would she hear me? And if she did, was I even worth her time?

At the award ceremony, I told an audience of about two hundred and fifty my story. I had not written a speech. I never do. I just told them what had happened and all I had witnessed, and my young translator, Giovanna, translated my words for the crowd. Then Mr. Mauro gave me a silver plaque in a navy velvet box.

After I received the prize, a long line of people appeared in front of me, wanting me to sign their books. I signed one after another until a young man in his late twenties stood before me and smiled. I waited for a book, but none was forthcoming.

"I have something for you," he said. I extended my hand and held it under his closed fist, and he dropped a blue-beaded rosary into my palm. I gasped. It looked almost identical to the rosary I took with me to Evin, the one I left at Ali's grave.

"From Medjugorje,"* he said.

"Thank you," I mumbled as he disappeared into the crowd.

Was this an answer to my prayers? Did this mean that the Virgin was watching over me?

In the afternoon, Mr. Mauro took me to the Church of Santa Maria delle Grazie to see Leonardo da Vinci's *The Last Supper*. Mr. Mauro's wife, daughter, and assistants accompanied us. I had

---

*Medjugorje is a town in western Bosnia-Herzegovina that has become famous throughout the world because of the six young people who, beginning on June 24, 1981, claimed to have seen visions of the Madonna there.

read online that one could spend only fifteen minutes in the room with the painting. Security was tight, and the guides and church workers were serious about the rules. Only twenty-five people were allowed in the room at a time; at the end of fifteen minutes, visitors were ushered out and a new group would enter.

In order to reach *The Last Supper*, we had to pass through several sealed chambers. The English-speaking guide with us explained that they provided climate control. Da Vinci had used a new, experimental technique to draw *The Last Supper* on the wall of the monastery dining hall, and this new technique had caused the painting to deteriorate significantly since its completion in the late fifteenth century. Measures such as the sealed chambers were put in place to slow the deterioration.

When I saw *The Last Supper*, I gasped. It was huge! Even though I knew it was a fresco, I had somehow expected it to be much smaller. Yet there in front of me were the life-size images of Jesus and his disciples breaking bread and chatting. The colours of the clothing had obviously faded with time, but the blues, reds, yellows, greens, and browns were still breathtaking in the light that poured onto the wall from left and right, while the room itself remained immersed in darkness. Like a small child given the most incredible gift in the world, I marvelled at the sight before me. My heart beat faster and faster. I felt that if I called out Jesus' name at that moment, He would look straight at me, and even though I wanted this to happen more than anything, I knew I wasn't ready for it. What would I tell Him I had done with the time given to me? I had to work even harder to set things right, and once I was satisfied with the results, I would return here and speak His name. But would I ever be ready? Would I ever dare assume I was ready?

I noticed that my group had moved away from me. They were gazing at photos placed around the room that told the history of the church and the fresco. But the photos didn't interest me. I just wanted to stand in silence and stare at the disciples long enough to understand their hopes and dreams. There was Saint Peter, unaware that he would betray Jesus. He actually believed that he would gladly give his life for his Master. Except, things didn't work out that way. His love for this world and what it had to offer was greater than his love for Jesus.

Betrayal of the one you love—I had been there. When Ali told me I had to convert to Islam, I didn't put up a fight. But I had another trial ahead of me. I believed that God expected me to forgive and love Ali. Love thy enemy. Once I opened my heart to Ali and tried to understand him, my resentment of him began to fade. Maybe if he had lived, I would even have come to love him. Maybe. However, I believe that my ultimate betrayal had nothing to do with my conversion or with Ali. It was my betrayal of my friends when I walked away from Evin, knowing that they had to stay and suffer, maybe even face death. How could I have left them behind? I was a young woman who had wanted to go home. Yet at what price? Back then, I didn't understand that the price I had to pay was far too high. Tears flowed down my face.

After our fifteen minutes expired, to my surprise our group was allowed to stay; Mr. Mauro must have made special arrangements. I stood in a corner and continued to stare at the image of Jesus.

The way I see Jesus has not changed much at all since I was a child, but my imprisonment and all that followed made me love Him even more. His being the Son of God makes sense to me, because I believe God to be loving, just, forgiving, and merciful. I also believe that He respects free will. After all, He has given it to us so that we can choose to love or hate Him, do good or evil. But is it fair for a loving God to sit on His throne in Heaven and let us struggle and suffer on our own? Would any good father abandon his children this way? It makes perfect sense to me that God decided to come among us, live like us, and die a horribly painful death after being tortured. This is a God I can love with all my heart. A God who sets an example. A God who has bled and whose heart has been broken. This is who Jesus is to me. I don't pretend that I understand the Holy Trinity. But I understand love and sacrifice. I understand faithfulness.

In prison, to make myself feel better, I sometimes compared my suffering with what Jesus went through. He was lashed and so was I. He had to wear a crown of thorns and carry a heavy cross through the streets; I was raped. He had nails hammered into his body and he died from that; I faced a firing squad, although I didn't die. I have tried to understand what crucifixion must feel like. I just know that the pain must be beyond what I have ever experienced. I respect, love, and trust the One who endured all this when He didn't have to. I understand Jesus with my heart, and the rest of the world can think of Him as it will. The historians and writers who argue about whether Jesus was married don't interest me. If He chose to marry, good for Him. This would only make Him more human, more like me, and I can appreciate that. I am a very unconventional Catholic. I believe that even though Jesus is the way to God, other ways to Him exist. I believe that a good Muslim, Baha'i, Jew, Zoroastrian, Hindu, Buddhist—anyone, for that matter—who follows his or her conscience and tries his or her best to do good will find eternal peace in God. What Jesus did was to make it easier for people to relate to God. My religion has only one rule: Love One Another. Even though this seems simple enough, life has shown me that it isn't easy to follow. Loving one's enemy is easier said than done.

After an hour with *The Last Supper*, we left the Church of Santa Maria delle Grazie. As we were about to step out, our guide took my hands in hers and told me that *Prisoner of Tehran* had affected her deeply. I gazed into her unfamiliar eyes, and I was consoled to know that the memory of those who suffered in Evin lived in her, a complete stranger from a foreign land who didn't even speak our language.

# A Star-Shaped Christmas Cookie

My grandmother taught me to pray and first told me about Jesus and Mary. She made sure I understood that even though she would not be around to watch me all the time, God would always know what I was up to. She took me to the very long Russian Orthodox Mass every Sunday, and to reward me for my patience and good behaviour, she bought me treats as we walked home. I loved the chocolate and candy, but Christmas cookies were my favourite. Christmas meant going for a much-longer-than-normal Mass and being terribly bored—but it was worth it, because after the Mass, *Bahboo* would rush me home and allow me to take a star-shaped cookie from the Christmas tree. My parents were not religious and never attended Mass with *Bahboo* and me. The Russian Orthodox were a tiny minority in Tehran, and most of the people attending Mass at our church were old women.

Christians have always been a tiny minority in Iran. Most Iranian Christians are either Armenian, Assyrian, or Chaldean—ethnic groups who have been present in Iran for hundreds of years and have churches in a few large cities, including Tehran, Tabriz, and Isfahan. Following the 1915 genocide of Armenians in Turkey, many of them eventually immigrated to Iran and their community became larger. During the time of Mohammad Reza Shah Pahlavi

(1941–1979), Armenians were allowed to have their own schools. Armenians played a significant role in the modernization of the country, and they became known as a hard-working, honest people. Throughout centuries, they have had a marginal status in Iran and have survived by paying homage to the leadership of the country in exchange for safety and protection from Muslim religious extremists. The majority of their population belongs to the Apostolic Church, but a small number of Armenians are Catholics and Protestants.

Whether Assyrians are an ethno-national group or a religious community* is not entirely clear. They fall into several denominations, including the Nestorian Church; its Chaldean offshoot; the Russian Orthodox Church; Protestant churches; and the Jacobite Church.

Iran's population is currently about seventy-four million. Close to ninety-nine per cent of the population is Muslim, of which approximately eighty-nine per cent is Shia and ten per cent Sunni. Baha'i, Jews, Christians, and Zoroastrians constitute the remaining one per cent of the population.

EVEN THOUGH *Bahboo* couldn't carry a tune, she was a member of the church choir. I keenly remember her standing next to the other singers, who were all at least as old as she was, her grey hair gathered into a tight bun at her nape, her white blouse and black skirt perfectly ironed, and a little red scarf tied around her slim neck. I watched her as she smiled, singing joyful hymns that had found their way out of her heart and were now dancing over the flickering flames of the candles, images of the Virgin and the Child, and members of the congregation. *Bahboo* was happiest at Christmas and Easter. She was a kind and generous woman who

---

*Sanasarian, *Religious Minorities in Iran*, 40.

had lived an arduous life and, as she had explained to me, had forgotten how to smile. Christmas became a miracle to me at a very young age because it was one of the two special days of the year that I could see happiness in *Bahboo*'s eyes.

*Bahboo*'s life in Iran in the twenties and thirties was vastly different from mine in the seventies. I grew up wearing what I wanted to on the streets, and during the time of the shah, I was never discriminated against because I was a member of a religious minority. I read Western literature and went to a good school. However, when *Bahboo* arrived in Iran around 1921, she was forced to wear the *hejab*, which at the time had to be the *chador*, and sometimes as she walked to the market, the neighbourhood children threw rocks at her, calling her a dirty Christian.

Then times changed. On February 21, 1921, Reza Khan staged a *coup d'état* and overthrew Ahmad Shah Qajar, the last king of the Qajar dynasty, which had ruled Iran since 1794. According to some sources, the British Empire helped Reza Khan come to power to stop the penetration of the Bolsheviks in Iran. Reza Khan was declared shah—king—in 1925 and began the Pahlavi dynasty with a vision of modernizing Iran. During his sixteen-year reign, he built the trans-Iranian railway, connecting the north of the country to the south. He constructed many roads, introduced modern education to the country by establishing the University of Tehran, and erected many modern industrial plants. At the beginning of his reign, all women in Iran observed the *hejab* in public, because this had been their religious tradition for hundreds of years. In another attempt to modernize Iran, in the late thirties Reza Shah declared the *hejab* illegal. He believed that it held women back and prevented them from taking an active role in the progress of the country. After Reza Shah's decree against the *hejab*, if a woman wore the *chador* in public, the police would forcibly remove it or even arrest her if she resisted.

Reza Shah was a dictator. He had no tolerance for criticism and created a system where freedom of speech did not exist and anyone who dared criticize him was arrested, imprisoned, tortured, even killed. He arrested many political leaders, including Mohammad Mosaddegh, and gave the order for the killing of others, such as Teymourtash (his minister of court from 1925 to 1932). He confiscated land from the Qajars and his rivals and added it to his own estates. Corruption continued under his rule and became more and more widespread. He closed down Armenian schools in 1938–39 and threatened the internal autonomy of the Armenians. Many villages in Iran's Azerbaijan Province had ancient Armenian names, but Reza Shah changed them to Persian ones.

Article 13 of the Constitution of the Islamic Republic of Iran states: "Zoroastrian, Jewish, and Christian Iranians are the only recognized minorities, who, within the limits of the law, are free to perform their religious rites and ceremonies, and to act according to their own canon in matters of persona, affairs, and religious education."

The phrase "within the limits of the law" has certainly been open to interpretation by Iran's regime. Even though the recognized religious minorities in Iran are allowed to have their temples, synagogues, and churches, they cannot advertise their religion openly because they would be suspected of encouraging Muslims to apostatize. In Iran, conversion from Islam to another religion is punishable by death. The government of Iran has been particularly vigilant in recent years in curbing proselytizing activities by Christians whose services are conducted in Persian.

In 1985 and 1986 I worked with a group of Catholic Armenian nuns who ran an all-girl school in Tehran. Although the Catholic Armenian Church still appeared to own this school, the government had significantly limited the nuns' authority.

The government had assigned a Muslim principal and many Muslim teachers to the school, and the nuns were not permitted to teach the students from Christian catechism books. Instead, the Islamic government had designed and written religious education books for Christian students, and these books had nothing to do with the teachings of the Church. These amended and distorted catechism books had to be in Persian instead of Armenian so the government would have complete control over the teaching material. Soon, all religious minorities were banned from teaching their language in their schools. A decree prohibited having a school on church, synagogue, or temple grounds. Purportedly, the purpose of this new rule was to keep the Muslims who attended these schools from being exposed to other religions. In his letter to Ayatollah Montazeri, published in *Iran Times* on July 6, 1984, Archbishop Manukian wrote, "Despite your comforting words, not only did the problems raised in connection with the schools remain unresolved, but recent orders have actually worsened the situation: the unwarranted replacement of school principals, the dismissal of several teachers of the Armenian language and religion, and the closure of a number of schools."*

The Baha'i remain "non-recognized" in Iran and do not have legal status. The authorities have classified them as "unprotected infidels." They are subject to systematic discrimination because of their religious beliefs and have been, and are still, prosecuted in Iran. They have suffered more than any other religious minority in the country. In 2008, seven leaders of the Baha'i community were arrested in Iran and taken to Evin prison. As I am writing these lines, they remain behind bars. This latest sweep recalls the wholesale arrest or abduction of the members of two national

---

*Sanasarian, *Religious Minorities in Iran*, 77.

Iranian Baha'i governing councils in the early 1980s—which led to the disappearance or execution of seventeen individuals.*

*BAHBOO* DIED when I was seven, and with her death, Christmas changed for me. There were no more Christmas trees and star-shaped cookies. However, Alik saved the day a couple of times by giving me a gift. One year, it was a doll with black curly hair and blue eyes; another time, it was a toy train set. I had never received gifts for Christmas because *Bahboo* believed that toys spoiled children, so Alik's kindness delighted me, but I still missed the Christmas tree and the cookies. When I turned four, Alik moved to the city of Shiraz in central Iran to attend university, and I rarely saw him. His short visits were always exciting. I loved the smell of his cologne hanging in the air. To me as a young child, he was like a hero from a book who would materialize every once in a while, then disappear in an air of mystery and intrigue.

Christmas has never been a holiday in Muslim Iran, so I had to go to school on Christmas Day. But this didn't bother me, because I was used to it. After the Islamic Revolution of 1979, when I turned fourteen, I felt a strong need to resurrect Christmas and have it back in my life. Christians were an accepted minority in Iran, and even after the revolution, going to church and celebrating Christmas wouldn't get us in trouble as long as we abided by the Islamic rules that governed the country, didn't try to convert Muslims to Christianity, and didn't criticize the government.

In the summer of 1980 I began saving my money to buy a Christmas tree, and when the time came, I told my mother that I needed her to go with me to help me carry it home. She didn't mind. Buying a Christmas tree in Tehran wasn't easy, since only a

*From a letter released in May 2008 by Ms. Diane Ala'I, Representative, Baha'i International Community, United Nations Office, Geneva.

handful of vendors sold them across the city, but luckily, there was one within walking distance of our apartment. Once the tree was in its stand, I pulled the old dust-covered boxes of ornaments out of our basement, but was disappointed to see that they had faded and looked rather ugly. I decorated them with ribbons from the store until they appeared almost brand new.

Christmas changed again for me in prison. When Ali forced me to convert to Islam, I felt like a traitor. In solitary confinement, one has a lot of time to think, and I talked to God for hours at a time. I apologized to Him over and over, explaining that I didn't have a choice, that if I didn't do what Ali wanted me to do, he would arrest my mother, father, and Andre, and I just couldn't live with that. If they arrested my family, I would not have a home to go back to one day. I expected God to say something to me, but He never said a word, and many times, I wondered if He had abandoned me. But there were moments in the night, somewhere between sleep and consciousness, when I could feel the darkness of the cell wrap itself around me like a grave—and then I would feel a presence. It wasn't a voice or something I could see or touch, but it was warm and kind, and it refused to let me go.

On Christmas Day in 1983, it snowed. I had been moved out of solitary and was again in a cell with many other girls. Early in the morning, through the barred window, I watched feathery flakes glide back and forth on the wind. Soon, the clotheslines in the courtyard and all the clothes hanging on them were frosted with white. When our time to use the yard arrived, most of the girls came back in immediately after collecting their laundry, because the air was too cold. Our rubber slippers didn't offer much protection against the elements. I volunteered to bring in the clothes of two of my friends. It was chillier out than I had thought, but I liked the touch of snowflakes on my face. There was no one outside. I took off my socks and slippers and stood as motionless as possible. The white curves of winter took me in, covering me, filling the small spaces between my toes. Christmas Day. The day Christ was born. A day of joy and celebration, of singing carols, eating big meals, and opening gifts. How could the world go on as if nothing had happened, as if so many lost lives had never existed?

After a while my feet began to hurt, and then they went numb. Evin had taken me away from home, from the person I had been; it had taken me to a realm beyond fear; it had shown me more pain than any human being should ever witness. I had experienced loss before; I had grieved. But in Evin the never-ending grief kept its victims in a perpetual state of suffocation. How was one supposed to live after such an experience?

When we came to Canada in 1991, I was thrilled to see that Christmas was actually a holiday here. To go to the mall, look at the decorations, and watch the shoppers delighted me. The last Christmas before my arrest, I had knitted scarves for friends and loved ones, but here in Canada, even though we didn't have much money, I could go to the store and buy them something much nicer. All the scarves I had knitted were black, because wearing bright colours could get one in trouble. The Revolutionary Guard issued warnings to anyone not wearing only black, brown, grey, or navy.

Since I began writing in 2002 I have been thinking more and more about my Christmases in Iran, and I have decided that I want Christmas to be as simple as it can be. The tree is essential for me, but I don't want new ornaments. I want to sing carols, even though I know I can't sing. I want to remember the loneliness I felt in the prison and the presence that kept me alive when all light had faded from my world. I want to remember my friends who suffered in Evin and those who lost their lives. And I want to remember the baby who was born more than two thousand years ago and told people to love one another.

If it were up to me I would ban Christmas gifts at my house, but I know that if I did I would have a rebellion on my hands. I do not give useless knickknacks to the letter carrier, co-workers, or teachers, among others. Instead, I give money to charities. What I want for Christmas are star-shaped cookies, a Christmas tree, and my family to surround me—because I know how unpredictable life is, and that we might not have another Christmas together.

# A Jar of
# Folic-Acid Supplements

For years, I avoided folic-acid supplements, even though my family physician had instructed me to take them because of a genetic blood disorder that I have. I always had a jar full of them, but I kept it out of sight at the back of my medicine cabinet. For the longest time, I didn't think about why I avoided them—I did not want to revisit the memory. But during a trip to Greece, that memory came back to life in an unexpected way. Once I returned from that trip I put the folic-acid jar on my kitchen table, where I could always see it. As with my grandmother *Bahboo,* who kept her jewellery box on her kitchen table, the ghosts of my past have moved into my kitchen.

On May 30, 2008, in Thessaloniki, Greece, I dragged myself out of bed at 8:00 a.m. I had arrived there the previous evening and was exhausted. After drinking three cups of strong black coffee I walked to the Thessaloniki Book Fair, where I would speak. My event was not until 1:00 p.m., but I wanted to go to the Canadian booth first. The Canadian Embassy in Greece and my Greek publisher had together arranged my trip.

I walked around the fair grounds and looked at books for a few minutes. As I made my way to my fellow Canadians, I spotted the Islamic Republic of Iran booth. I decided not to speak to the two Iranian men behind the counter—I knew quite well that the people the government of Iran sent to international events were individuals they could trust. There was a good chance those two had connections to the Ministry of Information and were not exactly the kind of people with whom I would want to chat.

The Canadian booth was only steps away from the Iranian one. Many copies of the Greek translation of my book sat on display, and a copy of the fair's newspaper featuring an earlier online interview with me was taped to the wall. As I shook hands with Denys Tessier, the Canadian political and public affairs counsellor, I noticed one of the men from the Iranian booth striding toward us. He marched right past me, went to the bookshelf, picked up a copy of my book, and flipped through it. Then, as I was still chatting with Mr. Tessier, he interrupted us and asked, "Are you the author of this book?"

"Yes," I answered, smiling my biggest smile, my heart beating as fast as if I were halfway through a hundred-metre dash.

The man stared at me.

I was not going to let him think that he had intimidated me, so I said, "Please, would you like to sit down with us?" and I pulled two chairs forward as Mr. Tessier pulled one out for himself.

"I'm sorry—I missed your name," I said.

"Ali," he responded.

He was playing a game with me. Maybe his name *was* Ali, but Iranians never introduce themselves by their first name. They always say only their last name—for example, I would say that I am Nemat—or they say their first *and* last names. My heart was beating even faster now.

The silence was getting uncomfortable. I had to say something. Anything.

"So ... how is the traffic in Tehran?" I asked. "Is it still as bad as I remember it?" Tehran residents complain about traffic the way Canadians complain about the weather.

"Terrible," the man said. "When were you there last?"

"1990."

"It's much worse now. We have a terrible mayor, and he hasn't done anything to improve it. The streets downtown are like parking lots."

Silence again. We all just looked at one another.

"By the way, I have an event here today at 1:00 p.m.," I blurted, "and if you'd like to learn more about my book—"

"I know," he interrupted, getting up. "We know all about you. We've been watching you," he added, and was gone before I could say another word.

Mr. Tessier turned to me and asked, "What the hell was that?"

"I have no idea," I responded.

Zoe Delibasis, the cultural, media relations, and public affairs officer at the Canadian Embassy, came up to us. "That guy was circling our booth for a couple of days," she said to me. "I think he was waiting for you. I should have told you. Are you okay?"

"I'm okay. They just want to intimidate me."

I was shaken, but I was still in control. The way the Iranian had gazed at me was horribly familiar. He reminded me of Evin's interrogators. He had tried to demonstrate that he was in a position of power. He would have been able to upset me much more when I was sixteen and a prisoner, but I had grown up and learned a few lessons. I was now a free woman.

In Athens the next morning, my Greek publisher, Athanassios Psichogios, showed me many of the city's famous sites. Athens reminded me of Tehran. Its streets, with their four- or five-storey concrete or brick apartment buildings, were similar to those of Tehran. Even the air smelled like the air in Tehran, polluted and saturated with exhaust fumes. Athens was the closest I had been to Iran since I had left it so many years ago. In the afternoon, I wandered the city for hours, and when I got blisters on my feet, I went to a pharmacy to buy ointment to relieve the pain and prevent the blisters from worsening. The pharmacy's cluttered shelves, poor lighting, and friendly staff also reminded me of pharmacies in Tehran, especially the one Ali had taken me to. Until that moment the convenient distance of Canada had helped me ignore my longing for my homeland, but now it was as if I could reach out and touch my memories of Iran.

IN LATE AUGUST of 1983, fourteen months after my marriage to Ali, I started to feel terribly sick and began vomiting. After a few days, Ali drove me to see his mother's physician, a woman in her early fifties. She ordered some tests, and later told me I was eight weeks pregnant. That I might be expecting had not occurred to me. When I agreed to marry Ali, I only considered the effects of my decision on my own life, my parents' lives, and Andre's. I had never thought about children. Now another life would be affected: an innocent child's. A child would need me, rely on me, and, whether I liked it or not, would need its father. This baby was the absolute end of the person I had been before Evin.

When the doctor gave me the news, she also told me that according to the tests, something was wrong with my blood.

"The results are definitely not normal," she said. "But I don't know the cause. You must see a specialist."

She wrote the specialist's name and number on a piece of paper and handed the paper to me, making me promise I would phone for an appointment. Ali was waiting for me in the car. When I told him about my pregnancy, he was overjoyed. Then I gave him the paper from the doctor and told him she thought something was wrong. He looked very worried and said he would make the appointment.

A few days later, Ali drove me to the specialist's office, located off Kakh Avenue.

"You'll be fine," Ali said after he turned off the engine and took my hand in his. "Whatever it is, it's not important. You'll be fine. The baby will be fine, too."

I nodded. I didn't want that baby. I was ashamed of my feelings, but I couldn't help it. Deep inside, I wished I had leukemia and that both I and the baby would die soon.

The doctor ordered more tests, and after the results came in, she called Ali to say that she needed to see us. Apparently, I had thalassemia minor, a genetic anemia. She said the condition was like a very mild form of blood cancer, and it would get neither better nor worse nor would kill me. I had always had thalassemia without knowing it, and I could keep on living as I always had. Even though there was no cure for it, folic-acid supplements could help a little. She said that my condition could cause complications only when having children.

"I'm pregnant," I said.

"We'll have to test your husband," she said thoughtfully, looking at Ali. "If he has the same illness, which is relatively common in Iran, your children may die from anemia very early in life."

Ali went for the test, and it showed that he didn't have thalassemia. He was relieved, but I felt as if I were watching the blade of a guillotine drop closer and closer to my neck. With a baby, I would never have a way out. Even though I had been able to avoid telling my family about my marriage, I couldn't hide it now. I had to face them and disclose the truth. Would they disown me and hate me forever?

Ali drove me to the pharmacy, and we picked up all the folic-acid supplements that I needed. When we got back in the car, Ali didn't move, just stared ahead.

"You look so sad and miserable," he finally said.

I gazed down.

"What's wrong?" he asked

I laughed.

"What's so funny?"

"That you ask me what's wrong," I said. "Everything is wrong! Everything! You! Me! This marriage! Evin!"

I was crying.

"Marina, you're pregnant. Pregnant women get like this. Life is tough. I know. But I'm really trying, and I need you to try, too. Please."

I was cornered and there was no escape. Despite everything, I had kept up hope. It was time for me to accept reality. The Marina I had been was dead, and this other woman I had become had a husband and soon a baby who would need her.

"It must be the pregnancy," I said, sobbing. "I don't mean to be this way."

"I have to cheer you up," Ali said. "Look over there. Next to the pharmacy. See that little shop? It's very popular with women. Akram [Ali's sister] sometimes shops there. I have driven her here a few times and waited forever for her to do her shopping. Here ... let me give you some money. Just go in and buy yourself something nice."

He passed me a handful of bills. I stepped out of the car and walked to the store. There were a few nice towels and an embroidered pink bathrobe in the store window. They appeared so delicate. I walked inside. The female clerk, who was wearing a lot of makeup, greeted me. I wondered how she could dare walk in the street like that, but maybe she washed off her makeup before heading out. I avoided eye contact with everyone in the store. A few robes and nightgowns hung from a rack, all of them lacy and beautiful. I chose a pink nightgown and a matching robe and asked the clerk if I could try them on. She directed me to the change room. I put them on and glanced at my reflection in the mirror. I didn't look pregnant at all. My stomach was as flat as ever. I imagined myself sitting in a solitary cell, wearing my new things.

Someone knocked on the change-room door. I jumped.

"Yes?"

"Do you need a different size?" the clerk asked.

"No. This is fine," I said.

"May I see how you look in them to make sure they fit right?"

I opened the door.

"Beautiful!" she said. "Your husband will like them."

If only she knew.

WALKING AWAY from the pharmacy in Athens, I thought of the baby—whom I had been sure was a boy. I miscarried when Ali was assassinated. If our son had lived, he would have been twenty-four years old now. A young man. Would he have resembled Ali or me? Would he have ended up working for the Iranian regime, or would I have been able to teach him right from wrong? If he had survived, I would have told him that even though I blamed his father for his terrible job in Evin and for forcing me into marriage, I was proud of him for quitting his job shortly before his death and for his efforts to take care of his unborn son and me.

A year after my trip to Greece, I received an email from a young man named Nima, who told me he had been born in Evin prison in 1981. He had never known his parents. He had read my book three times and felt that his mother could well have written it. I was heartbroken. I asked him if he knew what had happened to his parents. He responded that he would tell me when he was ready. How many children had been born in Evin? How many of them had been fathered by guards and interrogators? We had a pregnant young woman at 246. She and her husband had both been condemned to death. Executing a pregnant or breastfeeding woman is against Islamic law, so Evin officials postponed her sentence. She gave birth to a beautiful son. We watched him grow. He became a toddler while I was in prison. His mother eventually sent him home to live with her parents, even though parting with him devastated her. But he had never seen a tree or a flower. His world had been made of concrete and barbed wire.

"They tried to rob us of everything," I wrote to Nima, "including the possibility of ever being happy again. I wish you happiness, even if it has to be incomplete."

He wrote back, "I wish you happiness, too, Marina, as it is our only revenge."

This was exactly what Shahnoosh had told me when I dreamed of her.

AFTER MY RELEASE from Evin and before I married Andre, my secret marriage to Ali and my pregnancy came perilously close to being exposed.

I sometimes had very heavy menstrual bleedings, and one month after I got out of Evin the bleeding was so severe I couldn't climb out of bed and my pads became soaked after only a few minutes. My mother phoned a family friend who was a gynecologist. She stopped by our house and gave me an injection to control the bleeding, and then she ordered some blood tests. After the results came back, she said I had to see a specialist. I had not told her or anyone at home about my marriage, pregnancy, or the miscarriage, so I couldn't tell her I knew I had thalassemia minor. I was shocked and terrified when she referred me to the same specialist the physician of Ali's mother had sent me to.

Andre told me he would take me to see the specialist. There was a good chance that she would recognize me and ask about Ali and the baby. I couldn't let this happen. Two or three days before the appointment, I went to her office. I told her secretary that I needed to see the doctor for only a few minutes and I was willing to wait as long as necessary. I was quite distraught, so the secretary told me she would send me in as soon as she could. After an hour or so, the secretary showed me into the doctor's office. I reminded the doctor who I was. She remembered Ali and me. I told her that Ali was dead and that I had miscarried. Colour left her face. I told her that I had been a prisoner when I had come to her office the previous time. Her eyes grew larger by the second.

"My family doesn't know anything about Ali and my relationship with him," I said. "I beg you to keep my secret. They will disown me if they find out. I'm going to marry the man I love very soon. I just want to put the past behind me. We have an appointment with you in two days. Please pretend you don't know me when I come with him."

"I'm your physician," she said, her voice trembling. "Everything I know about you is confidential, and I assure you that it will remain that way. Dear girl ... I had no idea ... you looked so normal ... he looked so nice ..."

I breathed a sigh of relief.

The doctor played her role perfectly when I went to see her with Andre. Andre didn't suspect anything. He, too, was tested for the disorder, and he didn't have it. We could have children.

ONE NIGHT IN ATHENS, I had dinner at the Hotel Grande Bretagne with two friends. We ate at the rooftop restaurant, with its magical view of the Acropolis. The Greek ruins made me think of those at Persepolis, which I had visited when I had been five or so. Both ruins are wondrous reminders of a time when different superpowers ruled the world. Persians call Persepolis *Takht-eh Jamshid,* or "Throne of Jamshid." It was the ceremonial capital of the Achaemenid dynasty. The army of Alexander of Macedonia set fire to it around 330 BC.

As the sun set, the lights came on and the Acropolis became a vessel of yellow light floating in darkness. I could almost see Persepolis in the desert. Each one of its molecules held a story in its nucleus. Its empty doorways were like the eye sockets of a strange skull, and its dusty skeleton seemed to stare into the sky, remembering what the rest of the world had forgotten. Above Persepolis, the full moon rested in its gauzy halo, white and pale and ghostly, watching a severe land where day and night chase each other with a vengeance and mirages are the only threads that weave hope into reality.

*Bahboo* sometimes said, "I'll go back home to Russia one day. Those Communist murderers will be gone, and I'll go home."

She never went back. Eventually, the Communists were banished, but she was long gone by then, her bones decaying in the earth. Yet I have faith that her soul is at peace. I have not dreamed of her even once since she died.

Now it is my turn to fantasize about going home. Will I live to see the end of the Islamic Republic?

# My Happy-Daisy Slippers and a Broken Umbrella

Even though I might see the end of the Islamic Republic, my father might not live that long.

In the winter of 2009, at the age of eighty-eight, my father developed an infection in his right toe. At first, the infection didn't seem serious, but it spread and turned into cellulitis, and he had to be put on intravenous antibiotics. Although he slowly recovered, his health began to deteriorate in other ways—a mini stroke, high blood pressure, arthritis. He was holding up, but he had grown visibly slower and more fragile. Still, every morning, he did basic ballet moves for about an hour. He told me that without exercising, he would never have been able to remain relatively healthy for so long.

After his mini stroke, my father became more aware of his mortality. I had been taking him for his doctor's appointments, buying his groceries when he was unwell, and making sure that he was comfortable. One day he gave me an envelope, and when I opened it, I found one thousand dollars inside. I refused to accept the money, but he told me if I didn't, he would get upset.

"I'm going to die soon, Marina, so what use will money be to me?" he said.

Since my mother's death, my father had gradually turned into a different person. Before me was the same person who had refused to lend me the money that would get me out of Iran and probably save my life. I took the envelope and thanked him, asking myself if my father facing his mortality was the only reason he had changed. He and my mother had been married for fifty-eight years when she died. Her death was an enormous loss for him. Early in my teenage years, I became aware that friends and family seemed to like my mother more than they did my father. She was popular and had many friends; my father preferred to be alone. He had two or three friends, but altogether, he disliked socializing. His idea of fun was going to the cottage and spending hours watering trees and shrubs. Since I can remember, he and my mother had had one fight after another, and during most of them, my mother would burst into tears and threaten to leave. Her threats terrified me when I was very young, but soon after I turned twelve, I began to realize that I could take care of myself and didn't really need my mother. This was an important stage in my life when I became independent and stopped worrying about what my mother might do. By then, I had also found ways to escape my father's critical and severe watch. I had learned to hide from him things I knew he would not approve of—for example, my friendships with boys and my religious beliefs, which were growing stronger every day. Years later in Canada after my parents moved in with me, my mother initiated most of our fights and my father just followed her. Now that I've been married for twenty-five years, I know that after such a long time of living together, husband and wife become almost one entity, affecting each other in a constant, profound way. As I saw in my parents, once one of the pair dies, this entity ceases to exist, and the living part has to redefine itself.

I always feel connected to those who acknowledge death and accept it as an inescapable reality. If we manage to survive an encounter with it, death has the amazing ability to teach us how to live. We begin to put our life to good use only when every moment becomes a universe to explore and cherish.

In May 2007 when I was in Amsterdam, a journalist named Kim Moelands, a young woman with a big warm smile and long honey-coloured hair, interviewed me about *Prisoner of Tehran*. Every so often she would pause in mid-sentence, overcome by a severe cough that came from deep within her chest. It sounded like pneumonia.

"Are you okay?" I asked her. "Would you like me to order some tea?"

"No, thank you," she said and smiled. "I have cystic fibrosis. I'm thirty now, and doctors informed me that I'd die before the age of thirty, but I'm still here." Then she added that her husband, who had also had cystic fibrosis, had died a year earlier.

I was at a loss for words.

She told me how she had related to my book, to living with death, to fighting a seemingly impossible-to-win battle.

After the interview, we stood by one of the room's large windows, which opened over a narrow street and a canal, and watched the world go by. It was late afternoon. The water shimmered, and the white, brown, red, blue, and grey reflections of the old townhouses across the street quivered on the water's dark-green surface. Two cyclists, young men who were speaking and laughing loudly, rode by. A white tour boat was making a U-turn, and surprisingly, it succeeded, even though its length was only slightly less than the width of the canal. Kim and I both took in the beauty around us, very much aware of life's fragility. We had both looked straight into death's eyes and had accepted that it was coming for us soon. Acknowledging death doesn't mean giving up on life; on the contrary, this understanding makes every moment in this world more meaningful and precious. Kim and I now had no time to waste. At that intimate moment, I felt a strange sense of peace, and I knew that Kim felt the same.

Kim and I remained in touch after I returned to Canada. She told me she had decided to write a memoir, and I encouraged her, explaining that even though writing about my traumatic experiences had been very difficult, it had also given me an exhilarating sense of freedom. Kim's book, *Breathless*, was published to great critical acclaim in the fall of 2008 and became a bestseller in Holland.

The last time I saw Kim was in November 2008, on my way to speak at a conference in Milan. She had just been released from the hospital, where she had faced many complications. She had told me that she had met a man named Jan, a journalist who had interviewed her, and they had fallen in love. I was ecstatic when I heard the news. Kim said that Jan understood very well that their time together was limited. I reminded Kim that everyone's time is limited. None of us knows how long we have. The difference in Kim's case is that her disease is a constant reminder of life's fragility to all who love her.

Amsterdam was cold and damp at that time of year, and I spent most of my time indoors with Kim. We talked about books, life, and death for hours. She gave me a pair of cozy yellow Dutch-style slippers with smiling red daisies on them. She had bought two identical pairs at the hospital: one for herself and one for me. They had made her smile during painful procedures, and she was sure that they would be good for me, too. I had thought of buying Kim a gift and I had looked for one as soon as I knew I would be able to see her on my way to Italy, but the more I searched, the more I realized that buying her anything was impossible. I wanted to give her health. Except, how could I do that? I wished I could find Jesus, grab Him by the arm, and take Him to Kim. I prayed for her on a regular basis, but my prayers didn't seem to accomplish much. So I decided to give her my rosary, the one the young Italian man had put in my hand in Milan when I was there to receive the Human Dignity Prize—the rosary from Medjugorje. It had already performed its miracle for me; it had reminded me that the Virgin was watching over me. Since I had received the rosary, I had taken it everywhere with me, but it was time to give it away. It was time for it to perform another miracle.

I have told my father about Kim, and he asks me about her every time I visit him. Kim is constantly in and out of the hospital, and I pray for her and keep her in my heart. I beg God to cure her, but she is not getting any better. Do I understand the world well enough to know why people like Kim suffer? No, I don't. All I know is that Kim has shown me a special kind of strength and courage. In her, I see a unique beauty that I have rarely seen before. If she had lived a comfortable and "normal" life, would she be the Kim I have come to admire and respect? Probably not. So I am going to stick with what I know for sure: I love Kim and I want her to be well. And, like a stubborn child who refuses to take no for an answer, I am going to keep on begging God.

ON THE PLANE on my way to the conference in Milan, I thought of the Angel of Death. I had dreamed of him at the age of seven after *Bahboo*'s death. In my dream, he was a handsome young man with curly black hair; he was wearing a white robe, and he told me that he was my guardian angel. When I asked him why he didn't have shoes on, he said that there was no need for shoes where he came from. He held me in his arms and made me feel loved and secure. Ever since, whenever the world became too much to bear, I thought of him. As I lost loved ones, I felt comforted to know that he waited for them in the next world.

Milan was unseasonably cold, even colder than Amsterdam, with the temperature hovering around 0°C. Early in the morning of my second day at the conference, when I looked out the window of my room, it was snowing—a relatively rare sight in Milan. The snow was accumulating, and the flakes were the largest I had ever seen. In keeping with my morning ritual, I took a shower, got dressed, and went outside for a little walk. I didn't want my hair to get wet and frizzy, so I opened my umbrella. The wind wasn't too strong at that point, and I enjoyed the fresh, crisp air. I stood by a large fountain with little angels in the middle of it. Dressed in snow, they appeared even more heavenly. The wind grew stronger, so I turned back to go for breakfast, but a strong gust suddenly blew my umbrella inside out and tore it out of my hand. Years earlier, something similar had happened to me in Iran. Now it was as if a hand grabbed me and pulled me back in time. Tears fell down my face and burned my frozen skin. I couldn't move.

I was at a memorial service for Arash, the boy I had first met at the Caspian Sea. I didn't know how passionately he believed in the need to fight the shah's regime. In September 1978, only a few months before the success of the revolution, he was killed at a street demonstration. His family didn't know where his body was. He was eighteen when we met, and had finished his first year of studying medicine at the University of Tehran. We spent a lot of time together that summer, and he was the one who first told me about the Islamic Revolution in progress in the country. I had never heard the name Ayatollah Khomeini before Arash mentioned it to me. I was only thirteen and interested in books and music, not in the news. Even though a five-year age difference stood between us, we became close friends quickly and our friendship turned into love. Arash told me that the shah was a dictator and imprisoned those who opposed him. He said that the people of Iran were revolting against the shah because they wanted democracy. I didn't know what to make of it. From my perspective, we had good lives and didn't need a revolution. Arash disagreed with me, telling me I was too young and naïve.

In December 1979, Arash's parents finally gave up their search to find his place of burial and had a memorial stone made for him. Friends and relatives accompanied them to his aunt's cottage by the Caspian Sea, a place he loved dearly. There, on a miserable, freezing, rainy day in January 1980, we held a memorial service for him. My face was numb from the cold. My eyes moved from face to face, from one black outfit to the next, from the grey landscape to the grey sky, longing for hope. The rain suddenly changed to snow. I had never seen it snow at the Caspian. As Arash's brother, Aram, put a bouquet of red roses next to the memorial stone, a strong gust of wind turned my umbrella inside out and blew it out of my hand, away into the trees.

Arash's mother began to scream. Her cries seemed to rip open her chest, exposing her pain and her helplessness. Everyone was sobbing.

After the service we returned to Tehran, and the first thing I did was find a cardboard box that I hoped was large enough to hold my memories of Arash. I had to cure myself of the agonizing pain I felt, and it seemed that the only way was to forget. Walking from room to room, dragging the cardboard box behind me, I gathered souvenirs, clothes, music tapes, books—anything that even slightly reminded me of Arash. When the box was full, I closed it, taped it securely, and kept it in our basement for a while. In March 1980, during the Iranian New Year holidays, I took the box to our cottage with me. There was a special place on the property where, as *Bahboo* had taught me, I said the Our Father every morning. From a distance it resembled a big moss-covered rock, but as you approached you could see that it was made of many small stones. It stood about four feet high and six feet wide, and a thick, rusty metal bar reached out of one of its corners. It belonged to ancient times when the sea covered most of the land. Once useful as a place where fishermen tied their boats, it looked strange and out of place when I discovered it in a forgotten corner of the property. I loved to stand on it, open my arms to the gentle breeze, close my eyes, and imagine the sea surrounding me, its glassy surface transforming the sunlight into a golden liquid that glided toward the shore. I had come to call this strange monument the Prayer Rock. I found a shovel, dug a large hole in the sandy earth, and buried the box next to the rock.

After Arash's death, I became close friends with his brother, Aram, until he left Iran shortly before my incarceration in Evin. I lost touch with him and didn't hear from him until April 2000, when I received a phone call.

The winter of 2000 had felt longer than any other I had spent in Canada. It had seemed as though spring would never come, that it had frozen to death somewhere deep in the ground, buried inside an eternal shroud of glittering ice. On April 22, 2000, my thirty-fifth birthday, I checked my flower beds. The deep-green leaves of my tulips had broken the surface of the soil, but the landscape was still grey. The wind whipped against me. It started to rain, and although I hated being cold and wet, I stayed outside, breathing in the scent of the waking earth. A group of returning Canada geese filled the sky with their joyous, urgent cries; their graceful, dark wings arched, stretched, rose, and descended, bearing them back home.

I went inside the house. I had taken the day off work because of my birthday, but the kitchen floor was a mess and the bedrooms were upside down. I decided to have a cup of tea before attending to housework. As soon as I sat down, the phone rang.

I picked it up.

"Hello?"

"Marina?"

"Yes."

Silence.

"Hello?"

"It's me ... Aram."

"Aram?" Speaking his name sounded unreal, like hearing a vague and scattered echo.

"Arash's brother."

"My God. Where ... where are you?"

"New York."

"You live there?"

"No. I'm here for work. I live in Australia."

"How did you find me?"

"Long story ... It took a long time."

"Yeah. About ... nineteen years."

I told him that I had married Andre in 1985, and we had two sons. Aram said he was divorced and had one son. His parents had both died a few years back, within a year of each other. He asked me about my parents, and I told him that my mother had died a few weeks earlier, but my father was well.

"Sorry to hear about your mother," he said. "You know, she wrote to me and told me you had been arrested ..."

"I was in Evin for two years."

"I lost touch with your parents in early 1984. My letters began coming back."

"My parents moved."

"It took me years to find out you had been released and left Iran."

"We came to Canada in 1991."

"Marina, I was so angry at you. Didn't I tell you to be careful?"

After nineteen years, had he called me to say "I told you so"?

He said he could come to Toronto to see me. My heart sank. I wasn't sure if I wanted to see him. Actually, I realized I didn't. That part of my life was over and I didn't want to step into it again.

"Aram ... let's not go back ..."

Silence.

"Aram?"

"I understand."

"Stay in touch."

"I will."

I hung up and stared out the window. A black squirrel was sitting on the fence, staring back at me. I sat down. A part of me was telling me to call him back, to say that I had been wrong in not wanting to see him, but I knew what that would mean. For sixteen years, I had avoided the past at all costs. The bubble I carried on my shoulders, the one that held the memories of my life in Iran, had been secure for years, but now cracks were forming on its surface.

Aram called me again about three months later, and after that, we emailed each other every so often. When I decided to publish *Prisoner of Tehran*, I asked for his permission to write about his brother and about him. He gave it but requested that I protect his identity. He still had friends and family in Iran and travelled there about once every two years. I had to be discreet enough that Iranian authorities wouldn't easily recognize him from my book and cause him trouble.

After *Prisoner of Tehran* appeared in print, I considered visiting Aram. Before my arrest, I had *really* liked him. We were simply compatible. Except, I had been his brother's girlfriend. After Arash's death, we couldn't be more than friends. Then I fell in love with Andre in 1981, shortly before Aram left Iran.

We have a word in Persian that does not have an exact translation in English. It is *mehr*, which could be translated as "love." But in Persian, the word for love is *eshgh*. However, *eshgh* is the dramatic, hormonal kind of love, when *mehr* is even-handed, strong, and gentle. It implies friendship and trust. During all the years we had lived together, my *eshgh* for Andre had evolved into *mehr*. Seeing Aram could put what Andre and I had in jeopardy.

In so many ways, Andre and I could not be more different. I love literature, and he reads books only about his work. I love movies, and he watches only the news, sports, or the weather channel. I love to dance, but he has never danced in his life. I love to travel, and he always wants to stay home. I am easygoing and believe in not sweating the small things, but he is a perfectionist and expects everything—for example, even making the bed—to be done flawlessly. He has been loyal to me, and I have been faithful to him. We became one in front of God. When I considered seeing Aram, Andre and I had been married for twenty-two years. We were—still are—committed to each other. I knew I had to protect our marriage. I had to take care of Andre the way he had taken care of me. Till death do us part. This is the reason I decided not to see Aram, even after I faced my past.

AT THE END of that snowy day in Milan before I fell asleep at night, my last thoughts were of Arash and Aram. I had emailed Aram before going to bed to tell him about my umbrella and how that small incident had drawn me back in time. The next day, I found an email from him in my inbox:

> You won't believe this, but I dreamed of Arash last night before reading your email. The two of us were standing on the beach by the Caspian, watching you swim in the distance. Arash was holding an umbrella. It was a beautiful day, so I asked him why. He said it was yours, and that he had promised to keep it for you.

# A Dream Catcher

When I was a child, I sometimes saw angels, monks, or ghosts as I lay in my bed at night. As I grew older, the line that separated dreams from reality became more and more clear, but there were still instances when I found myself in a world I can only describe as in-between sleep and consciousness. A friend of mine who has had quite a few traumatic experiences told me that his nightmares sometimes make him get out of bed in the middle of the night and try to defend himself and the people he loves. Unlike him, though, when nightmare and reality become one, I never react. My nightmares pull me into the dark ocean of silence and paralyze me.

Occasionally, I have recurring nightmares. In one of them, I am on a relaxing holiday or a day trip with friends or family. We are strolling along, laughing, and having a great time. I'm wearing a bright, floral summer dress. Suddenly, a hand grabs me and drags me into a semi-dark room. There I find myself tied up to a bed. I struggle to scream, but I have been gagged. A man is always in the room, but I can never clearly see his face. I wake up in a cold sweat.

When my two boys were very young, I bought them each a dream catcher and hung it in their bedrooms. I explained how the dream catcher, which is a willow hoop with a woven web in the middle and is decorated with personal and sacred items such as feathers and beads, would catch their nightmares so that they would have only sweet dreams. Dream catchers originated with the Ojibwa nation, but during the sixties and seventies, Native Americans of a few different nations adopted them. Some consider the dream catcher a symbol of unity among those nations.

WHEN, in the fall of 2008, I was in the city of Cosenza, Italy, to receive the Grinzane Prize for *Prisoner of Tehran*, I met a woman named Giuliana Sgrena. She was one of the judges for the prize and sat next to me during a dinner party. I felt at a total loss because I didn't know anything about her, but she had read my book and, as a result, knew me very well. She was about an inch shorter than I was, probably in her late fifties, and weighed no more than ninety-five pounds. Her shoulder-length blond hair was carelessly combed, and she wore no makeup. Her eyes were a colour I didn't have a name for—a shade between amber and grey. She appeared tired. Very tired.

"Do you speak English?" I asked her, trying to make small talk.

"Yes," she said, "but not very well."

"I'm sure your English is better than my Italian," I said, and smiled. "What do you do?"

"I'm a journalist."

"Do you travel abroad a lot?"

"Oh, yes ..."

"Have you ever been to the Middle East?"

"Yes, to Iraq, Afghanistan ..."

"When were you in Iraq?"

"Many times. Last time in 2005."

"How was your trip?"

"I was kidnapped and held hostage."

I felt like an idiot. How didn't I know this? She did look a little familiar. Maybe I had seen her on TV.

"I'm so sorry ... I didn't know. What happened?"

"They kidnapped me outside a mosque in Baghdad where I was interviewing refugees from Fallujah on February 4, 2005, and they let me go a month later. I don't think they were fundamentalists. They were probably members of the Bath Party or something like that."

"How did they treat you?"

"They didn't beat me or really mistreat me. What bothered me more than anything was that I never knew if I was going to be alive in five minutes. It was a state of constant terror."

I knew exactly what she meant. A place between life and death.

"What was their demand?" I asked.

She said they wanted Italy to pull out its troops from Iraq. She told them that she was against the war, and that she was there to interview Iraqis to show the world how the war had affected the average person in Iraq. But they didn't care. They said they didn't want any foreigners in their country. They couldn't see what good she could do for them. She had dedicated her life to getting people heard. Real people. Victims of violence. But they didn't care. She believed this was what war had done to them: killed any possibility of communication.

I asked her how they had let her go and she explained that the Italian military secret service negotiated her release. One day, her kidnappers took her out in a car. They had blindfolded her, and she couldn't see where they were going. They told her not to move or make noise and then they left her in the car. About twenty to thirty minutes later, a friendly voice called her name. It was Nicola Calipari, an official from the Italian military secret service. He said she was free and he was taking her to the airport to go home. Another man was with him. They escorted her to a car and Nicola sat next to her in the back seat because he knew she was disoriented and scared. He was talking to her and comforting her all the time. They drove toward the airport in Baghdad. They were only a kilometre from it when an American armoured vehicle parked off the road behind a bend opened fire on them.

"The *Americans* opened fire on you?" I asked, shocked.

"Yes, the Americans," she said.

"Was this at a checkpoint? Did you fail to stop?"

"No, no, it wasn't a checkpoint. There was only an armoured vehicle. No signs. No warning. They just opened fire. As soon as we heard the guns, Nicola pushed me down and lay on top of me. He died right there. I was shot in my left shoulder. The bullet exploded in my body and my lung collapsed."

I could see the scene she was describing, and it was terribly familiar. Ali. I could see Ali. He pushed me down and lay on top of me, shielding me from the bullets that killed him. He drew his last breath in my arms. I shoved away the memory.

"The driver was yelling 'We're Italian! We're Italian! Don't shoot!' And the Americans finally stopped," Giuliana continued.

"This is horrible! What did the Americans say? Why did they shoot at you?"

"They just said that this was war, and took no responsibility."

They had shrugged off the incident as acceptable loss. War is supposed to justify anything and everything. How many innocent Iraqis have been killed at checkpoints? What about those massacred in the violence between Sunni and Shia that erupted after the U.S. invasion? How many lost innocent lives are too many? When there is no accountability, there will be no justice.

I asked her if she was still working as a journalist, and she said she was. She had been a war correspondent for many years. This was what she did.

She told me that some people said she should have stayed home and never gone to Iraq, that what happened to her was her own fault.

"It's always easier to blame the victim," I said, "especially if the victim is a woman. I've been blamed for what happened to me, too. This is just the way it is. How are you now? Do you have any health problems?"

"Yes, I do ... and I can't sleep ... I've become an insomniac."

I said that I didn't know how her experience had affected her, but mine had made me look at my life differently. I now lived in the moment, and imagining what things could be like in a month was hard for me. Every night before I went to bed, I considered that I might not wake up the next day or that I might lose the ones I loved.

She said that she was the same.

The distance between Giuliana and me had disappeared as if it had never existed. She and I had been strangers only a few minutes earlier, and now I felt as though I had always known her. I felt her emotions, and I knew she felt mine.

I told her that I might have seen her briefly on TV when she was kidnapped, but that I'd never heard about the Americans shooting at her. She said that she had published a book about her ordeal. The book had been translated into English and was available in the United States. Later, I read *Friendly Fire,** in which she explains that an American military inquest into the shooting incident that killed Nicola Calipari ended with full absolution for the soldiers who had opened fire on the car. The U.S. military concluded that the car was speeding at forty to fifty miles an hour and did not stop despite repeated signals, so the soldiers were forced to shoot. This conclusion went against the testimony of Giuliana and the driver

---

*Published in 2006 by Haymarket Books, Chicago; translated from Italian by Lesley Freeman Riva.

of the car, Agent Carpani, who both testified that the car hadn't been speeding and there had been no warnings.

Giuliana worked for a newspaper called *Il Manifesto*, an independent communist paper. The word *communist* always leaves me with a strange, uneasy feeling in the bottom of my stomach, because most—though not all—communists I have met have been dogmatic people whose idea of a dialogue is not letting others speak, pushing their ideology on others, and mocking the religious beliefs that others hold. But I liked Giuliana, and I could see that she was a highly intelligent, compassionate woman. I believe in real dialogue and sharing human experiences; clearly, Giuliana and I had connected in this way. I despise political boundaries that separate human beings as if we are from different species. "Religious" and "left" seem mutually exclusive, but are they really? I am a Catholic who doesn't agree with all the policies of the Catholic Church and many of my views are "left." What does this make me? I am tired of being categorized, and I believe that in general, all ideologies have proven to be dangerous political tools that usually divide people into "us" and "them." I have never blindly followed the Catholic Church.

Very early in the morning when it was still completely dark, a cab picked up Giuliana, two other people, and me to take us to the airport to catch our flight to Rome. Giuliana sat next to me in the back seat, and I wondered what she was thinking. We were both silent. I was sure that travelling in a car in darkness brought back terrible memories for her. Perhaps she replayed the shooting, again and again, each time trying to remember one more detail of the ordeal. This was what I did, and sometimes still do, even if not as frequently as before. I am afraid to forget, as if forgetting means dying a sudden, meaningless death.

"Look at the moon! It's so beautiful!" one of our companions said.

I glanced up and was surprised that I had not spotted the full moon. It was large and silver and perfect, and yet the darkness of the night felt heavy and absolute. I could feel the spaces between us, the occupants of the car. And then I remembered how Giuliana and I had connected. We lived distinct lives but had somehow shared a similar experience. And the spaces between those of us in the car grew smaller and smaller.

At the airport as we sat at our gate waiting to board the plane, I noticed that a man standing nearby was staring at Giuliana. The stare wasn't casual; it carried recognition. For Giuliana not to have noticed him would have been impossible because he stood directly in her view, yet her calm, serious expression didn't change at all. I was sure that she was recognized frequently, but one could never get used to that kind of attention. Her story had received a great deal of publicity in Italy, and her picture had been in newspapers, on TV, and on posters all over the country. I was proud of her for putting up a fight, for doing what she believed in, and for keeping her head up. I knew that she probably wished her ordeal had never happened. Except it had, and the experience had made her who she was—and she had chosen not to run away from that reality.

As the plane glided in the grey morning air that was slowly filling with light, I looked out my window and saw the deep blue of the Tyrrhenian Sea washing the western shores of Italy. I had flown over the Atlantic Ocean many times, but the Italian waters were the calmest I had ever seen; the surface of the sea was like blue silk. When I crossed the ocean for the first time in my life, looking forward to a new life in Canada, I could never have imagined that seventeen years later, I would go to Italy to receive an award for telling the story of my darkest days. What was Giuliana's life like when I was in prison? I tried to compare my time in Evin with hers in captivity. In order to expand my understanding of the world and feel that my experience transcended my limited life, I needed to understand others who had suffered trauma.

Unlike my experience, Giuliana's had been public from the start. Moments after her kidnapping, news agencies around the world reported the event, and most people in her country were openly concerned and wanted her to return home safely. For Iranian political prisoners incarcerated in the 1980s before YouTube and Facebook, things were vastly different. In a way, we were kidnapped, too, but by our own government; as a result, our disappearance remained a secret that our families and the local media could not discuss openly, or they would share our fate.

Just like Giuliana's abductors, ours had complete power over our lives. In her case, luckily, they chose not to physically harm her, even though the possibility of execution at any moment was excruciatingly real. What would have happened had Italian officials decided not to negotiate with the hostage takers? Giuliana could very well have been killed—maybe beheaded gruesomely, as other hostages had been. We, on the other hand, thousands of Iranian teenagers, were brutally tortured while we lived under the constant threat of execution by firing squad or hanging.

Giuliana told me that what gave her hope during her incarceration was knowing that the people of Italy were aware of her ordeal and were asking for her release. A few days after her kidnapping, her captors let her watch a report on the EuroNews Network. It showed a giant photo of her displayed at city hall in Rome. Later, the kidnappers were surprised when, at a soccer game, members of Rome's top soccer team wore jerseys that read Free Giuliana. Italians demonstrated for her release and made their voices heard, giving her strength. In our case the world, it seemed, had decided to forget about us. No one cared what happened to us, as if we had never existed. Our families cried silently and knew very well that they might never see us again, but their fears had to remain secret; in other words, *we* had to remain a secret. The terrible secret of the Islamic Republic of Iran. Our photos did not appear at city halls and were never published on the front pages of newspapers. We found hope in each other instead of in the outside world. The only way for us to survive was to remember that we were human, that we had families—brothers, sisters, mothers, and fathers—and that we used to go to school, celebrate birthday parties, read books, watch movies, and go on holidays. And by sharing these memories with one another, we created a collective hope that helped us believe that our nightmare would end one day and that we would somehow go home.

Once Giuliana was released, she fell straight into a media frenzy. Some regarded her as a hero, some a victim, and some severely criticized her, but her experience was known, and this mattered, even though she never received the attention she deserved in North America and the government of the United States did not take responsibility for the events that led to the death of Nicola Calipari. On the other hand, those who survived Iran's political prisons in the 1980s and were eventually released—in most cases after years—entered a world that was dominated by silence. We were forced to push aside our memories and deal with them alone. Giuliana dealt with her trauma immediately after her release, when we had to create new realities for ourselves from which the prison experience had to be erased. Only after twenty years did I begin the journey that Giuliana travelled right after her ordeal. I have a twenty-year hole in my life that is impossible to fill, but at least I have found my way to myself. I fear there are thousands of others like me who are still living false lives.

In June 2009, after the disputed presidential election in Iran, Maziar Bahari, an Iranian-Canadian journalist who worked for *Newsweek* magazine, was arrested in Tehran and accused of espionage. He was tortured, psychologically and physically, and forced to make false confessions. He spent four months in Evin. After he was released and returned to Canada, I listened to his interview on *The Current*, a CBC Radio One show. He said that his interrogator repeatedly asked him why no one in the outside world was mentioning his name. Didn't he have friends? Didn't he have anyone who cared about him and wanted him released? Bahari had been cut off from the world, so he had no way of knowing that in the West a great deal of publicity surrounded his case. Only when one of the nicer guards called him "Mr. Hillary Clinton" did he realize that a serious campaign to end his imprisonment existed. Bahari asked the guard what he meant, and said the guard replied that Hillary Clinton had mentioned his name in a speech that day. This gave Bahari a huge morale boost.

Bahari said that while in solitary confinement, he regularly thought of the Leonard Cohen song "Sisters of Mercy," and this helped him survive. He found it ironic that a song written by a Jewish Canadian gave him hope in the most notorious prison in the Islamic Republic of Iran. I had never heard "Sisters of Mercy," so I listened to it, and wished I had known it in Evin. Now I have it on my iPod and have memorized its words. The only song I sometimes hummed in solitary was *Soltan-eh Ghalbha*. It helped me remember Andre's face, the colour of his hair, and the love in his eyes. I had been in Evin so long that his image had started to fade in my mind.

One night, I dreamed that Giuliana and I built a huge dream catcher together, while Bahari and Leonard Cohen watched us, singing "Sisters of Mercy." The dream catcher was so big that we easily fit in its circle. Maybe it was big enough to save us all from nightmares.

# Jasmine's Poem about the Night Sky

During my incarceration in Evin prison in Tehran from January 1982 to March 1984, the guards regularly took my fellow prisoners and me to the Hosseinieh—the gym-size room on the prison grounds where hundreds of people could gather—to listen to propaganda speeches, attend group prayers, and hear the "confessions" of other prisoners. I hated the Hosseinieh, but I sometimes found myself willingly going there to escape the boredom of Evin's routines, if only in a minor way. Many of my friends got quite excited about going to the Hosseinieh because we were not blindfolded there, and they hoped to catch a glimpse of family members or friends who were prisoners in other cellblocks. Inmates from different cellblocks were not allowed to speak to one another, but just seeing loved ones was a treat. I had a friend named Jasmine whose only reason to go was to see the night sky. Jasmine was a Muslim and had grown up in the city of Yazd, in central Iran. Many times, the guards walked us to the Hosseinieh when it was dark. As we neared the building, they would tell us to remove our blindfolds. Jasmine would ask me to hold her hand to make sure she didn't fall, because she didn't want to take her eyes off the night sky. She was a poet and told me that stars were candles lit by angels. Stars made me think of my nights at the Caspian. I used to lie down on the beach in absolute darkness, count shooting stars, and listen to the whisper of the sea. Before the revolution, I knew next to nothing about real darkness, about the cruel acts that mark too many parts of the world.

One day, Jasmine recited one of her poems to me. We didn't have pen and paper, so she couldn't write it down. I cannot remember it word for word, but it went something like this:

> *Stars are candles lit by angels in the windows of heaven*
> *I see my friends run across the night sky, leaving trails of*
>     *light behind*
> *Why can't I be with them—please tell me why?*
> *Darkness holds me in its* dakhmeh
> *But I will escape. I promise*
> *I will dance across the night sky and sing and laugh and play*
> *I will bathe in the light of the moon and drink from the*
>     *Milky Way*
> *And I will never be alone or forgotten.*

Jasmine asked me if I knew the meaning of the word *dakhmeh*. I said that as far as I knew, it signified a dark, terrifying place, something like a dungeon. She said that even though many Iranians were unaware of the word's history, *dakhmeh* was what Zoroastrians had called cemeteries in the old times. Although I had gone to a Zoroastrian school, I didn't know anything about their burial customs, so she explained that Zoroastrians believed that death was not the work of God but the work of the Devil, a temporary triumph of evil over good, and this was why they considered the dead to be unclean. According to Zoroastrian belief, demons entered the body after death, so corpses could not be buried or cremated, for fear they would contaminate the world of the living. In the deserts of Iran, special raised structures named *dakhmeh*s, which Westerners called Towers of Silence, stood outside the walls of cities. On top of these towers, the dead lay exposed to the elements. Vultures ate the flesh from the bones and left them to the hot sun of the desert. The towers, which were fairly uniform in their construction, had an almost flat roof, with the perimeter slightly higher than the centre. The roof was divided into three concentric rings: the bodies of men were arranged around the outer ring, those of women in the second circle, and those of children in the innermost ring. Once sun and wind had bleached the bones—which could sometimes take months—they were collected in an ossuary pit at the centre of the tower. There, assisted by lime, they gradually disintegrated. Rainwater washed the remaining material through multiple coal and sand filters before eventually carrying it to the sea. In the early twentieth century, Iranian Zoroastrians gradually abandoned this tradition and began to bury or cremate their dead.

Jasmine told me that the moment she stepped into Evin, she felt that it was a *dakhmeh* for the living. The thought made me shudder.

ONE OF MY REASONS for writing *Prisoner of Tehran* was to reclaim my past. Now I wanted to reach out to my prison friends with whom I had lost contact. I asked people who I thought might know something and searched various publications and the Internet. I eventually created a website, where people could easily get in touch with me. The time my school friend Shaadi found me through my American publisher, she gave me the good news that when she had travelled to Iran a couple of years earlier, she had seen a few of our classmates who had been arrested around the same time as I; they had survived and were living their lives. However, I was unable to find my best friends in Evin, and I consoled myself by believing that ultimately they had been released. But in late 2008,

I found information on a website that Jasmine had been executed. The information came from a report—published by a reputable international organization—that listed her and tens of others as persons executed in the Islamic Republic of Iran in 1984–85. Jasmine's real name is quite unusual, so I doubted that this could be a case of mistaken identity.

I read each line of information on the website many times, and my computer screen blurred before my eyes. This couldn't be true. But her name was in the report, so it had to be true. Executed in 1984. I was released in 1984. The execution must have happened after my release or I would have heard about it. Or would I have? Officials had moved us to different parts of the prison. I don't even know where Jasmine ended up. In 1983, we had spent a few weeks together in the same cell.

I could see Jasmine: she was about an inch shorter than I, a petite girl with a serious face. Her sad eyes seemed so large, but I think this was only because she was extremely thin and pale.

I read the information again. Why was it so incomplete? Was this all that was left of her—only a name and a date? I tried to remember all I knew about her, but twenty-five years had gone by and my memory had gaps. She was about my age and had been a high-school student at the time of her arrest.

I contacted Amnesty International, and they confirmed that the website I had visited was reliable. I contacted the people who had set up the website, and they said that all they knew was that Jasmine's name was on a list of the executed, but there was no way to find out how accurate the list was. The person I spoke to told me it was a good sign that Jasmine's name was on only one list. *Only one list?* I felt terribly frustrated.

What if she really was dead? Had they hanged her or shot her? Some guards and interrogators in Evin believed virgins went to heaven when they died, and I had heard that they raped young girls before killing them. Had they raped her before her death? I should have somehow protected her. I should have died instead of her. But everything and anything I said after all these years wouldn't change the fact that she had died and I had lived. Now all I could do was to tell the world what a beautiful person she was. She did not deserve to go to prison. She did not deserve to die. I wished I could reach back in time and bring her back. I loved her, but my love wasn't enough. I wished I could do something significant, but all I could do was to write and make sure that people remembered her.

Every day, Jasmine read the Koran and prayed for hours. Her tears soaked her prayer mat as she said her Namaz. We used to talk and talk. We daydreamed about all the wonderful things we would do once we went home. We wanted to go for walks on the beach and read the books we loved. We wanted to cook elaborate meals and eat until our stomachs hurt. We wanted to go to the movies, dance, laugh, and sing.

The Internet was always the last resource I used to try to find my friends, as it is usually a source of bad news; it won't tell you that your friend was released, went back to school, got married, and had kids, but it might tell you that her name is on a list of the executed. I had Googled other friends before Jasmine, leaving her out—and I'm not exactly sure why. I think it was because she was the quietest, kindest, and most loving person I had known in Evin. Why would they have killed her? I had made the same mistake with Shahnoosh, but I had not learned from it; a person's goodness and innocence do not protect her in Evin.

Jasmine was one of only two of my cellmates with whom I ever talked about death. For Evin prisoners, death was the elephant in the room; we lived with it, but we never mentioned it. Jasmine and I also spent a lot of time reciting poetry to each other, especially the works of Forugh Farrokhzad and Rumi.

I had begun reading Forugh a few months before the 1979 revolution. I owned and treasured three collections of her poems. She was one of the greatest Iranian poets of the twentieth century and had a very strong feminine voice that was quite controversial for her time. She was born in 1935, married at sixteen or seventeen, was divorced two years later, and died in a car accident in 1967. After Arash was killed I buried myself in books, including hers. In Evin—in solitary confinement and in 246—I tried to recall Forugh's words. I had not entirely memorized any of her poems, and I could remember only parts of each of them, including one about death, which I one day recited for Jasmine:

> *My death will come one day*
> *In a spring bright with waves of light,*
> *A winter dusty and distant,*
> *Or a fall void of sound and joy ...*

> *... They will come to put me in the earth,*
> *Oh, perhaps my lovers*
> *Will lay flowers on my sorrowful grave ...*

That was all I could remember.

"Come on!" Jasmine protested. "That is it?"

"I've never been good at memorizing things. I'm surprised I remember this much."

"Maybe you'll remember more later."

"You know ... years ago I almost took a full jar of my mother's sleeping pills," I confessed.

"You say 'years ago' like you're thirty!" she said, smiling.

I laughed. "I wonder if I'll ever be thirty. It sounds so strange."

"You didn't take your mother's pills."

"No."

"Why?"

"I didn't want to be a coward."

"If you had taken them, you wouldn't be sitting here with me, reciting poetry."

"No."

"I would have missed you, but you wouldn't have missed Evin."

"I would have missed you, too," I said.

"Are you afraid of death?" she asked.

"I guess ... but I don't know what death really is ..."

"No one does."

"I trust God, though," I said.

"Me, too."

"Are *you* afraid of death?"

"Not really. Even if God decides to turn us into nothing, it's not so bad."

"No, it's not."

Jasmine's death came much sooner than mine, and I would never even know if she left this world in spring, summer, fall, or winter. Her friends and family would not have put flowers on her grave—they had probably not been allowed to. Had the guards even told her parents where she was buried? Many of the executed are buried in a cemetery the government calls "The Land of the Cursed,"* which the families of the victims have renamed "The Flower Garden of Khavaran."** A barren piece of land located on Khorasan Highway on the outskirts of Tehran, it has mass and individual graves, many of which are unmarked. Families of the executed sometimes go there to celebrate the Iranian New Year or other occasions. Many of them can only guess that their loved ones have been buried there. The Revolutionary Guard have attacked

---

*Lanaat Abad.*
**Golzar-eh Khavaran.*

several of the peaceful gatherings of the families. Some of the executed have also been buried in marked and unmarked graves in Tehran's main cemetery, Behesht-eh Zahra.

I couldn't stop thinking about Jasmine. Even though she was most probably dead, a part of me refused to believe it—and this angered me. I was mad at myself for being in denial. It frustrated me to the point of madness that my friend might have died twenty-five years ago, and yet she might be alive—I just had no way to know for sure. And if I wasn't sure about her death, I couldn't write about it, because if she was alive and still lived in Iran, writing about her would cause her a great deal of trouble and could draw the attention of the authorities to her.

I talked to a friend of mine, Steve, about my dilemma. Because of his job, he knew a great deal about human rights and victims of torture. He, too, had had a difficult past, and he understood my state of mind. He asked me if I was familiar with *los desaparecidos*— "the disappeared"—of Argentina and Chile. I had seen photos of Argentine and Chilean mothers holding the pictures of their lost sons and daughters, pleading for information about their fates. Steve said he could only imagine how terrible it was to know a loved one had been arrested and never to hear any news, never to learn if the person was dead or alive. He reminded me that thousands of people around the world have suffered like that. He believed that I should write about Jasmine. Not knowing what happened to her was an important part of my suffering and the suffering of many others like me. He believed I should honour her with my words; in so doing, I would be making my readers aware of *los desaparecidos*. He said he had no doubt I knew what was best.

But I didn't. I had hit a dead end.

IN EARLY MARCH 2009, I finally decided to join Facebook. This was a big step for me, because I am technologically challenged.

Andre believes that I would have been happiest had I been born in the Stone Age, which is probably true. Technology has always intimidated me. When we came to Canada, I refused to learn how to drive, and it took Andre years to talk me into taking driving lessons. I never failed a driver's test, but for months after getting my licence I shook with fear every time I sat behind the wheel of our car. When I decided to publish *Prisoner of Tehran*, it was obvious that I had to type it, but I knew absolutely nothing about computers and found them scary. Even moving the cursor around the screen was difficult for me. To help me out Andre bought some voice-recognition software, but that only frustrated me more, because the program didn't understand my pronunciation. I eventually learned to type, use Microsoft Word and many other programs, and surf the net. Friends kept inviting me to join Facebook, but to me it was another computer skill that would take me months to master. However, after being unable to confirm the news about Jasmine's execution, it occurred to me that I could use Facebook to find old friends.

In the beginning, my Facebook page showed only my name and date of birth, but I soon began receiving messages from readers of mine who wanted to contact me. I was encouraged and put more information on my "wall," and then I began looking for people. I connected with a few high-school friends who had never been arrested and had eventually left Iran, and then I started searching for my prison friends. But I failed in every case. Finally, I typed Jasmine's name in the Search box. I didn't really expect any results, but I had to try. Her name came up. I froze. This was impossible. It couldn't be her. A small profile photo sat next to her name. I looked at it and my heart almost jumped out of my chest. Even though the woman in the photo didn't look like the Jasmine I'd known, her smile was familiar. I tried to enlarge the photo, but it didn't work. So I decided to write to her. But what should I say?

"Hi! I was wondering if you and I were in prison together ..."
If this woman was not my Jasmine, she would think me a mad
person who was harassing her. So I worded my message carefully:

> *Hi: My name is Marina Nemat (maiden name Moradi-Bakht)*
> *and I'm an author living in Canada (you can Google me). I'm*
> *looking for a friend with the same name as yours. Are you the*
> *one I lost touch with in 1984?*

For the next few hours, I sat in front of my computer and kept
busy, but I constantly found myself staring at my Google Notifier.
Would this woman write back to me, saying that she was not the
Jasmine I was looking for? Or would my Jasmine write to me that
she was alive and well?

The next morning, I opened my laptop before doing anything
else and found this message:

> *Oh, my God! Of course I know you from those terrible times! I*
> *can't believe it ... I remember you and even your nightmares ...*
> *remember you told me about them? How wonderful that you*
> *found me ...*
>     *Jasmine*

The world stopped. I read her words again and again. She was
all right. Tears rolled down my face. I had found her. The dead
had come back to life. I had so many things to ask her, so many
things to tell her. Did she know that her name was on a list of the
executed?

> *Jasmine! This is a MIRACLE! Where are you? When did they*
> *let you go? I've been looking for you forever. Please do me a*
> *favour and Google yourself. There's a website that says you*

*were executed in 1984! I saw it in December '08, and I had a*
*nervous breakdown. I even contacted Amnesty International ...*
*I also contacted the people behind that website, and they said*
*there was no way to verify the info. My God! I thought you were*
*dead! I'm a writer now, and I even wrote a chapter about you*
*to include in my new book. It's like a eulogy of some sort. I was*
*devastated because it looked like there was nothing left of you*
*except a name and a date ... So many terrible things happened.*
*I'm so happy you're okay!*

As I waited for Jasmine's response, I thought about the strange
situation we were in. Even though she didn't seem to think that I
was dead, my message must have shocked her. I had spent the last
few years thinking and writing about Evin, but she had probably
tried to forget it—and now the ghost of the past was looking
straight into her eyes. I didn't want to be a reminder of pain and
suffering; except, remembrance was all I had left. Jasmine and
I were alive, but many others like us were not. Also, those who
had survived Evin needed to be acknowledged in a human way. I
realized I had to give Jasmine time to deal with the avalanche of
memories she now had to face. But how I longed to hear her voice.

That evening, Andre came home from work and we sat at
the dinner table to eat. I had not called him to tell him about
my finding Jasmine. I had felt exhausted all day, staring at my
computer screen, thinking.

"How was your day?" he asked.

"You first."

"To tell you the truth, not that great." He went on to describe
his workday, and I listened impatiently.

"Your turn," he said.

"I don't know where to start. I'm still in shock."

"What happened?"

"Nothing bad. It was great, actually. Miraculous. But I still haven't been able to get my head around it."

"What?"

"I found Jasmine. She's okay …" I told him the whole story. He was thrilled.

The next day I felt like pulp. I hadn't heard back from Jasmine. But I had to be patient. Too much was coming at her too fast. I was like a bomb that had just exploded in her world.

Jasmine wrote two days later and told me that she'd been released two years after me. She still lived in Iran. After Evin, she went back to school and got a university degree, and then she got married. I had so many things to ask her. Was she in touch with any of our cellmates? Had she talked to her family about Evin, or had she remained silent? Did her family ask her about what had happened to her behind bars? I desperately wanted to know every detail about her life after Evin. Yet she could be arrested because of her connection to me. I had heard that email was a safe way of communicating with people in Iran. But even though technology had become an effective tool in the hands of dissidents, the regime could use it against the people. I decided to stop writing to her, and she agreed that we should keep our communication to a minimum. I was not going to take any chances with Jasmine's life. I wanted her to be safe and happy, and the truth was—I was a danger to her.

# Letters from
## My Cellmates, and
## My Barbie Doll

Since the publication of *Prisoner of Tehran,* I have met many ex-prisoners from Iran, but most of them are not ready to talk about the past. They have approached me at events to offer a few words of encouragement, or they have emailed me and wished me the best of luck. One woman wrote to me saying that as a teenager she had been in Evin. She later immigrated to Canada and became a psychologist, but she had never talked about her prison experience with anyone, not even her husband and children. Once she read my book, she told her children that they had to read it. This was as far as she was ready to go. But I didn't lose hope. I knew that others would come forward sooner or later. The truth cannot remain buried forever.

In December 2008, an Iranian woman—whom I will call Anamy here—wrote to me through my website. She said that she had been in Evin between the ages of sixteen and nineteen, around the same time as I was. After her release she had gone back to school and received a degree. She had remained in Iran until just recently, when she had begun to feel the urge to tell her story. She wanted me to help her publish her memoir. I wrote back to her, explaining my writing process and the difficulties I had faced, and I shared what I knew about the publishing world. I noted that in order to be taken seriously, she needed to finish her manuscript and then enrol in creative-writing classes to perfect it. Once that was done, I promised that I would read it and give her feedback. We communicated regularly:

> *Dear Marina,*
>
> *Just like you, I was sentenced to silence for years … I cannot remember anyone asking me about my experience in the prison … No family member, no friend or boyfriend, not even my husband … Whether they want it or not, this silence makes our loved ones one of "them." I think the best way is writing, but in the meantime, I guess talking has its advantages … I had a tough time reading some parts of your book. Especially the parts about interrogations and 246. It took me back there, and I was literally gasping for air …*
>
> *There are major gaps in my memory. I was not aware of them before. I do not at all remember the room I was in Bandeh yek [a cellblock in Evin also known as 240]. I was there for months. How is this possible? In the meantime, I clearly remember the wet grasshopper I saw sitting on the windowsill the rainy night they forced us to evacuate 246 and move to Bandeh yek. I was desperate and hopeless … I think I remember everything that was somehow meaningful to me …*
>
> *A couple of nights ago, I had this feeling that I would not have much time, like I would not stay alive for long. I don't know whether it is an intuitive feeling or a hidden desire. I think, as you said in your book, I have been sleepwalking, too. I have always been somehow distracted from life, more like a witness and not like someone really involved in it … I have never been passive in my life, but I was doing it all from a distance. I always knew it had something to do with the prison. It is just like you have gotten off a train, and then after a couple of years, you once*

*again want to catch up with it! What you said in the interview on*
*the last pages of your book about the effects of writing your*
*memoir on getting back into life was really interesting to me. I*
*had never thought of it like that before ...*

*I cried a lot reading your email, and I had a very hard time*
*replying. What you said about having the same feelings about*
*death while writing your book had a very profound impact on*
*me. Not just because it was so unbelievably exactly the same as*
*mine, but because it made me start to think that many things*
*that I considered to be my personal problems, now seem to be*
*symptoms that all ex-prisoners are experiencing in the silent*
*cells we are still in ... It is so unbelievable to have this much in*
*common with someone you do not know. In Evin, you and I*
*lived literally metres away from one another for many months*
*and maybe more than a year and still far away and unknown to*
*each other. Now we live miles and miles away, yet this close and*
*connected ...*

*Marina, a part of me is still in Evin. By letting sixteen-year-*
*old Marina speak, you have not only shown her to me, but you*
*have also helped me see the sixteen-year-old me, still in prison,*
*squatting in silence near a wall, looking straight into my eyes,*
*and begging me to give her voice back.*

*I want to speak. I need to.*

*Anamy*

After Anamy, a few other ex-prisoners from Iran got in touch
with me and told me that they wanted to write their memoirs
of the prisons of the Islamic Republic. Anamy and my other
cellmates who have decided to break the silence are my beacons
of hope. I relied on my friends in Evin to find a ray of light in
absolute darkness; I now look again in their direction. I am not
alone in my journey of trying to document the human experience

of those who have suffered at the hands of the Islamic Republic. My cellmates are out there, and they will sooner or later raise their voices. I hope that we will one day stand at a memorial for our lost friends in Iran. However, we will not wave our fists in the air, demanding revenge. No. We will want justice, but if too many years have gone by and justice for our dead friends and for us seems impossible, we will cry and grieve, but we will refrain from resorting to violence, because if not, we will become victims of the never-ending cycle of hatred and injustice that has already destroyed too many lives.

ON SEPTEMBER 22, 2008, I had a meeting with Dr. Rosemary Meier to discuss the effects of torture on children. Dr. Meier is a geriatric psychiatrist, an assistant professor at the University of Toronto, and a member of the health committee and network of the Canadian Centre for Victims of Torture.

Dr. Meier reminded me of *Bahboo*. When I entered the Common Room of Massey College at the University of Toronto, I spotted her sitting on a sixties-style brown leather sofa that faced a wall-to-wall window overlooking a courtyard where tall trees towered over patches of green grass. She had a subtle smile on her face. Her thin, silky grey hair was gathered in a bun at her nape and a few strands fell onto her neck and shoulders. She was not wearing makeup, and her clothes were practical and simple. Her eyes were different from *Bahboo*'s, though. *Bahboo*'s eyes were full of shuttered sadness; Dr. Meier's, even though I had no doubt they held their own secrets, were like open windows. She was kind, but not in an artificial sort of way. She liked to get straight to the matter: "Tell me what happened. I'm interested."

Up to this point in my journey, I had relied on my own experiences and observations to understand how my two years in Evin had shaped me. I had not been able to trust those who had lived "normal" lives to analyze me and help me understand myself. But I finally felt I had arrived at a stage where I had achieved a good level of self-awareness, so it was time to discuss my findings with professionals.

I told her that for lack of a better term, my writing *Prisoner of Tehran* had been like throwing up; the story had exploded out of me when I couldn't hold it down any longer. It had been an urgent telling of events. In order to acknowledge and understand my past, I needed to see it on paper.

"Does this make any sense?" I asked.

"Yes, it does," she said. "One of the meanings of *catharsis* is 'a purging of the bowels.'"

I explained that I knew guilt was the engine driving me. Guilt was a negative emotion, but I believed it could have positive outcomes. It had made me write obsessively, as if I were living the last day of my life.

"Your experience reminds me of Holocaust survivors," she said. "Most of them couldn't talk about their experiences for years, until these people became old and frail. They never shared their memories. Yet their children wanted to know. They needed to know. The experiences of their parents were a part of these children and they wanted to understand them, but it was very difficult for their parents to talk about the past."

I know that silence, the silence of trauma quietly and carefully handed down to the next generation, I thought. A package of secrets that changes hands. The problem is that the giver of the package is aware of its contents, but the receiver is not. The receiver can only see how it disturbs everything it touches. And it comes with a warning: "Don't open me or I will explode!" So it sits in plain sight, staring at the children of survivors in its mute, threatening way. Silence saddens me. It breaks my heart. I want to scream, *Tell! Tell! Tell! The children can face it. They have to face it. They need to face it.*

*Please trust them. They need to understand the human experience of history before they start a war or genocide of their own.*

I asked Dr. Meier why she thought I was telling my story after such a long time. She said that life was not linear; it was spiral. The journey of life makes us who we are. Even our preverbal experiences are important. Events that we remember shape us, but so do the ones we don't. Unresolved grief manifests itself in many different ways. Some people spend a lifetime running from grief. Some finally face it at a certain point in their lives. Even though the human experience is more or less the same, and grief is grief and loss is loss, every case is different. Every case is unique.

I asked Dr. Meier about memory as I stared at the small pond in the courtyard. A little fountain shot a trembling dome of water into the air, creating ripples that turned sunlight into golden splatters. She told me that memory was like cosmology. The more we look at the universe and study it, the more we discover. The more we peer at a corner of the night sky, the more stars we find.

After my meeting with Dr. Meier, I reflected on our conversation. All roads in my life have somehow intersected the dark void of silence. After Evin, I lived in silence for so long that I almost forgot all about the world of voices. But one doesn't need to have been tortured or be a Holocaust survivor to be trapped in it. Almost any form of trauma can lead people there. A few months before the publication of *Prisoner of Tehran,* as I stared at its release date on my calendar, the date was like a wall. I felt as though I was going to hit it at the speed of light and disintegrate. That day *had* to be the day of my death. How could I possibly survive such exposure? But I reached that wall and walked right through it. It didn't kill me. On the contrary, it made me feel more alive than I had felt since I had been a teenager. The Tower of Silence had begun to fill with voices.

As I was writing this book, I had my editor Diane and her husband over at my house for dinner one night. As usual, some of our conversation revolved around my prison experiences. After we finished eating, we talked about torture—and I found myself fighting my tears. My younger son was sitting with us at the table. A couple of days later on the phone, Diane told me that she had never heard me speak about my torture in front of my children. I had, but she had not been present on those occasions. She also said that I had been more emotional than ever. She was right. Every day, I am able to feel a little more than the day before. The numbness that became a part of me in Evin is a formidable force, and I have to wrestle it on a daily basis. Every day is a small victory.

Why do we, the human race, make the same mistakes over and over? Why do we torture, abuse, wage wars, and commit acts of cruelty? I can't say it enough: the only way to stop the cycle of violence is to speak out. As long as victims do not bear witness, their suffering will be forgotten. Children should be encouraged to talk about all that is considered unspeakable. Torture should be discussed at dinner tables and in schools. In history classes, we should discuss human suffering and read the memoirs of those who have lived through wars, revolutions, genocides, and dictatorships.

On October 29, 2008, I had an appointment with Dr. Donald Payne. I was very excited about meeting him. Since 1979, Dr. Payne has assessed and treated more than fourteen hundred victims of torture or war. He has testified at refugee determination hearings, has provided in-service training to members of the Immigration and Refugee Board of Canada, and has made presentations and written articles on torture and the treatment of torture victims.

Dr. Payne greeted me warmly in his office. I'm not quite sure what I had expected a psychiatrist who had worked with hundreds of torture victims to look like, but the man in front of me was like someone's favourite uncle or a gentle grandfather one would meet at the park with a young child, a kind and simple man who has lived an average life. However, I knew that Dr. Payne's life could never be described as "average."

Dr. Payne invited me to sit down. I got straight to the point and asked him if he believed that torture affected teenagers differently from adults.

"There are so many factors here," he said. "Younger victims are more vulnerable, but they're also more resilient in some ways. Older people don't have much life ahead of them, and it's harder for them to begin a new life after a traumatic experience, but those who are in their late teens still have a future."

"What if the victim is fifteen or sixteen years old?" I asked.

"This can be very difficult, but it also depends on the young person's level of development and maturity. For example, an overprotected sixteen-year-old kid who's arrested because of a family member can feel completely devastated."

I explained that in Iran, thousands of teenagers were arrested in the 1980s because they had read certain books or newspapers, had pamphlets of illegal political groups in their backpacks, or had gone to protest rallies. They weren't exactly what could be considered "political." They didn't have the ideological or practical background to support them through torture. Older prisoners strongly believed in a certain ideology, but most of the young ones didn't. They rarely got angry at the guards and interrogators who hurt them. Instead, they blamed themselves and became shameful and withdrawn.

Dr. Payne agreed that self-blame was common in young victims, whereas the older prisoners who were politically involved had a strong sense of commitment that was like a religion to them and had become a part of their persona. If adults break under torture, they lose a part of who they are. However, this is not true for teenagers; ideology and political commitment are not fundamentally a part of them.

I talked about the silence surrounding political prisoners, and Dr. Payne told me about one of his young patients who had been in prison for four years. Later, she escaped and came to Canada. She didn't want to talk about her experiences with her friends because she wanted to be like everyone else, but she was aware that her not sharing her past with anyone affected her relationships and made them shallow. Her friends had no idea who she really was—but she wasn't ready to tell. Dr. Payne gave me another example of a husband and wife from Argentina. The husband had been detained and tortured. After his release, he left the country with his wife and they had children, but he didn't want the children to have any knowledge of his past; his wife, however, believed that it was important for them to know the truth. Dr. Payne also reminded me that many Second World War veterans never spoke about their experiences of war.

I explained that many Iranians, including me, were consumed with getting rid of the current regime in Iran, but the problem was that no one had a clear idea what would replace it. Thirty years ago we had a revolution whose results were catastrophic. We wanted democracy, so we deposed the shah and brought Khomeini into power—and one dictatorship replaced another. I disagree with those who say things cannot get worse. Neither Marxism nor Marxist-Islamism nor any other ideology can bring democracy to Iran. Like the Islamic regime, they have proven that they have no tolerance for those who think differently. We, the Iranian people, are suffering from some form of traumatic stress disorder. I believe that the same way an individual can suffer from it, so can a country as a whole. We Iranians lived through the terrible 1980s: not only were we at war with Iraq and people were dying in cities as a result of Scud-missile attacks or young soldiers were being killed at the front, but thousands of teenagers, boys and girls, were being tortured and executed in prisons. We were a nation destructing from the inside and the outside, and our cemeteries were getting bigger and bigger.

After the war, people talked about its horrors. This dialogue could take place because the war had been a collective experience: we had been attacked and we had fought for our sovereignty. But the suffering of political prisoners was never publicly discussed—at least, not until the unrest that followed the 2009 presidential election in Iran. Yet even then, the discussions were limited. To openly bring up the issue of torture is, of course, painfully difficult. In homes during private get-togethers, no one ever talked about prisoners. It was as though the country was suffering from some form of collective amnesia. Before the unrest of 2009, members of a few political groups in exile in the West wrote about the horrors of Iran's political prisons, but their publications had tiny print runs. Most Iranians chose to look the other way and ignore the situation altogether. The majority of ex-prisoners are still silent because they are traumatized. Even though torture has a political aspect, it is also terribly personal and isolates its victims. On the other hand, like my friends and family, "normal" people want the prison experience forgotten, as if it had never happened. Because not only do they wish to be safe from the pain of remembering atrocities, they also wish to avoid any responsibility associated with acknowledging that an atrocity like torture occurs. Someone might ask, "Where were you when it happened? Why didn't you stop it?" No one likes facing tough questions like that.

I told Dr. Payne that I feared for the young generation in Iran, the children born after the revolution. They have always lived a double life. The middle and the upper classes in the country are well educated, and their kids love Western music, movies, fashion, and technology, but the government constantly tells them the West is "evil." The kids don't care. They listen to Western music and they want to dress like Western pop-culture icons. In Tehran, more women enter universities than men. Many Iranians have satellite dishes, and they watch the latest foreign films. They connect to the West through the Internet, even though the government tries to control it. At home, most young people can listen to music, read all sorts of books, and watch movies, but when they go to school and are in public, they have to behave the way the government expects them to or they will be punished severely. Even very young children have adapted to this duality.

I was trying to understand post-traumatic stress disorder, so I asked Dr. Payne about it: "Like the American soldiers who come home from Iraq, do many PTSD sufferers have a tendency to become violent?"

"No," he said. "Soldiers are trained to be violent. It's their job. They're supposed to kill, and they're rewarded for killing, but once they return home, they can't be violent anymore. Their violent behaviour is not a symptom of PTSD but a reaction to it. The symptoms of post-traumatic stress disorder are usually quiet. They're nightmares and flashbacks that refuse to let go."

"But can there be a gap?" I asked. "I mean, can an individual who has experienced extreme trauma begin having nightmares and flashbacks years after the event?"

"Yes," he said. "This is quite possible. Actually, it's common."

I told Dr. Payne about how normal I had seemed for years— how I had been a dutiful wife, a good mother, and an attentive waitress. No one could have guessed anything was wrong with me.

"Yes," said Dr. Payne. "The false self."

He didn't need to explain the concept; I had lived it. After the prison, I created a new "Marina," a carefully constructed fictional character. She had never experienced torture, rape, and humiliation, and she was going to live happily and normally ever after.

I told Dr. Payne that I didn't go to the Canadian Centre for Victims of Torture when we first came to Canada because for a long time after we arrived, I was not at all ready to admit that I was a torture victim. He agreed that most victims didn't go there, and noted that the main aim of the CCTV was to assist victims with their settlement issues—learning English and finding a job and proper housing—not give them psychiatric help.

"It's very difficult for victims of torture to trust anyone," he told me, "except for those who were in prison with them and who share their experiences. I worked with a young woman for a while. One night I was driving her and a few others home, and she was the last one for me to drop off. I asked her what her address was, and she refused to give it to me. Even though I had been helping her for a while and she seemed to now trust me, she still didn't feel comfortable enough to tell me her exact address and wanted to be let off at a corner."

I agreed that trust was a serious issue. Many ex–political prisoners from Iran don't even trust one another. Even now, they carry with them the political disagreements that plagued them in prisons. I have heard that after my release from Evin, ideological conflicts between prisoners gradually became so severe that some prisoners boycotted the others. Supporters of different political groups refrained from speaking to one another in prisons. These divisions became quite destructive and drained a great deal of the prisoners' energy.

Dr. Payne—or Don, as I came to call him—and I remained in touch. We had lunch together a few times and talked about recovery from torture and trauma, good and evil in the world and in individuals, and God and religion. One day, Don surprised me by bringing me cookies he had baked himself. The cookies were moist and delicious and my favourite—oatmeal cranberry and chocolate chip. I enjoyed them so much I decided to try to bake more often, because nothing is more comforting than the scent of freshly baked cookies on a cold day. Don's cookies made me think of all the things that gave me a sense of peace and happiness: books, rosaries, prayers, the sea, mountains, being close to Andre, my Prayer Rock, our cottage by the Caspian Sea ... and my Barbie doll.

As a child I had always wanted a Barbie, but my mother believed that dolls were a waste of money. I had only two dolls: one I called "Lucy," after Lucy Pevensie, the youngest Pevensie child in *The Lion, the Witch, and the Wardrobe*; my brother gave her to me as a Christmas gift when I was about nine. The other was a nameless one that my father's closest friend, whom I called Uncle Partef, had brought for me when I was five. She was almost as tall as I was and wore a pink princess dress. I was scared of her, so I asked *Bahboo* to hide her in our basement.

When I was twelve, a year before the revolution, I saved up some money and bought a Barbie, even though I was too old to play with her. She had brown hair and came dressed in a long blue dress and white high heels. I kept her on my bookshelf next to my favourite books. She made me smile.

After the revolution, my Barbie became one of my sources of courage when female members of the Revolutionary Guard replaced our teachers. Our new nineteen-year-old principal stood by the entrance of the school every day, inspecting all of us to make sure that we were not wearing makeup and that our head scarf completely covered our hair. If she suspected that a student had makeup on, she would wash that student's face in a bucket of dirty water. Every morning before leaving for school, I looked at my Barbie and promised myself that I would one day be as beautiful as she was without being afraid.

After my release from prison I discovered that my mother had thrown out my Barbie. She had probably thought that a young woman who had been a political prisoner had no use for something as silly as a doll, but I missed her.

Following the publication of *Prisoner of Tehran*, a friend gave me a Barbie for my birthday after I told her how badly I had wanted one as a child. My new Barbie is blond. She has blue eyes and a perfect smile and looks very pretty in her pink ballerina dress. She sits on my desk, keeping me company as I write. To me, she is a reminder of every child's right to enjoy beautiful things without facing imprisonment, abuse, or torture.

# An Elastic Band
## for Making a Ponytail

In February 2009, as I was working on this book and after I had found Jasmine's name on a list of the executed, I began having flashbacks again. I had not had any since late 2004, and they caught me off guard. I had been writing seven hours a day, had at least two speaking engagements a week, had taken on too many projects, and my father was ill. As a result, I was emotionally and physically exhausted.

After having flashbacks several days in a row, I decided to discuss them with Don, but he was away on holidays, so I waited impatiently, worried about my mental health. When I knew Don was back, I sent him an email, asking for advice, and he replied:

> *Sorry to hear that you had such upsetting experiences. I have known people to have vivid flashbacks many years later when under stress. They are usually isolated incidents and related to general stress. One Argentine woman, more than twenty years after her detention and torture, reported that when she was under the stress of preparing for her PhD thesis defense, she had a flashback of her detention while she was teaching a class ...*

*I would agree that your flashbacks were related to your high*
*stress level and being exhausted physically and emotionally ...*
*The intensity of the content of your book would also be a factor.*
*You should get enough rest and try to cut down on some of your*
*stress. Very much easier to say than to do, especially when some*
*things get thrown at you without control over them.*

*I hope and expect that they will not recur. If any do, accept*
*that it is a flashback, rather than anything to be realistically*
*afraid of, and that it will pass. Again easier to say than to do*
*when you are feeling very fearful.*

*Do not hold back in contacting me if it would be helpful.*

I felt much better after reading Don's words. Being reminded that other people in the world had gone through experiences similar to mine helped me put things into perspective.

One of the flashbacks that haunted me seemed benign at first, and its appearance puzzled me. The first few episodes were not exactly visual: I was gathering my hair into a ponytail without a mirror in front of me, so I couldn't see myself, but I could feel my fingers going through my hair. Every time, my heart would race. The memory was upsetting, but I couldn't place it. It was like a blurry, forgotten photo, without a past or a future and disconnected from the flow of time. Why would I be afraid of making a ponytail? I couldn't sleep. Where was the memory coming from? The more I thought about it, the more it recurred. But I still couldn't understand its meaning. I decided to do what Don had suggested: control my fear and tell myself that it was just a memory. Maybe if I wasn't so terrified, I would discover its origin. I gradually remembered more and more. Slowly, I managed to see my surroundings. I was in a cell at 209 in Evin. I dug deeper, asking myself, "Do I hear anything? Do I see anyone?"

*"Tie your hair back," Ali says. "I don't want it to get in the
way." He is standing over me.*

*My hands go toward my head and my fingers comb through
my hair. I pull off the elastic that sits on my wrist like a bracelet,
gather my hair, and make a ponytail. I close my eyes and tears
fall down my face.*

The past has a way of catching up with us. No matter how fast
we run, we cannot escape it. One of the reasons I finally confronted
my past was that I needed to prove to myself it could not control
me. The large gap between the day I was released from prison and
the day I started to write created a buffer that helped me keep my
balance as I travelled back in time. I began almost to believe that
I was in charge and in complete control. What I sometimes forgot
to bring into account was that nothing in this world is absolute. I
had never considered the possibility that what had happened years
earlier could come back to life and haunt me.

In September 2009, I accepted a radio interview on a Persian-
language station based in Canada. The host, whom I will call
Setareh here, phoned me, and during our pre-interview talk, she
told me that she had not read my book because she feared it would
be too upsetting for her, but she *had* watched my TV interviews
and read articles about me. I told her that I understood how she
felt, but I believed that we had to face our past in order to have
a better future. She asked me if it would be okay for listeners to
email their questions to her, and I said it was fine. The interview
went well and I answered all the questions, which were similar to
the ones I had been asked many times before. There was one odd
comment from a woman who claimed that *Prisoner of Tehran* had
been published in Canada by a small publisher first and then by
Penguin, and that on page 19 of the first edition I had mentioned
that my father's name was Gholamreza and my mother's Roghieh,

which are very Muslim names. I couldn't understand why she was making a false claim about my publisher, but I suspected that she somehow believed she had found some form of discrepancy in my work. I said that my book had been published in this country only by Penguin Canada and that I had never had another publisher here. Then I explained that during the time of Reza Shah when my grandparents obtained official identification papers for themselves and their children, Iranian citizens were not allowed to have foreign names, even if they were not Muslim. My parents' names had never been a secret. After the interview, Setareh said that she had received many questions from her listeners, but there was not enough time for them all. I mentioned that people could post any other questions they had on my Facebook wall, and I would respond to them all.

Three days later, I checked my Facebook page shortly after I awoke at 6:30 a.m. Setareh had posted a comment on my wall, claiming that she had a "solid source" who said Ali was alive in Iran.

I could not believe my eyes. Ali was alive? This was ridiculous. I was there when he died. No one could bleed that much and live. He stopped breathing in my arms. He was dead. He had been dead for twenty-six years. I got up and paced the room. Was this a mistake? A malicious attack? Pain knifed my chest. I had had this before. My family physician had run tests and had found nothing wrong with my heart. She recommended that I breathe slowly and deeply when pain occurred. I sat down, did that, and felt better. Then I went to my computer and read the comment again. Setareh had said that her information came from a "solid source." To post something like that in such a public way, she must have been sure the information was valid. I had met many journalists during the previous two years, and gotten to know a few of them very well. They would never risk sharing information without enough research. Why hadn't she called me first? Why did I have to read about this on the Internet? My mind raced back in time. I went through all my memories of the night Ali died.

*On Monday, September 26, 1983, at eleven o'clock at night, Ali and I say good night to his parents and step out of their house. It is a cold night, so they don't come out with us. The metal door connecting their yard to the street creaks as Ali pushes it open, and its lock clicks loudly as it closes behind us. We walk toward the car, which is parked about eighty feet away where the street is a little wider. A dog barks in the distance.*

*Suddenly, the loud sound of a motorcycle fills the night. I look up to see the bike come toward us from around the corner. Two dark figures are riding on it, and as soon as I see them, I instinctively know what is about to happen. Ali also knows, and he pushes me. I lose my balance and fall to the ground. Shots are fired. For a moment that stretches between life and death, a weightless darkness wraps its smooth, silky body around me. Then a faint light spreads into my eyes and a dull pain fills my bones. Ali is lying on top of me. Barely able to move, I manage to turn to him.*

*"Ali, are you okay?"*

*He moans, looking at me with shock and pain in his eyes. My body and legs feel strangely warm, as if wrapped in a blanket.*

*His parents run toward us.*

*"Ambulance!" I yell. "Call an ambulance!"*

*His mother runs back inside. Her white chador has fallen on her shoulders, revealing her grey hair. His father kneels beside us.*

*"Are you okay?" Ali asks me.*

*My body aches a little, but I am not in pain. His blood is all over me.*

*"I'm okay."*

*Ali grasps my hand. "Father, take her to her family," he manages to say.*

*I hold him close to me. His head rests against my chest. If he hadn't pushed me, I would have been hit.*

*"God, please, don't let him die!" I cry.*

*He smiles.*

*I had hated him, I had tried to forgive him, and in vain I had tried to give him love.*

*He struggles to breathe. His chest rises and falls and then is still. The world moves around us, but we have been left behind, standing on different sides of an unforgiving divide. I want to reach beyond the dark depths of death and bring him back.*

*The flashing lights of an ambulance ... A sharp pain in my abdomen ... And the world around me disappears into darkness.*

I sat on my bed and tried to take slow, deep breaths again. Ali was alive? Why would he do this? How dare he just disappear like that after all that happened? Pretend to be dead? But he *was* dead. I was there. I saw it. Could they have revived him after I passed out? After the shooting, I was taken to the hospital and then to the prison. For months, I didn't have contact with anyone except his family. I was still a prisoner, and his family could keep me in the dark if they wanted to. But they mourned him. I watched them cry. I witnessed their pain and devastation. No one can fake that. No one.

I calmed down a little. But I needed to know the truth. The absolute truth. I had to email Setareh. I sat at my computer and wrote to her, asking for proof. How did her source know this? Did the person who had claimed Ali was alive know him personally? Did that individual have a recent photo of him? My chest began to tighten. I had to breathe slowly and wait. Should I call Andre at work and tell him? No. That was crazy. Tell him what? I had to wait for proof.

The day advanced in slow motion. Even though the simplest chore overwhelmed me, I attended to my duties. I drove my son to school and listened to him tell me about his plans for the day. I had yoga that morning, the first class of the fall session. I visited my father at noon—I had promised. I had been away the week before and not seen him in ten days.

Back at home, I checked my emails again. Nothing. My heart raced. I needed to talk to someone, but I couldn't talk to my family until I had proof—why upset them over a claim that could be entirely false? Who could I call? Steve. I had to call Steve. I knew he was usually very busy at work, so I emailed him, briefly telling him about the claim and asking him to call me. He phoned early in the afternoon.

"Marina," he said, sounding concerned.

"I can't believe I'm even considering this, Steve, but what if he's alive?"

"Marina, let's deal with the facts. You were there when he died. Journalists do this sometimes. Not all of them, but some of them jump at things before corroborating the facts because it's a good story. She should have phoned you. She shouldn't have posted it on Facebook. It's so irresponsible."

"What if they revived him after I passed out, and he went into hiding because there were people who wanted to kill him?"

"Okay. But wouldn't he have contacted you? He loved you, Marina. Do you really think he could have stayed away for so long?"

"No."

"What's the worst thing that can happen if he's alive?"

"I don't know … nothing, I guess."

"Write to the journalist and insist that she reveal her source. She owes you that."

"I have written to her. I'll write again. But if he's alive … Steve, do you realize what it would mean? That I have two husbands! What would I tell Andre? I have put him through so much. He's been so good …"

"Marina, you don't have two husbands. You didn't give your consent. You were coerced. Your marriage to Ali was illegal."

"I know … I know … But he believed I was his legal wife … According to Iranian law I was his legal wife …"

"Is Andre the jealous type?"

"Yes. Very much. Steve, put yourself in his shoes. How would you feel if you discovered your wife had another husband?"

"If she went through the hell you went through, I would support her."

"I'm going to wait until there's proof. I have to protect Andre."

"But would he think you were hiding it from him? As a man I would rather know the truth."

"I can't do this to him now. He gets paranoid sometimes. He might think Ali is hiding in the neighbour's shed to come and get me or something."

"Really?"

"Really."

"Call the journalist. Her information is probably hearsay. You need to verify her source."

"If Ali's alive, should I talk to him?"

"Absolutely not!"

"No, I shouldn't. But there are so many things I have to ask him. Why did he do the things he did?"

I told Steve about my ponytail flashbacks. I needed Ali to know how he made me feel. Still, could I bear being in the same room with him? No. Could I bear hearing his voice on the phone? No.

"Steve, if this is true," I said, "I will become a nun. You know, one of those cloistered nuns in one of those distant convents on a mountaintop or something ..."

He laughed.

"Marina, hang on to your logic. I know what-ifs are unavoidable and there's always a conspiracy theory. But you saw what you saw."

"Yes. I saw what I saw."

Steve was right. I had to hang on to my logic. Except, I had emotions, too. All is well when logic and emotion coexist. However, when they go at each other, they create an explosion. The truth is that what happened to me in Iran had nothing to do with logic, so why should the aftermath be logical? I wrote to Setareh again; if she had a "solid source," I needed to see proof immediately.

I began making dinner, but I couldn't stop thinking about Ali. I never wanted him to die. Never. I have never wished death upon another human being. But his death was a fact that I accepted, a fact I could not change. I returned to the possibility I had mentioned to Steve: what if medics had revived him after the shooting? Maybe he then decided to take the opportunity to let me go. He knew he made me miserable. He knew I didn't love him. He had believed that I would eventually get used to him, even fall in love with him, but what if, after facing death, he realized that this would never happen, and he chose to do the right thing?

If this was true, it would mean that he truly loved me—more than I had ever imagined.

I felt panic rise in my chest. A terrible scream was forming in my throat. I ran to the bathroom, turned on the shower, covered my face with a towel, and screamed. Thomas was in his room, playing video games, and he could not hear me.

Once my screams ebbed to sobs, I took off my clothes and stepped under the shower. Ali would never have let me go. He was a torturer ... But he, too, had been a victim.

"Ali is dead." I said. "He died in my arms."

Warm water mixed with tears filled my mouth. I spit it out. I couldn't bear the thought that he might have sacrificed so much for me. He didn't have the right to be so good. Where would this leave me? I was terrified that Ali might have been a better man than I had believed him to be, and this broke my heart. Had I been cruel to him? Why was I losing my sanity over mere possibilities? Why was I feeling so guilty?

My hair dripping wet, I sat in front of my computer and stared at the screen. A few minutes later, Setareh finally wrote to me:

> *Dear Marina: I only sent you the message. Believe me that I gave you the news exactly as it was given to me. I never thought that it would upset you so much, my dear. I sent your message [to that individual, asking for proof]. Please remain assured that I will inform you of any news that comes my way.*
>
> *Please don't be upset about this.*
> *Yours truly,*
> *Setareh*

How could I *not* be upset?

Half an hour later, she wrote again:

> *Dear Marina: Now this individual is saying that he never said Ali was alive ... I can't believe it. What can I say? I only gave you the message of a listener. Now this person is saying that this was about another interrogator ... I am terribly shocked. I took my comment off your [Facebook] wall ... Sorry for the inconvenience. I was just simply relaying a message.*

Her "solid source" was a listener she didn't even know? I needed to have a stiff drink and go to bed. I was trembling.

Some events change everything in our lives. I have had a few of them. The Islamic Revolution in Iran was one. Going to Evin was another. Marrying Ali was the third. And his death was the fourth. After he died and I went back home, I built the foundation of my new life on the fact that he was gone. Then, twenty-six years later, I came face to face with the possibility, even though slim, that he could be alive. And my world collapsed. It was as if the ground had disappeared from under my feet and I was falling into the unknown. I had lost control.

It took me a few days to collect my thoughts and put things into perspective. I had a new understanding of the power of the past, how it could easily become the present and redefine everything. Yes, I had faced my past and my demons, but I had to remember that the road ahead was still treacherous.

I went to the bathroom and found an elastic band. My hair was shorter than it used to be, but I could still pull it back. My hands shaking, I put the elastic around my right wrist, looked at my reflection in the mirror, and made a ponytail. Despite my weaknesses and my having lost many battles, I was a worthy opponent for the past. After all, I was still standing. Tears fell down my face. But it was okay. No one was watching.

I heard a key turn in the lock of the front door. Andre was home.

# Acknowledgments

First, I have to thank Margaret MacMillan for her kind support and opening the doors that I didn't even know existed. Margaret: I am forever in your debt.

My heartfelt gratitude goes to John Fraser for offering me a fellowship at Massey College and to Peter Munk and the Aurea Foundation, whose generous grant made it possible for me to give this book all my time and energy for a year.

Diane Turbide, my editor and friend: a day doesn't go by that I don't thank God for you. You have an amazing ability to shed light on the road ahead when I lose my way. You saw the potential of this book even when it was terribly raw and disjointed. Thank you for having faith in me.

Beverley Sotolov: you are the most meticulous copy editor I have ever had. Thank you for your attention to detail, patience, and availability.

Also, I'm grateful to everyone at Penguin Canada. You have all become like family to me.

Beverley Slopen: you are much more to me than just my agent. Thank you for your sound advice and precious friendship.

Sister Mary Jo Leddy: thank you for trying to help Anamy; also for sharing books, thoughts, recipes, and stories with me.

Steve: our friendship has taught me a great deal about the world and myself. Thank you for always being there, for your thought-provoking emails, advice, funny jokes, favourite poems—and for your being you. Thank you for reading my manuscript at an early stage. Your comments and editorial insights have been a great help to me. Your kindness, compassion, strength, and humanity make the world a better place.

All my friends at the School of Continuing Studies at University of Toronto, especially Nory Siberry, Lee Gowan, Ed Carson, and Marilynn Booth: your continuous friendship and support mean a lot to me. Thank you for giving me a very special sense of community and belonging.

Dearest Hoda, my strong, beautiful friend. The difficulties I have faced are nothing compared with yours. The Islamic Republic murdered your mother when you were only three, and after her death you still suffered tremendously as a result of more tragedies and injustices, but you managed to maintain your dignity and humanity. The love in your heart astounds me. You told me that your only memory of your mother is her feeding you rice with her fingers. Your story will be told. The world will know.

Dear Elena: you are one of my best friends, yet we have never met! Thank you for your uplifting emails that make me laugh when I need a boost. And thank you for your insights. I would never have been able to organize this book effectively without you.

Martha, my talented and hard-working friend: thank you for the Barbie and for all the laughter you bring into my life.

E.H., my long-lost classmate: thank you for finding me and for remembering all those little things that I never thought anyone would remember. And many thanks to all my schoolmates from Anooshiravan-eh Dadgar High School who have written to me. As a few of you mentioned, we are all survivors. Our dreams turned into nightmares, but we kept going. I hope we can have a reunion one day and a memorial for our friends who did not survive. They are loved and remembered. Their courage and sacrifice are like lights that will shine forever.

My darling A.R.: you have a permanent place in my heart, and I wish you all the happiness in the world. I hope never to lose you again. You have always been a true friend, even when our paths separated.

Crystal Loszchuk, a singer and songwriter from Calgary, sent me an email in 2008. I didn't know her. She had read *Prisoner of Tehran* and loved it. It had inspired her to write a song for Iran's political prisoners—"Lift Your Voice"—which she attached to her email. I listened to it with tears in my eyes. It was absolutely beautiful. Then Crystal came to Toronto to visit me and sang her song at one of my speaking engagements at a high school. "Lift Your Voice" is now available on iTunes. Crystal, I don't know how to thank you. You are a beautiful, talented young woman with a very big heart.

Ambassador Alex Himelfarb, Nicoletta Barbarito, Simonetta d'Aquino Allder, Peter Egyed, and everyone at the Canadian Embassy in Rome: thank you for your help, hard work, and hospitality, which made my trip to Rome a very memorable one.

Ambassador Renata E. Wielgosz, Zoe Delibasis, Denys Tessier, and everyone at the Canadian Embassy in Athens: without your help, I would not have been able to visit Greece. Thank you for your kind support and attention.

My sincere gratitude also goes to Foreign Affairs and International Trade Canada and the Canada Arts Council for providing me with travel grants.

I'm not easy to live with, and without the support and patience of my husband and children, I would never have been able to write and travel. They are my pillars of strength and hope, and I love and appreciate them more than they can ever imagine.

Last but not least, I would like to thank all my readers, especially the ones who have written to me or come up to me at events to say that I have made a difference. What more can a writer ask for?